Country Houses of Louisville

1899-1939

Restrevor, the Ross Todd estate, 2011. (Blackburn)

COUNTRY HOUSES OF LOUISVILLE

1899-1939

to Steve —
Warm regards
Winfrey Blackburn

WINFREY P. BLACKBURN, JR.

R. SCOTT GILL

Foreword by Mark Alan Hewitt, FAIA

BUTLER BOOKS
LOUISVILLE

ISBN 978-1-935497-45-5

Book design by Scott Stortz

Printed in Canada

Butler Books
P.O. Box 7311
Louisville, KY 40257
Phone 502-897-9393
Fax 502-897-9797

To order additional copies of this book, or to see the entire Butler Books catalog, visit us online at www.butlerbooks.com

Endsheet image: Garden elevation of *Kanawha*, the William S. Speed house.
Office of Charles A. Platt, undated. (Private Collection)

To Dr. Winfrey P. and May Viehe Blackburn
with gratitude.

and

To Robert E. and Virginia G. Gill
Thank you for encouraging curiosity, rewarding
persistence and instilling the desire to share.

Photo: Detail, living room mantel, *Lincliff*, 2010. (Nation)

Contents

Homewood, the estate of Mrs. Thomas Underwood Dudley, 2011. (Blackburn)

FOREWORD

A country house is always intimately tied to its environs. Louisville, with its picturesque setting along the Ohio River, was ideally suited for a renaissance in house and garden design at the turn of the 20th century. Families such as the Nortons, Ballards, Coxes, Allens, Speeds and Todds constructed elaborate and elegant houses in Cherokee Park and along the bluffs of the river, employing the skills of not only local architects and landscape designers, but also national figures such as Carrère & Hastings, Charles A. Platt, and the Olmsted Brothers. For the first time, this handsome book documents the story and architectural achievements of this unique chapter in Louisville's history.

The country house of Kentucky and the South presents a unique problem for the modern historian because ante-bellum plantations were well-established institutions in America based upon the English model of the landed gentry that died out with the abolition of slavery. Those not destroyed in the Civil War were often left to deteriorate when family wealth dissipated in the latter half of the 19th century. Most of the houses built during the rise of the modern American oligarchy were constructed with new wealth acquired prior to the Great Depression. Surprisingly perhaps, Louisville's turn of the century wealth often came from similar industrial and commercial enterprises to those of New York and Chicago plutocrats. Thus, the country house of 1900 was very different from that of 1820. As the authors point out in their introduction, "What set the American country house apart from its transatlantic progenitor ... was the simple fact that the American version was built as a symbol of culture, taste, status and affluence—an icon of accomplishment and luxury from which very little, if any, income or political authority was derived."

The styles and types of houses built overlooking Louisville's lush river banks and encircling Frederick Law Olmsted's Cherokee Park track very closely the standard models developed elsewhere in the United States during the country place era. Georgian, Mediterranean, Tudor, Colonial Revival, and even Shingle Style variants exist today, surrounded by gardens in both formal and informal modes. What is most extraordinary about these places, to this observer, is the quality of the surrounding landscape, a verdant, rolling topography that is the hallmark of the Ohio River valley. The genius loci that is neither wholly of the South nor of the North, with a population drawn from the North, South and East, gives a continental flavor to these houses that otherwise tend to confound expected regional types.

Every one of the several dozen houses featured in this book shares an expansiveness and sweep characteristic of this unique part of America. Among the best examples, ranking with any in the Northeast, Midwest or West, are *Rostrevor*, the Italian inspired house of James Ross Todd in Cherokee Park (Carrère & Hastings, 1908-10); *Edgecombe* (John Bacon Hutchings & Olmsted Brothers, 1910-13), *Gardencourt*, for the Misses Norton (Shepley, Rutan & Coolidge, 1905-08), *Bushy Park/Melcombe* (John Bacon Hutchings, Olmsted Brothers, Marion Coffin, and Carrère & Hastings, 1909-30), and the William Speed estate, *Kanahwa* (Charles Adams Platt and Ellen Biddle Shipman, 1917-22). In each, the house and garden are designed as an ensemble, taking maximum advantage of the site. *Melcombe* has its monumental Greek theatre, designed by Carrère & Hastings. *Gardencourt* radiates from its expansive classical facades a formal elegance reminiscent of England. *Edgecombe* marries an English Arts & Crafts cottage with a soft-edged garden layout right out of the pages of *The Studio*. And *Kanahwa* uses scholarly Georgian colonial details to paint a picture of patrician grace appropriate to its distinguished patron.

Country Houses of Louisville is that rare combination of splendid book design and spritely narrative that should delight any fan of southern history or art. Winfrey Blackburn and Scott Gill weave the fascinating lives of Louisville's first families into their text, and the brilliant color photographs fill out the story of this bygone era of gentility and generosity of spirit. Their book is a joy to read and a feast for the eye.

– Mark Alan Hewitt, FAIA
Bernardsville, New Jersey

Ledgelawn, the Attilla Cox summer residence in Mockingbird Valley, ca. 1926. (Private Collection)

INTRODUCTION

THE COUNTRY HOUSE

There has been in recent years a migration to the country among the well-to-do in Louisville that has caused one prominent woman to be quoted as saying that none of the 'society people' live in town. While this may be an exaggeration it is undeniable that encircling Louisville are colonies of beautifully situated country houses which in picturesque location, charming furnishings and genial hospitality are extraordinary.[1]

America's era of the great country house was a felicitous 50-year period when unusually talented artistans and architects joined with patrons of remarkably substantial means and willpower to create expansive estates with magnificent houses and enchanting landscapes. The number of undertakings was prodigious, and the breadth of design exceptional. Before this prolific and all too brief era came to a close, countless richly imaginative, beautifully crafted and, of course, unquestionably impressive country residences came to dot the suburban hillocks of virtually every city of size in the United States. It was a period without precedent, and once over, without reprise.

The progenitor of the American country house was found overseas, most particularly Great Britain, France and Italy of the 18th and 19th centuries. In those countries, it was customarily a vast working estate, an economic entity that underpinned the wealth as well as political power of its owner. The house itself was typically a grand affair, designed to connote the stature of its landlord, who was usually a hereditary member of the aristocracy. Quite often, ownership of the land – and the house, in one form or another – extended back for generations within the same family. At the dawn of the 20th century, the European country house was inextricably associated with an image of substantial old money, refined culture, longevity and prestige, an image that proved irresistibly alluring to a burgeoning class of new industrial millionaires across the Atlantic.

America's extraordinary economic expansion in the late 1800s has been well documented, and the story of the country's dramatic shift from a passive agrarian economy to a system of aggressive industrial and commercial enterprises is well known. Rapidly growing railroads, banking, manufacturing, shipping and countless other endeavors of the new industrial era found their innovators and backers in the unbridled, laissez-faire atmosphere that was the United States. Untethered by the firmly established social, political and economic customs of their European counterparts, the new American entrepreneurs created affluence on a scale and in a timeframe hitherto unprecedented. As noted by architectural critic and political thinker Herbert David Croly, these "Great American Millionaires" had "amassed fortunes far surpassing any in history, simply for the pleasure of making money – so much money that new ways had to be invented for spending the excess."[2]

With few satisfactory indigenous models for living sumptuously with

Living room at *Rostrevor*, the Ross Todd estate, ca. 1910. (Private Collection)

great prosperity, America's millionaires turned to Europe for inspiration. Members of the country's upper class, possessing vast amounts of discretionary capital, traveled extensively to such cultural centers as Paris, London, Vienna and Rome, collecting art, buying elaborate clothes and absorbing architectural sights unseen in the United States. Fortuitously, their architects, many of whom came from privileged backgrounds, were engaged in similar activity, learning their field through a pattern book comprised of the grand edifices of princes and dukes. Such a propitious convergence of financially enabled client and appropriately trained and prepared architect had never before been so well timed.

At first, America's capitalists chose to celebrate their success through the construction of extravagant city residences, lined up proudly side-by-side along preferred downtown thoroughfares. New York's Fifth Avenue,

"Putting at Old Lansdowne," 1902. (Rogers Clark Ballard Thruston Photo Collection, Filson Historical Society)

Boston's Commonwealth Avenue and Louisville's Third Street all bore testimony to the hegemony of this new elite. As communications became easier with the advent of the telephone and transportation improved through local rail lines and the automobile, the prospect of a "place in the country" became decidedly more practical. In the United States, as in Europe, land was the oldest standard of wealth and status, and prosperous businessmen and their families soon flocked to the suburbs, competing – as they had in town – to build the grander house with the more elaborate gardens on the yet better-located piece of property.

The preferred model for the American country house was unquestionably drawn from the persistent English ideal of the noble aristocrat and his stately country manor. The British country house as a social, economic and political enterprise was still very much intact at the time, as was the prestige of the attendant monarchical system that forever fascinated the rising capitalists of the former colonies. What set the American country house apart from its transatlantic progenitor, however, was the simple fact that the American version was built as symbol of culture, taste, status and affluence – an icon of accomplishment and a luxury from which very little, if any, income or political authority was derived. Ultimately, the American estate was identified with leisure as well as romantic notions of cultural refinement and an appreciation of natural and man-made beauty. It was, in short, a commodity to be enjoyed.

Third Street, Louisville, 1912. (University of Louisville Archives and Records Center, Louisville, KY)

Barnard Hall, the Louis Seelbach residence, undated.
(Image used by permission of Archives and Special Collections, The Southern Baptist Theological Seminary)

Initially, as the idea began to take hold in the 1880s, the American country house assumed the form of a very large cottage, most often in an exuberant Queen Ann or Shingle Style, a blend of wood and stone or brick with towers, balconies and filigreed porches. However, as travel to Europe became easier and more comfortable with ever larger and more luxurious steamships, and architect and patron indulged increasingly in the luxuries of the continent, the thought of imitating the great villas, chateaux and Tudor mansions of the Old World became inescapably seductive. By the end of the century, the more modest and picturesque styles of the past two decades had become noticeably out of fashion and were soon abandoned in favor of grand European models.

The American country house as a type arguably had its beginnings in New York, where the nation's remarkable new commercial and industrial wealth was centered and where a steady influx of skilled immigrants made creating and staffing such places possible. The concept quickly spread to the west and south, however, as industrialists and others emulated what their peers were doing elsewhere. In Louisville, the era dawned as the 19th century came to a close.

LOUISVILLE

> Alluring to merchant and manufacturer, stranger and friend, lord or lady, hospitable Louisville sits snugly on the southern bank of the Ohio River and the northern verge of Kentucky. Too far north to be a southern city, and yet too far south to be a northern city, the place has the progressive wide-awake, enterprising spirit of the north, and the social generous, home-loving traits of the south. Where else can so ideal a combination be found? [3]

Louisville owes its existence to the limestone outcroppings that create the only obstacle to navigation along the entire course of the Ohio and Mississippi Rivers. It was this Falls of the Ohio that gave rise to a city that in the beginning served as a portage stop for trade heading south to New Orleans and north to Cincinnati and Pittsburg, and later as a toll booth for a year-round canal that bypassed the falls. George Ross Leighton, a writer for *Harper's* magazine, years later described the heyday of the bygone river trade era.

> The position of the town beside the falls was of decisive importance. In the days of river traffic, cargo had to break bulk there and the merchants of Louisville levied toll on shippers, became shippers themselves and suppliers of shippers. Round about lay a rich agricultural country. And it was in the middle; it lay between the old East and the Western wilderness, between the North and the South, a city of middlemen, acutely conscious of what transportation meant, taking tithe of every traveler. To Louisville came the southern planters to buy...cotton gins, sugar mills, pork, hay, and flour. Out of Louisville, northbound, went sugar, molasses, coffee, and cotton. It was a broker's paradise, a counting-house town where even the naturalist Audubon was pressed into service as a storekeeper... [4]

The rapid growth of the railroad following the Civil War sharply diminished though by no means eliminated the importance of river commerce to Louisville. Significantly, the city, which virtually

Ca. 1925 aerial showing, bottom to top, *Norton Hall* with stables at right; *Gardencourt*; and *Edgecombe* with stables at right. The James B. McFerran estate is at upper left. (University of Louisville Archives and Records Center, Louisville, KY)

alone among major Southern urban centers had survived the War unscathed, became a major rail hub through which passed so much of the trade between the rapidly expanding industrial North, the rebuilding Reconstruction South and the ever-opening expanses of the newly tamed West. By the turn of the century, it had also transformed itself from a town of merchants and intermediaries into a regional manufacturing and financial center, sending its products and services outward on the "ten great railroad systems" that passed through the city and on the steamers that "reach 33 navigable rivers." In the 1920s, 192 industries were established in Louisville, which was home to eighteen of the largest manufacturing plants in the South, six of which were among the nation's biggest.[5]

The years following the Civil War and leading up to the Great Depression were marked by tremendous population growth. Between 1870 and 1900, the census grew from 100,753 to 204,731. By 1925, it had expanded another fifty percent to 305,935.[6] This period was clearly a heyday for Louisville, and one that with logical consequence gave birth to the city's golden era of the country house.

Following the pattern established in other major American cities, Louisville's builders of country estates drew their fortunes not from agriculture, but from manufacturing, finance and investments. They were brewers and distillers, and makers of hardware, leather, flour, cement, lumber, whiskey barrels, rope and paint. They were bankers, investors in oil and railroads, and brokers of real estate and grain. Many inherited their wealth from family members who had enjoyed tremendous success in the aforementioned enterprises, and several were descendants of old and distinguished Kentucky families. Surprisingly, few were direct immigrants, although many were second generation Americans.

LOCATIONS OF CHOICE: CHEROKEE PARK AND THE BLUFFS OF THE OHIO RIVER

There were two favored locales for country houses in Louisville, both of which rose to prominence simultaneously. The first was the area encircling Cherokee Park, not far from the city's downtown. The second consisted of a string of estates running from the urban core eastward along the ancient bluffs overlooking the Ohio River. While each already hosted modest summer cottages and a few farms, it wasn't until 1899 that their transformation into enclaves for the city's well-to-do began to take shape.

CHEROKEE PARK

In 1887, members of Louisville's Salmagundi Club, a "genteel literary and conversation group" whose roster included many of the city's prominent businessmen, inaugurated a campaign to create three large "rural-type" public parks that would be joined by a system of tree-lined parkways. The idea developed gradually over the next few years until 1891 when the leader of the effort, Col. Andrew Cowan, invited Frederick Law Olmsted, the famed designer of New York's Central Park and the grounds of George Vanderbilt's *Biltmore House*, to Louisville to discuss his thoughts about the project. On May 20, 1891, Olmsted made his presentation to twenty of the group's members at the Pendennis Club, and two days later was hired for the job.[7] Two weeks earlier, the newly constituted Board of Park Commissioners had purchased 250 acres for what would become Cherokee Park and thus, with site in hand, design work began immediately.

Although the park officially opened in 1892, work continued well into the next century with further land acquisitions,[8] road and bridge

The formal garden at *Gardencourt*, 2011. (Blackburn)

construction and the inclusion of various monuments, structures and fountains. In the end, Cherokee Park – one of the last large commissions by the great landscape architect – grew to a size of 409 acres, much of the additional land donated by adjacent residents. Unlike New York's Central Park, which needed time to grow into its desired effect, Cherokee Park required only Olmsted's careful editing to immediately enchant the visitor, as noted by *Art Work of Louisville* in 1897:

> It seemed as if Nature had expressly prepared a spot which was to become a Public park at Louisville. It is singular that this ground was preserved in almost a primeval condition through

Cherokee Park with *Norton Hall* in the distance, ca. 1903. (*Artwork of Louisville*, 1903)

Bernheim Memorial Bridge, Cherokee Park, 1930.
(University of Louisville Archives and Records Center, Louisville, KY)

Christensen Fountain, Cherokee Park, 2009. (Blackburn) The distinctive horse watering trough was designed by Arthur Loomis and completed in 1902.[14]

ALL THE LONG YEARS OF THE PAST, AND THAT JUST AT THE MOMENT WHEN THERE WAS A PLAN FOR MAKING PARKS, AND LAND WAS WANTED FOR THE PURPOSE, THIS CHOICEST OF ALL THE LANDS ABOUT LOUISVILLE, CAME INTO THE MARKET FOR SALE. ... THIS BEAUTIFUL TRACT OF LAND ... WAS PURCHASED AND NOW CONSTITUTES CHEROKEE PARK. IT LIES CLOSE TO THE CITY, AND STREETS AND BUILDINGS ARE RAPIDLY EXTENDING UP TO ITS FRONT, AND ALONG EACH SIDE. THROUGH IT FLOWS THE BRIGHT CLEAR WATER OF THE EAST FORK OF BEARGRASS CREEK, ENTERING AT THE FARTHEST BOUNDARY AND RUNNING BETWEEN THE HILLS AND RIDGES IN A SERPENTINE COURSE. ALONG ITS BANKS ARE GROVES OF GREAT OLD TREES IN GREAT VARIETY. WOODED SLOPES AND GRASSY VALES, SPREADING PASTURE LANDS, ADORNED WITH SHADE TREES, AND AN EXTENSIVE TRACT OF ANCIENT UNBROKEN WOODS ARE FEATURES OF THIS PARK. FROM VARIOUS ELEVATIONS, BEAUTIFUL VIEWS ARE OBTAINED, AND UNDER THE SPREADING BEECHES, WALNUT, LOCUST, ELM AND OTHER VARIETIES OF TREES ALL THE LUXURY OF THE GENUINE COUNTRY CAN BE FOUND.[9]

One of the first individuals to recognize the extraordinary investment potential implicit in land surrounding the new park was John Byrd McFerran. The son of James C. McFerran, whose renowned Glenview Stock Farm was noted for its prize trotting horses, John B. had built a sizeable meat packing business, McFerran, Shallcross & Co., which he sold in 1887, not long after his widowed mother sold the Stock Farm.[10] With his ear clearly attuned to the plans of the Park Commission, in June 1890 McFerran purchased 229 acres abutting the east boundary of Cherokee Park from the heirs of William Burke Belknap.[11] Shortly afterwards, he initiated correspondence with Olmsted's firm, the first step toward subdividing the property into large and estate-sized lots. However, the national Panic of 1893 seems to have led McFerran to postpone his plans, for it wasn't until 1898 that he resumed platting work with Olmsted and constructed the first house on the property, a large frame cottage for himself. In March 1900, McFerran released the completed Design Map for Alta Vista[12] and began offering building sites for sale.†

John B. McFerran house, undated. (*Artwork of Louisville*, 1903)

Mary P. Clancy house, undated. (*Artwork of Louisville*, 1903)

† The subdivision plat was completed by Frederick Law Olmsted's sons, operating under the name of Olmsted Brothers, the senior Olmsted having retired in 1895.

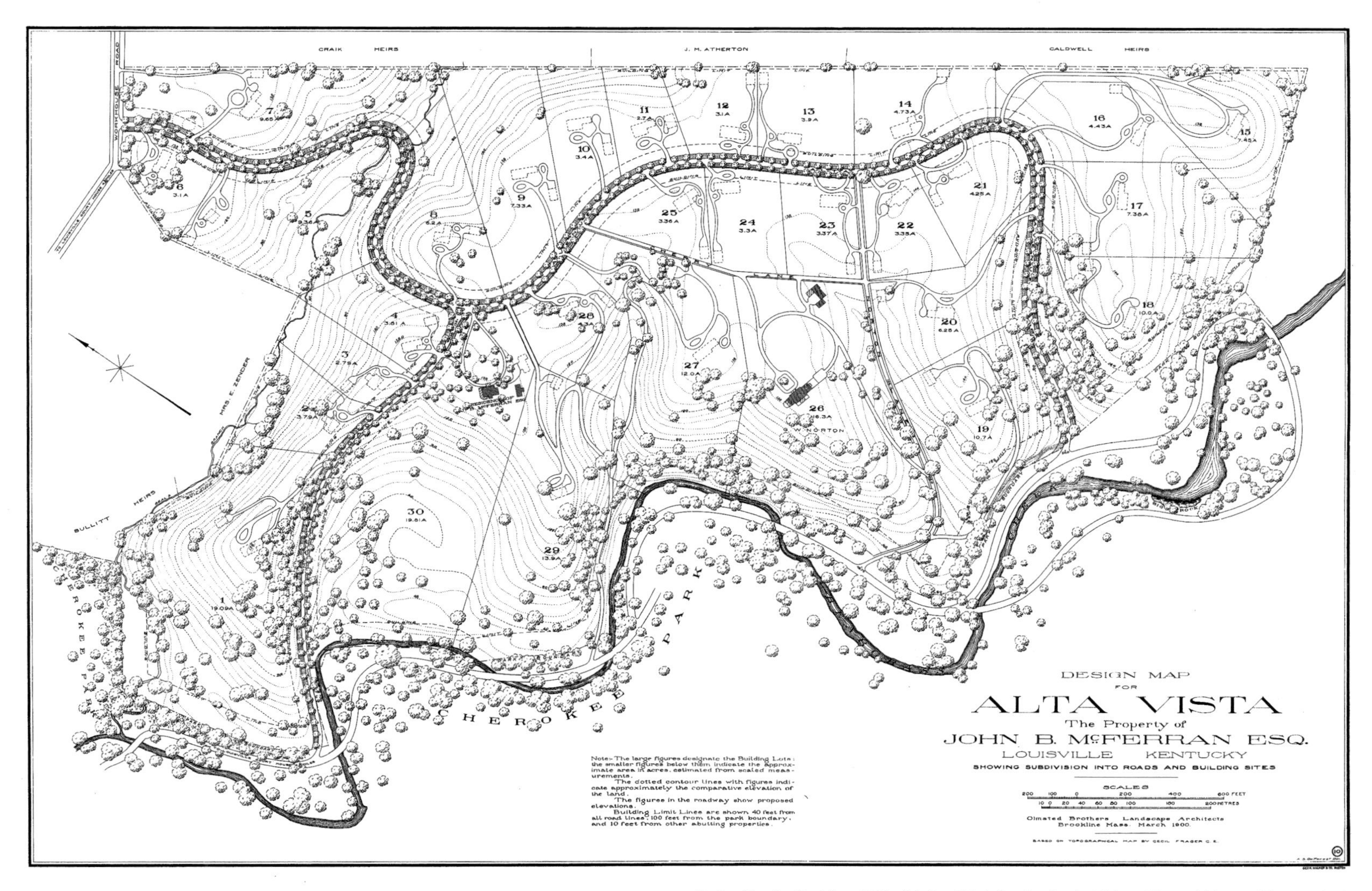

Design Map for Alta Vista, 1900. (National Park Service, Frederick Law Olmsted National Historic Site)

The development consisted of 30 lots, ranging in size from 2.7 acres to 19.81 (McFerran's own parcel), with the largest tracts located adjacent to the park. The first sale was evidently to George W. Norton, Jr., whose forthcoming grand residence, *Norton Hall*, was shown on Lot 26 – the largest site after McFerran's – when the 1900 Design Map was issued. McFerran's daughter, Mary P. (Mrs. W. P.) Clancy, followed Norton, building her own large Shingle Style house a year or two later near her father on Lot 5. With the construction of *Norton Hall* in particular, the tone was set not only for Alta Vista but for future houses surrounding the park: this was to be an enclave of exquisite country mansions and estates for Louisville's business and social elite.

Olmsted's work on Louisville's park system and McFerran's Alta Vista subdivision had a significant and lasting effect on the city. These commissions clearly established the firm as the landscape architect of choice, and led to more than a half century of additional projects throughout the city and county. By the end of its long design run in Louisville in 1963, Olmsted had platted at least 26 public parks, parkways and urban squares as well as numerous residential subdivisions (including Indian Hills and Cherokee Gardens), and had further executed work for over 90 smaller scale and estate-oriented residential clients.[13] In the early years, the builders of the great houses surrounding Cherokee Park employed nationally prominent architects in unusually disproportionate numbers. Undoubtedly it was Olmsted who, given the firm's relationships with such architects across the country, made these invaluable introductions, the legacy of which is a distinctly rich collection of architecturally significant country houses seldom seen outside of the nation's largest metropolitan areas.

THE BLUFFS OF THE OHIO RIVER

In 1899, Charles Thruston Ballard broke ground on his palatial Glenview estate, *Lansdowne*, inaugurating the transformation of unassuming summer cottages and simple farms along the river bluff into a strand of luxurious country houses to rival those sprouting up around Cherokee Park. The sites along the bluff offered Louisville's gentry an alternate choice of country environment. Whereas the park-side estates enjoyed a sense of pastoral serenity with views of a carefully nurtured landscape, those along the bluff were presented with opportunities for commanding, expansive vistas over the river to downtown and across to Indiana. And while the houses of Cherokee Park benefitted from a convenient proximity to downtown and its exclusive clubs, the mansions

View to the Ohio River and Indiana from *Ladless Hill*, the Alfred Brandeis estate, 2011. (Blackburn)

along River Road enjoyed comfortable access to two country sporting and social clubs, a welcome respite from the starched collar atmospheres of their urban counterparts.

Underpinning the enticing desirability of the bluff-top locations was a small train, which converted a time-consuming, dusty trek eastward from downtown into a comparatively easy, brief and pleasant journey. The Louisville, Harrods Creek & Westport Railway, fondly known as the "Interurban," was incorporated in 1870 by "persons who were prominent in the business activities of Louisville and the upper river road region." Initially powered by steam locomotives, the line originated downtown at First Street and ultimately terminated in Prospect, never quite reaching its namesake destination of Westport. For years, the train operated a schedule of four round-trips daily, with special runs in between for parties and other such events. Not only was it a convenient mode of transit for estate owners and their guests, it also served as a channel for transporting service and tradespeople to and from the great houses. The most noted service area of the line was the stretch between Louisville Country Club and Glenview, the bookends embracing the greatest concentration of sumptuous country houses along the River Road. The Interurban was electrified in 1901 and continued operations until 1935, when the Great Depression and the ever-encroaching automobile rendered it unsustainable.[15]

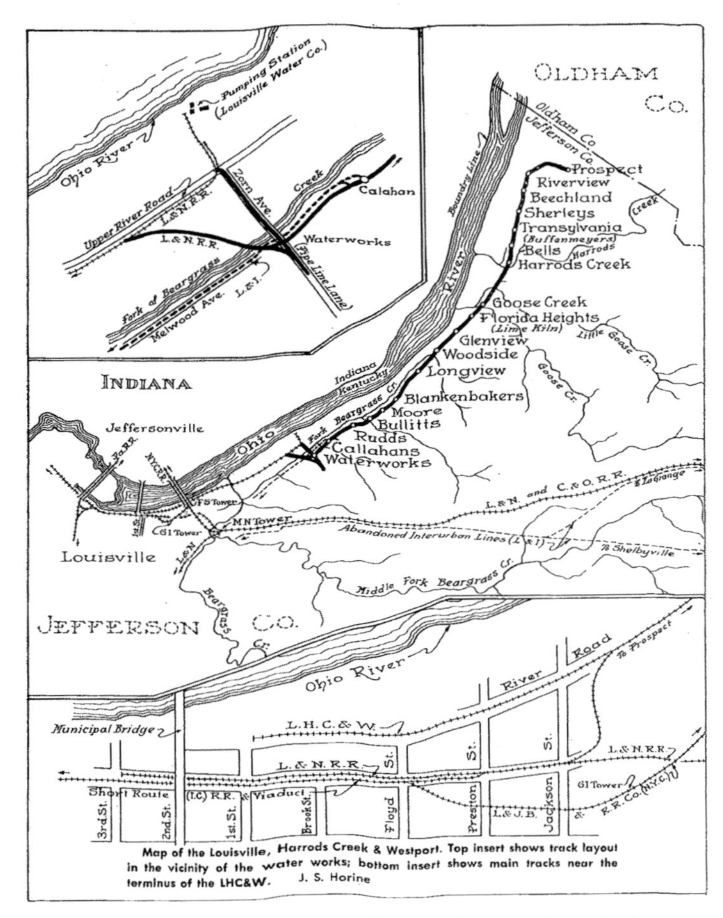

The route of the Interurban railroad, undated. (*Ghost Railroads of Kentucky*, by Elmer Sulzer)

Wealthy Louisvillians were first drawn to the far reaches of River Road with the creation, in 1887, of the exclusive Fincastle Club. Established as a summer colony of private cottages encircling a shared clubhouse and built on land from James C. McFerran's Glenview Stock Farm, the Fincastle membership included many of the city's industrial and commercial elite. Paradoxically, the club's allure – an ex-urban escape along the breezy hills above the river –

The Glenview Interurban station (now a post office), 2011. (Blackburn)

Entrance to *Malvern House*, the Attilla Cox estate on the river bluff, 2011. (Blackburn)

was likely its undoing, as a mere twelve years after its founding the club closed down, its members having elected to forego their small, on-site cottages for grand mansions set nearby on expansive estates. In time, the entire Fincastle property was subsumed within Robert Worth Bingham's *Melcombe*, the clubhouse replaced by Carrère & Hasting's imposing Greek theatre.

The country house movement nationally was accompanied by the development of the corresponding country club, which offered estate owners and their guests the opportunity to socialize and engage in sporting activities with members of their set in a less formal and more relaxed atmosphere than the traditional urban clubs allowed. Such clubs were typically organized around a golf course, a luxury that was impractical for all but the rarest of estate builders. As twilight settled over the Fincastle Club, its dining, guest, skeet shooting and tennis facilities easily supplanted by those constructed on new neighboring estates, the organization of the Louisville Country Club in 1895 introduced a desirable, conveniently located and exclusive golf and tennis alternative for the city's captains of commerce and industry. Not surprisingly, a permanent clubhouse was constructed in 1910 to the designs of Louisville society architects McDonald & Dodd, whose portfolio would ultimately include significant country residences for many of the club's members.

THE END OF AN ERA

The golden age of the country house in Louisville, and the United States, spanned the brief period between 1899 and 1917, a time of

Four Courts, the Mrs. Marion Taylor and E. Leland Taylor duplex residence under construction, 1923. (National Park Service, Frederick Law Olmsted National Historic Site)

Cobble Court, 1937 (foreground) and *Glen Entry*, 1911, two generations of Allen houses in Glenview, 2011. (Blackburn)

extraordinary prosperity, high immigration and low taxes. In Louisville, 77% of the great houses covered in this book were built or started prior to America's entry into World War I.

Wartime and post-War inflation of as high as 17% undoubtedly caused the city's well-to-do to hesitate before embarking on a project as expensive as a country house.[16] The size, scale and elaborateness of houses constructed after 1918 would never again match those of the preceding years. During the 1920s, only four of the thirty-five houses included in this book were built, all at a scale noticeably reduced from that of the grandest houses of the pre-War era. The "roaring decade," which enjoyed a period of extremely low inflation, nevertheless saw the personal income tax, first levied by constitutional amendment in 1913, rise to marginal rates of up to 56% in the first half of the decade, with a consequent dampening of country house construction.[17] In Louisville, very few significant new projects were started before rates fell to 25% in 1925.

Adding to the economic pressure on the creation and maintenance of the country house were, ironically, the expansion of automobile ownership and the thriving economy. Car registrations in Jefferson County alone increased from 6,500 in 1916 to 64,500 by 1928. This greater freedom of movement led to a burgeoning suburbanization with the result that prime parcels of land became scarcer and land values – and attendant property taxes – rose.[18] Further, the booming economy presented growing employment alternatives for domestic workers, enticing this indispensible service segment away from estate owners who had little choice but to pay more for the employees they were able to retain. As the 1920s progressed, wealthy families began to shun the expensive country estate and instead build impressive yet manageable residences on smaller lots within exclusive new suburban subdivisions.

Gate to *Rio Vista*, the J. H. Caperton estate, undated. (Private Collection)

The Great Depression, of course, reduced the rate of residential construction of all types to a snail's pace. During the decade of the 1930s, again only four of the houses presented in this book were constructed. In what was perhaps a genteel acknowledgement of the toll the times were exacting from the country house peer group, the most elaborate of the four estates, George W. Norton, III's *Fincastle*, was built remotely out of view from its compatriots, in stark contrast to the stately, high profile residences of Norton's father and aunts at *Norton Hall* and *Gardencourt* of thirty-plus years earlier. And the last house constructed on Maj. James Fox Allen's *Allenwood* estate, *Cobble Court*, reflected the comparatively modest, although still elegant, realities of this constrained era. In the end, Hitler's march into Poland and the onset of World War II closed the 40-year run of the great American country house. When the war was over, the economic landscape was forever altered, and the roster of Louisville's great country estates grew no more.

Of the 35 houses featured on the pages that follow, 28 still exist, virtually all in good or excellent condition and all but two in private hands, testimony to the enduring appreciation individuals and institutions have for irreplaceable works of architectural and landscape artistry. Indeed, these houses are different: they stand out in scale, in design and in craftsmanship; they are tangible if not nostalgic reminders of an era that existed before post-World War II residential development commoditized the built environment with the use of standards, catalogs and mass-produced components, and supplanted the trained residential architect with the bottom line-driven developer/builder. In Louisville, the houses remain as proud reminders that the city possesses an extraordinarily rich legacy of design by both local and outside residential and landscape architects, artists who drew on indigenous and regional influences and borrowed from a European past when creating their exceptional designs.

Homewood, the Mrs. Thomas Underwood Dudley house, ca. 1916. (Private Collection)

PRELIMINARY SKETCH FOR
BELKNAP BRIDGE
CITY OF LOUISVILLE PARK COMMISSION
SHEPLEY, RUTAN AND COOLIDGE, ARCHITECTS.

PART ONE

CHEROKEE PARK

Preliminary Sketch for Belknap Bridge, Cherokee Park. Shepley, Rutan and Coolidge, Architects, ca. 1900. (Courtesy Shepley Bulfinch Richardson and Abbott, Boston, MA)

NORTON HALL

THE ESTATE OF MR. & MRS. GEORGE W. NORTON, JR.

Shepley, Rutan & Coolidge, Architects - Olmsted Brothers, Landscape Architects

1899 - 1901

The first of Louisville's great country estates constructed after the completion of Cherokee Park was *Norton Hall*, designed by the prominent Boston firm of Shepley, Rutan & Coolidge for George W. Norton, Jr. An eclectic exercise in Colonial Revival architecture integrated into a calculated landscape, the project marked the first of many successful collaborations between the Olmsted Brothers and various nationally known architects that came to define the unusually rich nature of the city's park-side estates.

George Washington Norton, the father of George W. Norton, Jr., was a native of Russellville, Kentucky, who parlayed a nail manufacturing business into a series of enterprises encompassing banking and real estate (including the small town of Norton, Texas) to become, at his death, one of Louisville's – if not the state's – wealthiest citizens. Norton Sr. and his wife, Martha Stuart Henry, a descendant of Patrick Henry, were devout Baptists and played an instrumental role in subsidizing the Southern Baptist Theological Seminary's move from Greenville, South Carolina, to Louisville in 1877.

George W. Norton Jr. was born in 1865 in Russellville and graduated from Yale University in 1885. In 1889, he was named executor of his father's vast estate and, in 1897, married Margaret MacDonald Muldoon, the daughter of prominent monument maker Michael M. Muldoon.[1] One year later, he contacted the Olmsted Brothers to evaluate a site he had found for his new country residence, Norton Hall.[2]

The place Norton had in mind was a sixteen-acre parcel of land in John B. McFerran's proposed Alta Vista subdivision, which the Olmsted firm was then in the process of platting.[3] Norton was evidently the first to purchase a lot – No. 26 – as *Norton Hall* and McFerran's own house, together with their corresponding stables, were the only structures shown on the Omsted's final Design Map of 1900.[4] Because of the landscape architects' early involvement in Norton's acquisition, one can readily assume that the site was among the development's most desirable. One can also presume that the Boston-based firm, which had worked frequently with Shepley, Rutan & Coolidge, introduced the architects to Norton.[5]

Shepley, Rutan & Coolidge was the successor firm to famed Boston architect Henry Hobson Richardson who, upon his deathbed in 1886, called for the three partners to "carry on" his business.[6] The architects' early work included such well-known projects as the Art Institute of Chicago and the campus plan for Stanford University, as well as the design of numerous city and country houses, primarily in the East. After *Norton Hall*, the firm completed two additional projects in Louisville, the graceful Belknap Bridge in Cherokee Park and *Gardencourt*, the grand Georgian mansion for Norton's sisters.

Entrance elevation and forecourt, 1903. (Private Collection)

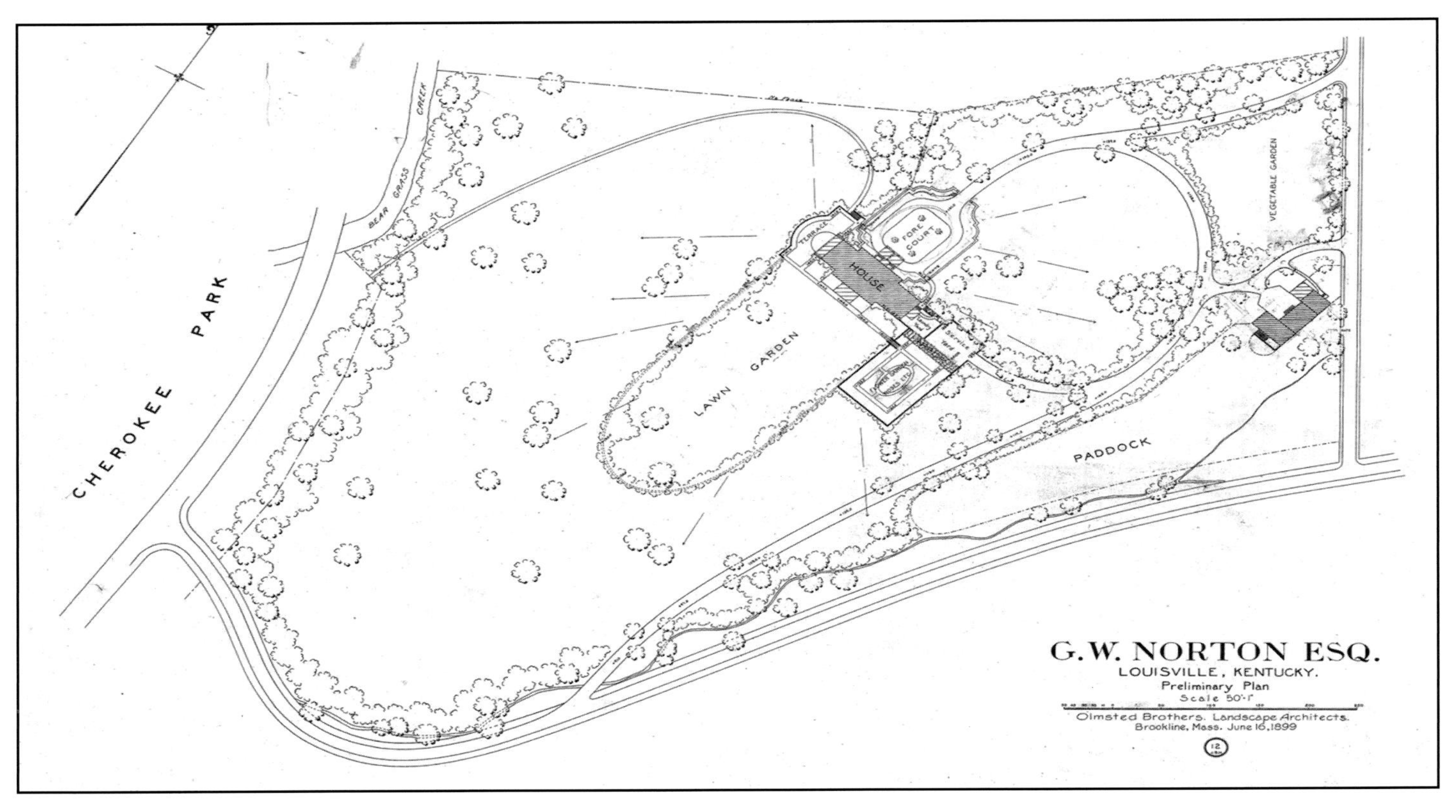

Site plan, 1899. (National Park Service, Frederick Law Olmsted National Historic Site)

Park elevation, 1943. (Private Collection)

Formal garden, 1943. (Private Collection)

Olmsted and Shepley worked hand-in-hand on the design of Norton's estate. The house was oriented along a north-south axis that followed a projecting narrow ridge; Olmsted would take advantage of this topography to create the tongue-like "Lawn Garden" that extended southward from the residence. The northern portion of the property was comparatively flat, which allowed for a broad driveway forecourt as well as for a nearby stable, paddock and vegetable garden. As with virtually all Olmsted's Louisville designs of this era, the dramatic experience was saved for the park side, where the sculpted natural terrain afforded spectacular views.

Staircase, 1943. (Private Collection)

The house as built reflected a distinctly New England type of Colonial Revival architecture, perhaps owing to the architects' Boston provenance. Constructed of brick in a Flemish bond pattern, it was essentially a Federal structure with several grand gestures that drew from the ascendant classicism of the Beaux-Arts. The tripartite massing of the house, flared stone jack arches above the windows, Ionic pilasters framing the center gable and white swagged picket fence of the forecourt were all reminiscent of late 18th century northeastern residential models. The impressive south and west porticos, columned entry carriage porch and star-patterned balustrade bore the unmistakable imprint of the Greco-Roman trends that had erupted after the enormously influential World's Columbian Exhibition of 1893 in Chicago.

The first floor plan of *Norton Hall* was organized around a pair of intersecting hallways that effectively divided the main block of the house into quadrants. The reception room, drawing room, dining room and

Dining room, 1903. (Private Collection)

Living room, 1903. (Private Collection)

Drawing room, 1903. (Private Collection)

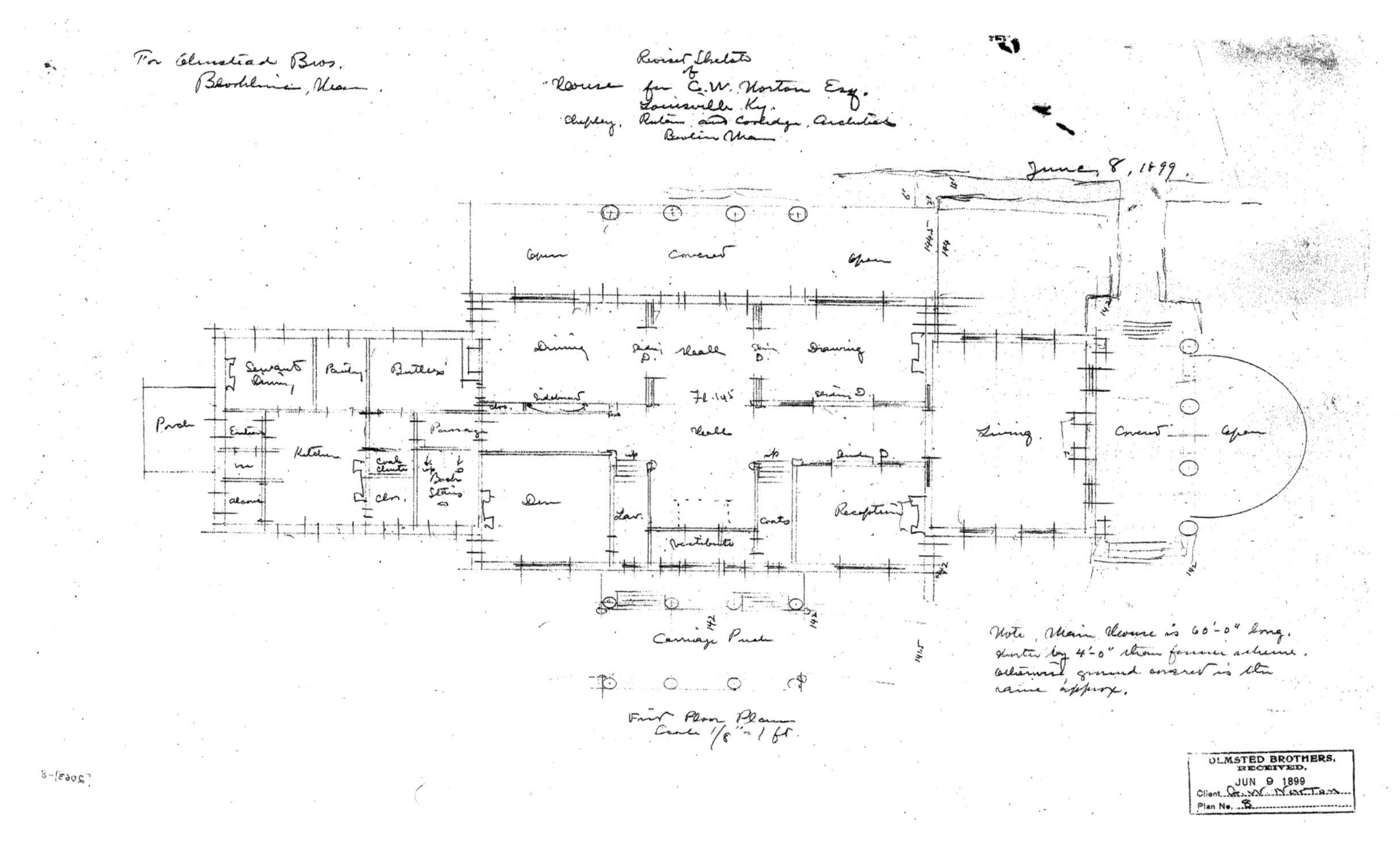

Sketch of first floor plan, Olmsted Brothers, 1899. (National Park Service, Frederick Law Olmsted National Historic Site)

den each occupied its own corner. At the west end of the transverse hall was the living room, which in turn opened to the grand west loggia; at the east end were the kitchen and related service functions. An impressive double stairway passed over the front door to the second floor and, at the rear, a great two story Ionic portico overlooked Olmsted's ridge-top lawn garden and Cherokee Park beyond.

The interiors were decorated and furnished using the services of several firms of note, including E.H. Brooks of Cleveland, William Baumgarten & Co. of New York and Earnest and Walter Thornton-Smith of London.[7] Of note was the French wallpaper in the second floor hall, which was made from Zuber blocks and offered an idyllic view of America, including scenes of Boston Harbor, West Point, Natural Bridge in Virginia and Niagara Falls.

When completed, the house and stable (which was subsequently rebuilt in brick) cost a total of $48,213.[8]

Olmsted, who continued to work on the estate until 1947, designed three distinct landscapes for *Norton Hall.* The first was an elevated lawn

Stables and carriage house, 1903. (Private Collection)

terrace that extended from the semi-circular west loggia and offered the most untamed vista down the hillside to Cherokee Park. The second was the lawn garden, a methodical grading of the property's prominent ridge into a gently sloping framed greensward that projected southward out toward the park. The third landscape Olmsted created was the formal rose garden, distinguished by an elliptical walkway inscribed within a sunken walled rectangle. While it was not unusual for Olmsted to include such a structured garden in its comprehensive designs, the almost incidental location abutting the residence's service court was highly unorthodox, representing a rare instance of treating such an element as a "found" rather than integrated place.

One of Olmsted's unique contributions to *Norton Hall* was the elegant set of gates the firm designed in 1926 for the Alta Vista Avenue entrance shared with neighboring *Gardencourt*. The result of numerous studies, the gates and accompanying wall enclosed both properties in an apparent effort for privacy and security following George Norton's death in 1924.

After her husband died, Margaret Norton continued to live at *Norton Hall* with various family members until she passed away in 1950. At her passing, the estate consisted of almost 22 acres, another six having been added to the original sixteen when the Nortons purchased Alta Vista lots 22 and 23 in 1902. Mrs. Norton bequeathed the property to the Southern Baptist Theological Seminary, which in turn used the house as a residence for the institution's president. In late 1959, having acquired the nearby Dudley house, *Homewood*, the Seminary entered into an agreement to sell *Norton Hall* to the Presbyterian Theological Seminary with ownership transferring in early 1961. Shortly thereafter, the house, gardens and outbuildings were demolished and a set of academic buildings constructed in a quadrangle around the former lawn garden, a chapel occupying the southern tip. With the exception of the entrance gates on Alta Vista, nothing survives of *Norton Hall* today.

Entrance elevation, 2011. (Blackburn)

ROSEHEIGHTS

THE ESTATE OF MR. & MRS. ALLEN R. HITE

D.X. Murphy & Brother, Architects - Olmsted Brothers, Landscape Architects

1901 - 1902

In July of 1901, Allen and Marcia Shallcross Warren Hite acquired lot 8 in John McFerran's Alta Vista subdivision, a 6.2-acre tract located directly across the street from McFerran's own residence.[1] The Hites joined George W. Norton and William Clancy as early purchasers in what was rapidly becoming one of Louisville's most exclusive enclaves.

Allen Rose Hite was born in Louisville in 1865, the son of William Chambers Hite and Mary Elizabeth Rose. Captain Hite, as William was known, built a fortune in the steamship business, and subsequently served as vice president of the Palace Pullman Car Company; Hite's mother had inherited "a considerable fortune" upon the death of her parents. Allen Hite earned his law degree from the University of Louisville, but never entered the legal profession, preferring instead to manage his own investment activities as well as the business affairs of his siblings.[2] Marcia Shallcross Hite was an artist of some note, and was instrumental in convincing her husband to bequeath almost $1 million to the fledgling University of Louisville art department. The Allen R. Hite Art Institute is the legacy of that bequest.[3]

The Hites hired D.X. Murphy & Brother of Louisville, architects of the famed twin spires at Churchill Downs, to design their new house and Olmsted Brothers as landscape architects for the grounds. Mr. Hite's instructions to Olmsted were quite specific:

"The site for the house and stable that we have selected is the one indicated on your Map made for Mr. McFerran, and [we have] agreed that this is by far the most desirable location for both buildings, as the front of the house will face the Park, and afford an unobstructed view between Mr. McFerran and Mr. Clancy's homes. ... When you are considering the laying out of the road ways, and walks around the house, and to the stable, I would like for you to divide the place up in such a way that I can have a kitchen garden, with a flower garden in front. This is to say, that when you enter the garden you pass through the flower garden, as Mrs. Hite and myself expect to make quite a feature out of this. ... If possible, leave a flat place for a Tennis Court. ... I also, wish a pasture lot for my horses and cows, and a poultry yard, where I can keep a few fancy chickens."[4]

The house Murphy designed was best described as a turn-of-the-century mixture of styles. The proportions of the two-story brick structure were almost Victorian in their verticality, and a neoclassical porch wrapped the ground floor in a manner reminiscent of the

Queen Anne and Shingle periods. Window headers on the lower level were decidedly Greek Revival, while those of the second floor came from the Georgian pattern book. A broad cornice of richly shadowed modillions supported a slate mansard roof atop which was a classical widow's walk, a combination which recalled both high Victorian and New England seaboard influences. Unusually large Georgian dormers punctuated the roof surface between surprisingly slender chimneys.

Detail of front door vestibule, 2011. (Blackburn)

Murphy's work on the house appears to have preceded Olmsted's work on the landscape, as correspondence from the latter to the architect focused on the exact positioning on the lot of the already-designed residence as well as the precise distance above grade for the porch and first floor:[5]

> We wish you would locate the house, and after placing yourself at the intended position of the front door of the reception room, twist the house, if necessary, to make the axial view strike the centre of the best view into the park."[6]

In their final design, Olmsted retained the general site configuration indicated on their conceptual layout for the Alta Vista subdivision, but added a formal terraced flower garden at the northwest side of the residence. A tennis court was platted but never constructed, supplanted by an expansive vegetable garden. In addition to a stable, the estate also included Mr. Hite's requested hen house.

Allen Hite died in 1941,[7] and Mrs. Hite passed away 5 years later. In 1947, Wilson W. and Anne D. Wyatt purchased the estate Hite had christened "Roseheights" (perhaps a play on his middle and last names) for the sum of $25,000. The house then entered what might be termed its golden age as Wyatt, who served successively as Mayor of Louisville, Lieutenant Governor of Kentucky and cabinet member to President Truman, entertained a veritable who's-who of Democratic politics and intellectuals, including Eleanor Roosevelt, Adlai Stevenson, Presidents John F. Kennedy and Jimmy Carter, and Carl Sandberg.[8] In their only major alteration to the property, the Wyatts replaced Olmsted's formal garden with a swimming pool. In the late 1960s, the northern reaches of the estate were truncated by the construction of Interstate 64, which passed between the neighboring Seelbach estate and *Roseheights*, taking in its path the adjacent mid-1860s James Speed/Maria Atherton mansion, *The Poplars*.

The Wyatt family lived at *Roseheights* until the mid-1980s. The house has since passed through several owners, and remains intact – albeit without its widow's walk - along with Hite's stable and the Wyatts' pool.

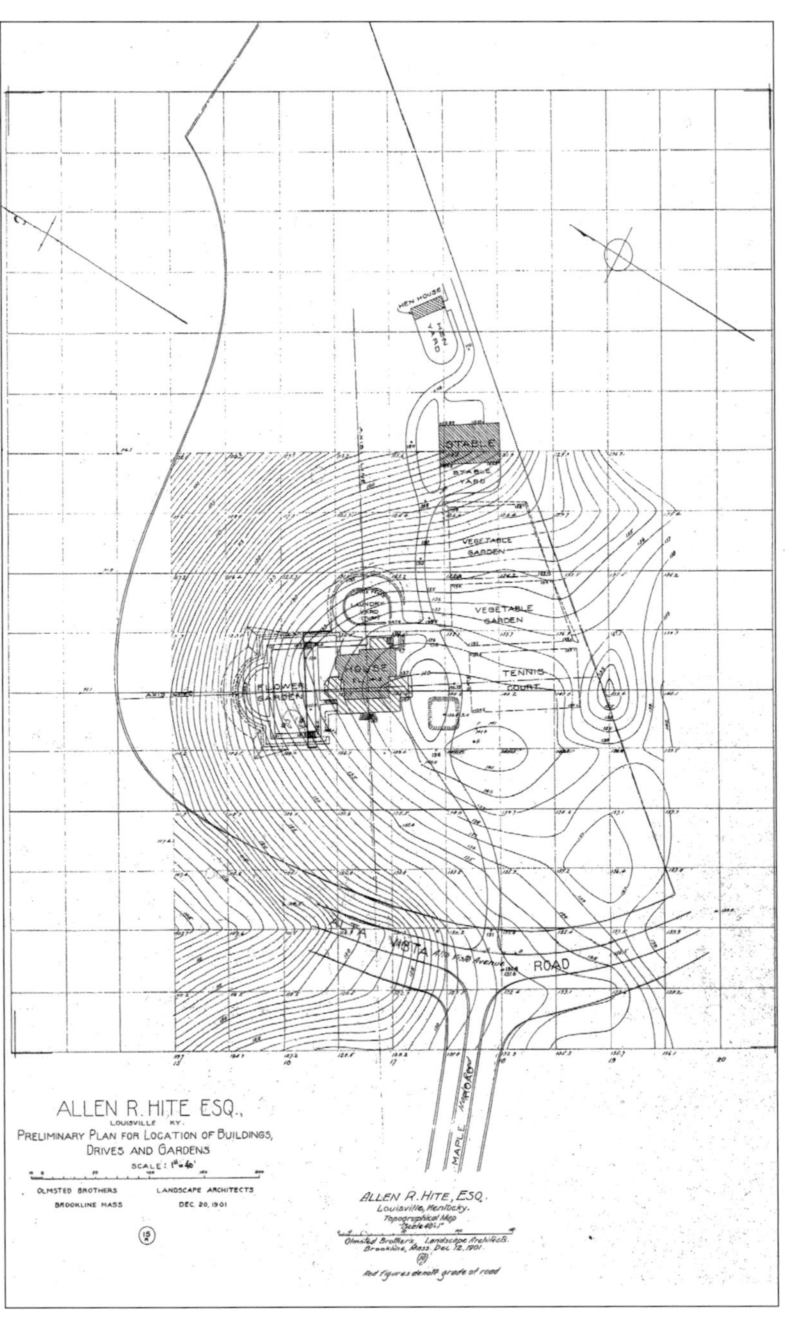

Preliminary site plan, Olmsted Brothers, 1901. (Private Collection)

Entrance elevation, ca. 1903. (*Artwork of Louisville*, Part 3, 1903)

Park elevation, 2010. (John Nation)

Colonial Hall

The Estate of Mrs. Ann E. Barret and Mr. Richard Montfort

D.X. Murphy & Brother, Architects

1901 - 1902

In the early summer of 1900, Richard and Henrie Montfort and their young son, Barret, boarded a ship for the British Isles, where the family planned to visit relatives in England and Ireland. Shortly after their arrival, Mrs. Montfort became ill with what was ultimately diagnosed as malarial fever. Despite the optimism of her doctors, 39-year-old Henrie died on September 20 at Castlebellingham, Ireland. Her devastated husband and son brought her body back to Kentucky aboard the Cunard liner *Campania*, and she was buried at Louisville's Cave Hill Cemetery.[1]

At the time of Henrie's death, the Montforts were living with her widowed mother, Ann Eliza Rodes Barret, and Ann's invalid sister, Amanda (Ammie) Barret in the Barret family mansion on Third Street in downtown Louisville. Undoubtedly prompted by the tragic loss of Henrie, Ann Barret and her son-in-law decided by 1901 to leave Third Street in favor the Barret family country house overlooking Cherokee Park. Before taking residence, however, Mrs. Barret sought to enlarge and improve the house so that it could be an appropriate full-time home. To accomplish this task, she engaged

Stair hall, 2011. (Blackburn)

the Louisville architectural firm, D.X. Murphy & Brother.

The existing Barret house was a relatively simple frame affair, likely on the order of a large Colonial farmhouse. While the precise extent of Murphy's work is uncertain, the architects clearly contributed three major changes to the residence. First and foremost, they appended a monumental Greek Revival portico, consisting of colossal fluted Ionic columns, to the park-side (entrance) elevation, which served to lend the house a grand and imposing stature. The second notable enhancement was the addition of a steep mansard roof, which raised the profile of the house while also allowing for a commodious third floor. The last significant alteration occurred within, where Murphy redesigned the entrance hall to allow for a gracious U-shaped stairway that rose up the north wall, crossed over a paneled rear door vestibule, and continued up the opposite side to the second floor. A large leaded glass Palladian window illuminated the stair landing.

Murphy's changes were not without precedent. At the same time the firm was remodeling the Barret house, it was overseeing construction of two additional sizeable residences. Across the park, *Roseheights* for Allen R. Hite was under way, and shared the architects' predilection for the Ionic order and mansard roof. In downtown Louisville, at the corner of Frederick Law Olmsted's Shawnee Park, Murphy was also completing a new mansion for tobacco manufacturer Basil Doerhoefer, the street façade of which was virtually identical to the park elevation of the Barret house. Furthermore, the design for the architects' new stairway for Mrs. Barret and Mr. Montfort was likely borrowed directly from William J. Dodd and Arthur Cobb's Gilmer S. Adams mansion of 1897. Located just steps away from the Barrets' Third Street residence, Murphy's clients would undoubtedly have visited the Adams house and admired the staircase that was the highlight of the mansion's interior.

Mrs. Barret and Montfort were clearly interested in completing the alterations to their new home as quickly as possible. The architects made this desire plain when awarding the renovation contract to the builder, Mr. A. N. Struck, on November 5, 1901:

Dear Sir:-

We are authorized by Mrs. A.E. Barret to accept your proposition in amount Twelve thousand Eight hundred and Ninety-nine ($12899.00) dollars for reconstructing residence and building stable and gardener's house, near Cherokee Park, in accordance with plans and specifications prepared for same.

This acceptance is based on the condition that residence, stable and gardeners house are compete in every particular and ready for occupancy on or before May 1, 1902.

Yours respectfully,
DX Murphy and Bro.[2]

After the inevitable change orders and delays, Mrs. Barret, Richard Montfort, Barret Montfort and Ammie Barret moved into their renovated mansion in 1903, selling the Third Street residence the following year.

Ann Eliza Rodes Barret was the daughter of Clifton Rodes, of Danville, Kentucky, and the granddaughter of William Owsley, governor of the state from 1844 to 1848. In 1855 she married John G. Barret, a graduate of the University of Louisville School of Law. In

Parlor, 2002. (stephenphotography.com)

time, John Barret became an important member of the city's business and philanthropic leadership, helping establish, along with William B. Belknap and others, the Citizens National Bank (of which he was ultimately president), as well as co-founding the Short Route Railway Transfer Company and the Bourbon Stock Yard Company, of which he was also president, and the American Printing House for the Blind. He passed away in 1890, leaving behind his wife, daughters Henrie and Amanda and a son, Clifton Rodes Barret.[3]

Richard Montfort was born in Ireland in 1854, a member of a distinguished family that traced its roots back to England and, before that, France. The son of a medical doctor, Montfort received his education at the University of Dublin, graduating with a degree in civil engineering in 1876, the same year he immigrated to Louisville. He initially worked for the Louisville Bridge & Iron Company before, in 1880, accepting a position as bridge engineer for the L&N Railroad. He would become chief engineer for the railroad in 1887, then consulting engineer in 1905, a position he held until he retired in 1930. He and Henrie Barret married, most likely in the mid-1880s, and produced one child, John Barret Montfort, who was born in 1890.[4]

Ann Barret passed away in 1915, and her daughter and son-in-law continued to live in the house until their own deaths in 1931. At some point in the 1920s, Montfort sold the western half of the estate to developers, who created an exclusive residential enclave consisting of Casselberry and Sulgrave Roads. By 1951, the property that had consisted of 30 acres in 1913 had been reduced to three acres; the stone gateposts on Barret Hill Road would subsequently be incorporated into architect Stratton Hammon's house for Abe Cohen in 1955.[5] The house had been altered, too, a service ell removed from the rear and a monumental portico identical to that on the park side added to create a new main entrance. In 1977, the estate – known for years as "Colonial Hall"[6] – was purchased by famed art collectors and philanthropists Wendell and Dorothy (Dottie) Cherry, he the co-founder of health insurance giant Humana, Inc. The Cherrys renovated and expanded the house and constructed a series of terraced and formal gardens. *Colonial Hall*, together with D.X. Murphy's gardener's cottage (now enlarged), remain meticulously maintained and in excellent condition.

Entrance elevation, ca. 1910. (Private Collection)

AYRSTEAD

THE ESTATE OF COLONEL & MRS. ANDREW COWAN

Wilson Eyre, Jr., Architect - Olmsted Brothers, Landscape Architects

1904 - 1905

Andrew Cowan was born in 1841 in Ayrshire, Scotland. In 1848, his family emigrated to the United States, settling in Auburn, New York. Young Andrew attended Madison (now Colgate) University until 1861, when he entered the Civil War, enlisting in the Union army. Over the course of the war, Cowan distinguished himself in numerous campaigns, including Gettysburg and Appomattox, and completed his service having earned the rank of Lt. Colonel.

Following the war, Col. Cowan moved first to Indianapolis and then, in 1866, to Louisville, where he entered the leather, railway and mill products business, a lucrative enterprise that capitalized on the extraordinary rebuilding activity associated with Reconstruction. In time, Andrew Cowan and Company became known as a leading manufacturer of leather and leather belting, jobbers of railway and mill supplies, and makers of saddlery hardware and automobile supplies. Col. Cowan was named president of the National Oak Leather Company, manufacturers of oak-tanned harness and belting leather; vice president of the Louisville Leather Company, makers of sole leather; and director of both the National Bank of Commerce and the Columbia Trust Company. He was married to Anna L. Gilbert of Utica, New York, with whom he had one son, Gilbert S. Cowan.

Perhaps Cowan's greatest achievement, at least later in life, was his pivotal participation in the civic effort to create Louisville's famous necklace of parks and parkways. It was he who first publicly argued for the healthful and economic merits of a system of parks, and it was he who led the acquisition of lands for Cherokee and Shawnee Parks. Elected as one of the city's first park commissioners, he was reputedly responsible for bringing Frederick Law Olmsted to Louisville in 1891.[1] It should come as no surprise, then, that he was in a position to secure a choice site overlooking Cherokee Park on which to build his country estate, *Ayrstead*.[†]

To design his new house, Col. Cowan selected Wilson Eyre, Jr., the Philadelphian who was considered one of the nation's leading domestic architects. While Eyre was adept at working in a multitude of revival styles, his preferred idiom was the Tudor Revival and related Arts and Crafts, which he found to embody "the epitome of home."[2] For someone of Cowan's immigrant background, the romantic architecture of Great Britain made sense: it represented ancestral and historical pedigree, and was "redolent of the literate, landed aristocracy of England, of Shakespeare and the old universities."[3] In short, the Tudor style conveyed immediate social, intellectual and economic legitimacy. How Eyre and Cowan came

† While *Ayrstead* appears to be the name Col. Cowan gave his estate, it is also known as *Alloway House*, a name derived from the Scottish village in Ayrshire where the famed poet Robert Burns was born. Whether Cowan used both names – perhaps dubbing the house "Alloway House" and the overall property "Ayrstead" – is unknown.

Park elevation, ca. 1910. (Private collection)

to meet can only be a matter of conjecture, but it is quite reasonable to believe that the introduction was made through the Olmsted firm.

The site Col. Cowan selected for *Ayrstead* was located at the far eastern terminus of Cherokee Park, and consisted of almost 50 acres of land, the highest point of which afforded a magnificent view northwestward through the park up the valley formed by Beargrass Creek. It was on this summit that Eyre, working in concert with the Olmsted Brothers, positioned the new house.

In massing, the house consisted primarily of two intersecting rectangular volumes represented by the main house and the service wing ell, the latter which extended forward from the east end of the entry façade and, when partially balanced by the screened veranda on the west, formed a sort of forecourt for the residence. In appearance, the front of the house was symmetrically composed in concept and

Living room, 1930. (*Herald-Post* Collection, University of Louisville Archives and Records Center, Louisville, KY and Records Center, Louisville, KY)

asymmetrically disposed in detail. A pair of intersecting gables formed a projecting central bay, yet the broad porte cochère indicated a shift of axis. The fenestration reflected Eyre's love of the picturesque Arts and Crafts style, as each window location tended to respond to the needs of interior function rather than the formal requisites of exterior composition, thereby serving as the antithesis of the order called for in facades of fashionable Colonial Revival houses. The house was finished in coarse stucco; only the gabled extensions of the structure, including the screened veranda and the service wing, were treated in half-timbering, a diagonal cross board to the east of the stair hall windows an apparent Eyre signature. The roof, indicative of Eyre's penchant for rich textures, was likely of ruddy shake shingles or coarse slate. Of note was the adze dressing (the deeply hand-hewn surface) of the half timbers and porte cochère arches that gave credence to Eyre's statement that "there is no use in giving a man modern tools and telling him to do a bad job … give him primitive tools, and tell him to do the best job he can." [4]

The rear or park side of the house was more loosely composed than the front: the elevation's triple gable with projecting sleeping porch, arched dining porch opening (another typical Eyre element) and asymmetrically disposed protruding dining room window supported the observation that:

> A Wilson Eyre house always had a sense of movement and asymmetrical massing that was meant to surprise and charm. His houses fit their sites in the way that many Edwardian houses do – they were to be appreciated as great overgrown cottages in an old garden, full of rustic texture and color, mellow with the patina of age.[5]

In 1895, Eyre had taken a brief "sketching trip to England," returning to the United States with a heightened awareness of the art of integrating house and garden.[6] From this point on, he was careful to design his houses together with their formal landscapes to ensure a cohesive unit. While such an integrated garden was never constructed for Ayrstead, the organization of the rear terrace and stairs would seem

Dining room, ca. 1910. (Private Collection)

LIbrary, 2010. (Blackburn)

to indicate that Eyre had allowed for such a possibility. A formal garden was eventually built on the estate, but at a fair distance from the house, and as a consequence was unlikely a design of Eyre's creation.

The plan of the house was comparatively informal, with each of the primary rooms – living room, library, dining room and dining porch – afforded a view to the park. The second floor enjoyed a similar arrangement, with the inclusion of a screened sleeping porch that sheltered the open veranda below. In finish, Eyre's interiors all but abandoned the antique English precedents of the exterior. With the exception of the broad stair hall with its heavy beamed ceiling, paneled

Detail, library ceiling, 2010. (Blackburn)

wainscoting and solid Arts and Crafts stairway that wound to the second floor past a tall stained glass window, the rooms both up and downstairs were detailed with Colonial and Georgian mantelpieces, door casings and crown moldings (the living room even veered toward the Beaux-Arts with its elaborate bracketed crown molding, which was quite possibly added later by the Reynolds family). The only other exception was the library, stylistically a more late Victorian-era interpretation of the Tudor Revival that nevertheless had very little to do with the romantic, somewhat rambling and less refined architecture of the house as a whole.

At the time of Col. Cowan's death in 1919, *Ayrstead* consisted of the main house; a large three-story stable and garage structure to the immediate east of the forecourt; a house with tennis court for his son, Gilbert Cowan; and additional caretakers' quarters. The property extended across Beargrass Creek to abut *Rostrevor*, the estate of James Ross Todd.

Not long after Cowan passed away his widow sold the property to Richard S. Reynolds, the co-founder of Reynolds Metals Company and cousin of R.J. Reynolds of tobacco fame. In 1921, Reynolds engaged

Bedroom, ca. 1910. (Private Collection)

Carriage house, 2011. (Blackburn)

the Olmsted Brothers to survey the property with the intent of selling land to the city for an expansion of the park system. Shortly thereafter, and in exchange for $12,862, he completed the sale of approximately 4 acres along Beargrass Creek, thus separating *Ayrstead* from *Rostrevor* and joining Cherokee Park with the new Seneca Park.[7]

In 1951 the Reynolds family sold *Ayrstead* to developers who divided the property into 35 lots, leaving the Andrew Cowan house on approximately an acre. The Gilbert Cowan house no longer exists, having been destroyed by fire,[8] but the stables, garages and other structures survive, modified into single-family residences. Having passed through several hands, Col. Cowan's British legacy remains intact with few alterations, enduring as Wilson Eyre's only commission in Louisville.

Park elevation, 2010. (Blackburn)

GARDENCOURT

THE ESTATE OF THE NORTON SISTERS:
MATTIE NORTON, LUCIE NORTON AND MINNIE NORTON CALDWELL

Shepley, Rutan & Coolidge, Architects - Olmsted Brothers, Landscape Architects

1905 - 1908

Of the fifteen or so estates that surrounded Cherokee Park, only a few were designed as a conscious integration of architecture and landscape. The first to approach but not fully realize this Renaissance ideal was *Norton Hall*, designed in 1905 by the celebrated Boston firms, Shepley, Rutan & Coolidge, architects, and Olmsted Brothers, landscape architects. Five years later, with the completion of their exquisitely conceived *Gardencourt* for Norton's sisters, the two firms created what was arguably Louisville's first true marriage of house and garden in the most formal idiom.

In 1898, the same year that George W. Norton, Jr., was corresponding with Olmsted about *Norton Hall*, his two unmarried sisters, Martha A. ("Mattie") Norton and Lucie Underwood Norton, along with their widowed sibling, Minnie Norton Caldwell, contacted the landscape architects about their own project.[1] By 1902, having acquired Lots 25 and 27, comprising almost fifteen acres, in John B. McFerran's Alta Vista subdivision, *Gardencourt* was well under way, with Shepley, Rutan & Coolidge on board as architects for the residence and stables.[2] Upon its completion six years later, it would be one of the most costly of the Cherokee Park estates.[†]

House from the approach drive, ca. 1910. (Olmsted Brothers photo at the Louisville Presbyterian Theological Seminary)

† *Gardencourt* was an expensive undertaking. The original estimate for the house was $90,000; when the final bill was tallied in July of 1908, the total was a significantly higher $127,172, excluding the $22,925 cost of the stables. This combined total of $150,097 was in eyebrow-raising contrast to George W. Norton's expenditure of $48,213 on Norton Hall but a few years earlier. *(From the ledger books held in the company archives of Shepley Bulfinch Richardson and Abbott, 2 Seaport Lane, Boston, Massachusetts.)*

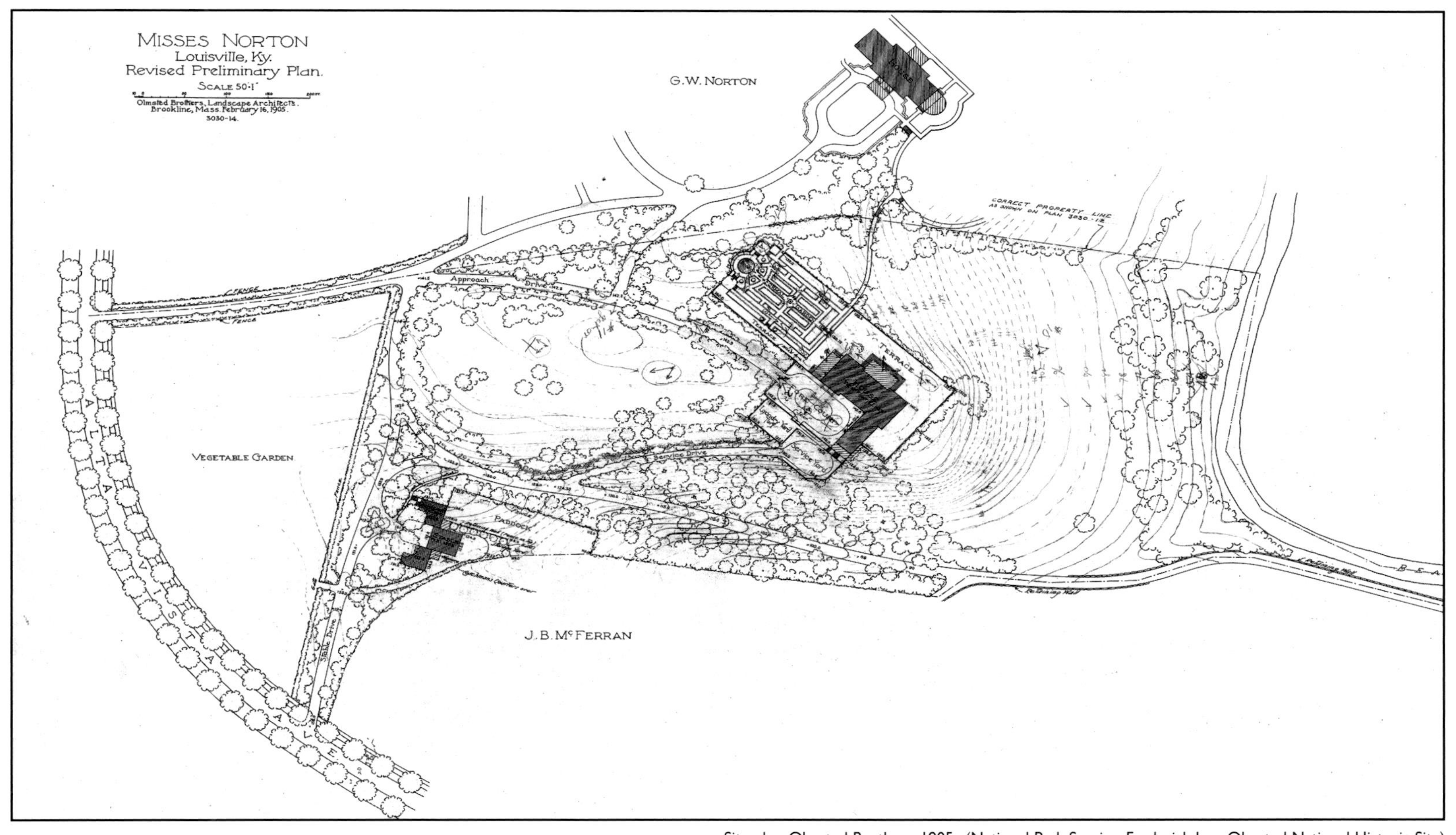

Site plan, Olmsted Brothers, 1905. (National Park Service, Frederick Law Olmsted National Historic Site)

The firms gave careful consideration to the site for the house, ultimately orienting it southward, as they did *Norton Hall*, and similarly placing it at the edge of a ridge from which the land rolled down toward the Park. As with their previous collaboration, the approach to the house was through a pastoral flatland past an expansive vegetable garden; however, at *Gardencourt* one arrived through grand iron gates into a walled forecourt, in contrast to the far less imposing picket-fenced front drive at *Norton Hall*. Once through these gates, the axis shifted ninety degrees and the visitor entered the house beneath a columned porte cochère. The mansion itself reposed on a substantial stone plinth, which, in a manner similar to *Norton Hall*, held an elevated lawn terrace that in turn afforded spectacular views over Cherokee Park. To the east extended a partially enclosed formal garden that likewise enjoyed open views to the south from its raised podium. Unlike Olmsted's later work at neighboring *Edgecombe* or Bryant Fleming's plans for Samuel Henning's *Cold Spring*, the house and formal garden were separated distinctly from the tamed natural hillock, almost in a manner of a theater box overlooking the stage from an aloof distance.

The residence was an exercise in high Georgian architecture enhanced with a number of Beaux-Arts flourishes. The design could very well have been modeled after New York architect Charles A. Platt's

Carriage house, 2009. (Blackburn)

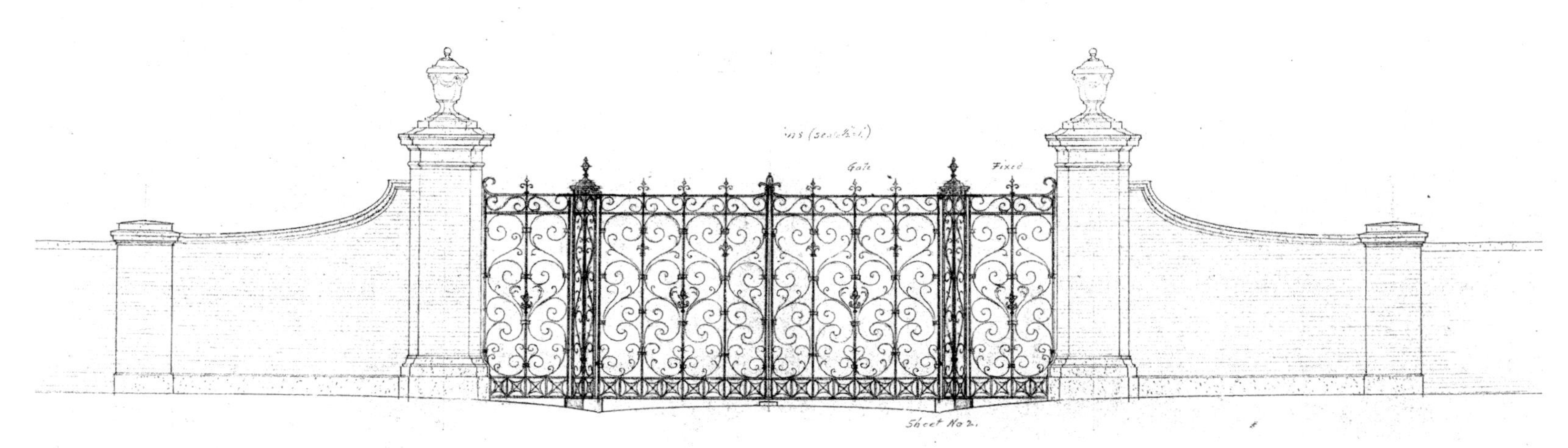

Final design, entry gates at Alta Vista Road, Olmsted Brothers, 1926. (National Park Service, Frederick Law Omsted National Historic Site)

House from the formal garden, ca. 1910. (Olmsted Brothers photo at the Louisville Presbyterian Theological Seminary)

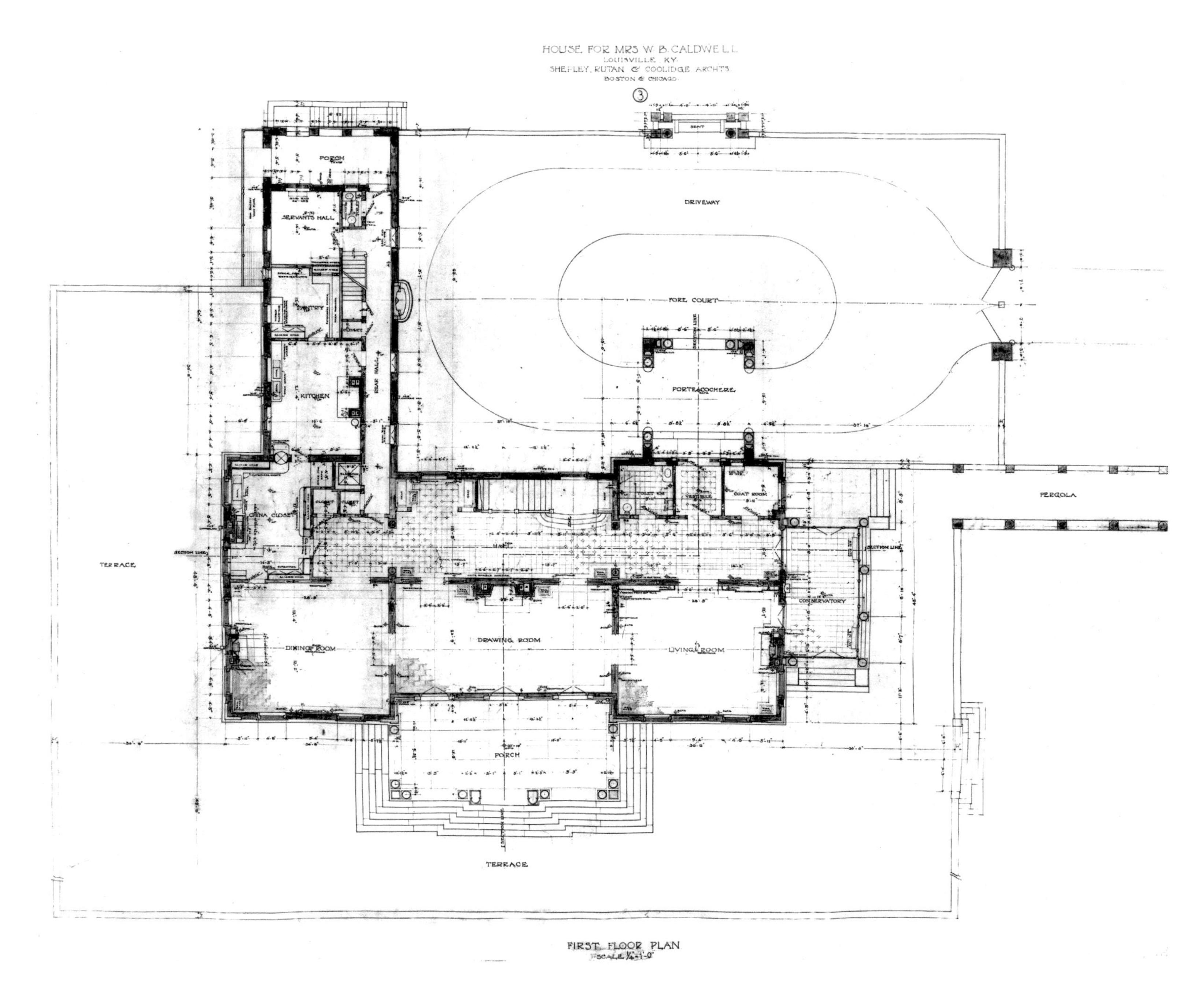

First floor plan, Shepley, Rutan & Coolidge, architects, ca. 1905. (National Park Service, Frederick Law Olmsted National Historic Site)

The hall, 2011. (Blackburn)

Maxwell Court in Rockville, Connecticut, which was featured extensively in the October 1903 issue of *House & Garden* magazine – a date when *Gardencourt* was in its early conceptual stages.[3] The south facades of the two houses were quite similar – particularly the great central portico with broken segmental pediment – as was the general disposition of entry court, elevated plinth and lateral walled garden. At *Gardencourt*, the house was executed in a deep red brick with limestone quoins, string course and porches; on the park elevation, recessed panels above the first floor windows and stone cartouches between those on the second floor combined with dark shutters (now sadly missing) to provide relief and pattern to the otherwise planar surfaces. Richly molded Tuscan Doric columns, classical balustrades and French-inspired dormers provided a robust sculptural quality to the entire composition. Symmetry ruled the day, including the east and west facades of the main house, where chimneys, windows, dormers and even downspouts were carefully organized into perfectly balanced arrangements.

Drawing room, with a view into the dining room, 1947. (© *The Courier-Journal*, courtesy University of Louisville Archives and Records Center, Louisville, Ky)

Within, the house was quite straightforward in plan and eclectic in finish. The primary first floor salons – conservatory, living room, drawing room and dining room – were all appended from one side of a great hall that extended along an east-west axis. The interiors were less stylistically pure than the predominantly Georgian exterior. The great hall was finished in a ponderous, dark and somewhat Jacobean manner, with oak wall paneling, beams and somewhat curious Doric columns setting the stage for a particularly Elizabethan stairway. Ornate gilded torchères, standing sentry on a black and white marble floor, illuminated the space, which terminated oddly at its west end in a rather prominent

Drawing room fireplace, 2011. (Blackburn)

Living room, 1947. (©*The Courier-Journal*, courtesy University of Louisville Archives and Records Center, Louisville, KY)

door to the butler's pantry. The living room also served as a library, and was distinguished by dark oak wainscoting, enclosed bookcases and a heavy plaster strapwork ceiling complete with pendants. The drawing room, which evidently also served as a ballroom, was the most feminine of the salons, and was graced with gilded mirrors and sconces, painted box moldings and, again, an Elizabethan strapwork plaster ceiling. Tall French doors opened to the lawn terrace. Beyond the drawing room was the dining room, the most Georgian in appearance with raised paneled walls, a heavy cornice and unadorned ceiling.

The second floor contained three primary bedroom suites – one for each of the Norton sisters – that were aligned with the primary salons below, as well as two smaller guest bedrooms and servants' quarters. Unlike the rooms on the first floor, the bedrooms were outfitted in a simpler Colonial Revival style, with painted moldings and fireplace mantles that were drawn more from early Kentucky precedents than the opulence of the Beaux-Arts.

The landscape at *Gardencourt* was conceived in four parts: the pastureland through which the driveway passed, the walled entry forecourt, the raised lawn terrace overlooking the groomed slope to the Park and the partially enclosed formal garden that extended eastward from the conservatory. Each of these landscape elements was integral to the house and together formed a cohesive design composition. The sylvan approach to the residence introduced the estate as a noble paradigm of the classic English country house: the manor set in the pastoral meadow. The forecourt, terrace and formal garden were created in the Italian Renaissance manner as outdoor rooms radiating from the residence, each architectural in form and linked directly to the house itself by walls of varying heights. The formal garden was planned as a partially sunken extension of the lawn terrace and

View from rose garden toward formal garden pavilions, ca. 1933.
(University of Louisville Archives and Records Center, Louisville, KY)

Rose garden, ca. 1933. (University of Louisville Archives and Records Center, Louisville, KY)

was bounded on the north by a long pergola and terminated at the east by two classical pavilions that framed a shallow reflecting pool. The views to the park reestablished the connection to the natural landscape that was first made at the approach to the house.

The Norton sisters continued their relationship with Olmsted Brothers for years following completion of the house. The last large commissions were executed in 1926-7, when the long wall and elegant gates (shared with *Norton Hall*) were constructed and a new terraced rose garden was added to the formal garden. The rose garden took the shape of a keyhole, and extended to the southwest using the southern-most garden pavilion as its axial point of origin. At the same time, Olmsted revised the layout of the formal garden, simplifying the original design.

Minnie Caldwell passed away in 1911, Lucie Norton in 1937. When Mattie Norton died in 1946, her executors donated *Gardencourt* to the University of Louisville for use by the School of Music.[4] The School made few alterations to the house and grounds, the most notable being the 1962 insertion of an auditorium into the forecourt.[†] Forty years later, in 1987, the University sold the estate at auction to a private developer who in turn sold it to the Louisville Presbyterian Theological Seminary. Following a multi-million dollar renovation, the property was combined with the existing neighboring Seminary facility (formerly the site of *Norton Hall*) to form a 67-acre campus. Today, the mansion, gardens and stables – all meticulously restored – remain in excellent condition, with the grand salons of the house serving as meeting and reception venues and the upper floors housing classrooms and faculty and institutional offices.[5]

† The Emily Davison Recital Hall, as the auditorium was named, was designed by William Wright Crandell and occupies about one third of the former forecourt. *(Joanne Weeter, Research Coordinator, Registration Form, National Register of Historic Places, "Gardencourt Historic District (Louisville: Louisville Landmarks Commission, August 12, 1988)).*

Entrance elevation, 2011. (Blackburn)

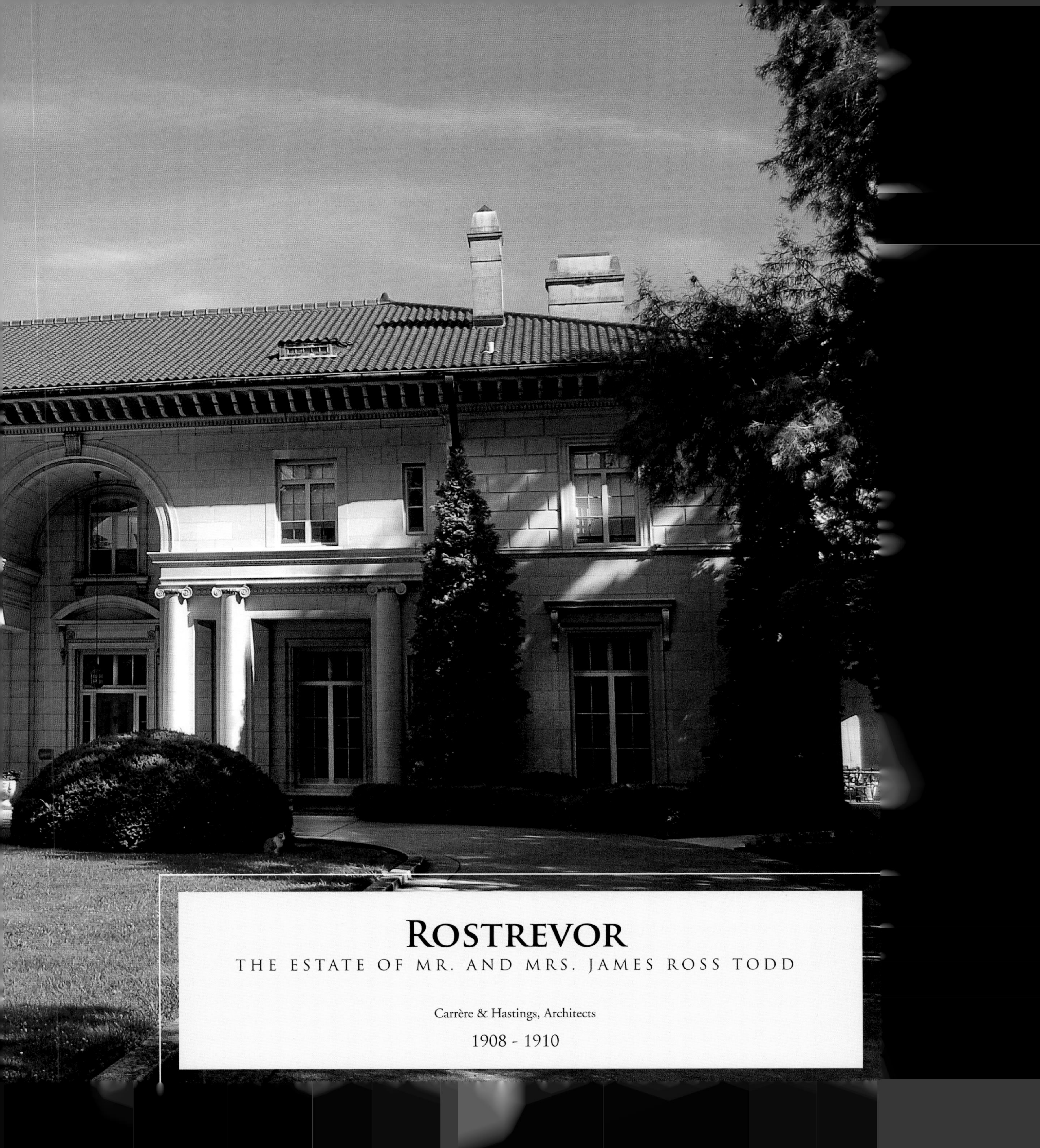

ROSTREVOR

THE ESTATE OF MR. AND MRS. JAMES ROSS TODD

Carrère & Hastings, Architects

1908 - 1910

In 1907, prominent banker James Ross Todd and his wife, Margaret Menefee Todd, purchased Lots 17 and 18 of John B. McFerran's Alta Vista subdivision overlooking Cherokee Park and embarked on building one of Louisville's grandest country houses, *Rostrevor*.[1]

To design his new estate, Todd engaged the distinguished New York architectural firm of Carrère & Hastings, whose roster of notable clients included Henry Flagler, Daniel Guggenheim, George Vanderbilt, Yale University and the New York Public Library. Educated at Paris' École des Beaux-Arts and apprenticed with New York's McKim, Mead & White, John M. Carrère and Thomas Hastings were exceptionally accomplished architects whose work reflected the disciplined rigor of classical training.[2] For Todd they would create an elegant, highly controlled and academically correct Renaissance Italian villa that would cost an estimated $70-80,000. [3]

Todd's 16-acre site was located at the eastern end of Cherokee park and abutted Col. Andrew Cowan's *Ayrsted* and the park to the south and what later became Alexander Witty's *Casa Mia* to the east. The house was located at the highest point of the estate along an east-west ridge, down from which three sides of the property rolled toward Beargrass Creek. The placement was logical and afforded not only exceptional views but the availability of cooling cross breezes necessary in a time before air conditioning.

The model for *Rostrevor*[†] was clearly Thomas Hastings' own house, *Bagatelle*, which the architect was simultaneously designing for a site in Old Westbury on Long Island, New York.[4] *Bagatelle* was virtually the same as *Rostrevor* in overall composition, plan and elevation; it differed primarily in scale (*Bagatelle* was a bit smaller), material (*Bagetelle* was built of brick, *Rostrevor* of stone) and formality. Both houses enjoyed similarly luxurious interiors. Of amusing note was Hastings' description of his thoughts about *Bagatelle* (and by extension, its cousin, *Rostrevor*), which revealed an almost Marie Antoinette-like Hameau vision of a gentleman's retreat:

> It is like an old Italian farmhouse, if such a thing exists. We did not want too much architecture; wanted to keep the house very simple...so that I can do things during the years to come. Wanted to be able to grow vines; have no repairs – house all masonry and no woodwork exposed outdoors except the window sashes. That was the program.[5]

Hastings' unconvincing pastoral depiction aside, needless to say neither estate remotely resembled an old Italian farmhouse.

In site plan *Rostrevor*, like *Bagatelle*, was arranged on a north-south axis, with the house at the south end and the garage/stable building at the north creating, together with the service ell of the house to the east, a semi-enclosed entry forecourt. The approach to *Rostrevor* was from a long drive that rose from the Park below, followed the south slope of the terrain upward and then turned back on itself at the top of the hill to head west directly into the forecourt. Just before the forecourt, smaller drives branched off to the service yard of the house to the south and the garage/stable complex to the north; a service road led to Alta Vista Avenue.

The house itself took the form of a Renaissance Italian villa as

† While the exact source of the name "Rostrevor" has not been documented, the name was undoubtedly borrowed from Rostrevor, a village in the Newry District Council area of County Down, Northern Ireland. Todd's father was born in Country Down and quite possibly Rostrevor.

House from the southwest, ca. 1910. (Private Collection)

Approach to the house, ca. 1910. The stables are on the right. (Private Collection)

Frederic Morgan–designed entrance gates, ca. 1950. (Private Collection)

interpreted by a student of the Beaux-Arts; that is, a romanticized hybrid of villa, palazzo and contemporary functionality. Imposing in its austere formality and symmetry, *Rostrevor* was distinguished by a monumental Palladian entry portico that extended two floors to the cornice line of the red tiled roof. Engaged Ionic columns were employed not only to contribute to the grandeur of the façade, but also to draw the viewer's eye away from the structural piers and beams that supported the second floor. A thin string course stretched from either side of the central entablature of the portico, theoretically demarcating the two primary levels of the house but also allowing for a change of wall surface from smooth limestone below to a dressed rusticated finish above. The symmetry of the front elevation was broken at the east by an elegant, slender window that revealed the location of the stair. The design of this window, complete with balustraded balcony, bracketed frame and segmented pediment, was undoubtedly drawn from the pages of Palladio's *Quattro Libri* or Serlio's *Architettura*, two classical pattern sources familiar to any successful architect at the turn of the century. The south façade continued the Renaissance paradigm – although more closely following urban palazzo models – while the service wing bore a much stronger resemblance to the 16th century country villa Hastings referred to above. Surprisingly, given its prominence opposite the forecourt from the entrance to the house, the stable and garage building was the most simple and farm-like structure on the property.

The plan of *Rostrevor* mirrored that of *Bagatelle* very closely. At *Rostrevor*, as at *Bagatelle*, one entered beneath the vaulted loggia into a long transverse entrance hall from which the public rooms extended. The hall at *Rostrevor* was finished in polished marble floors and plaster walls incised to resemble cut stone. Elegant fluted Tuscan Doric pilasters modulated the wall surface and supported a richly sculpted frieze and cornice of classical modillions. Three pairs of French doors, each elaborately framed in carved casings surmounted by richly detailed pedimented overdoors, led to the three main public salons. The center room, opposite the front door, was the reception room, a decidedly feminine salon decorated in the Louis XVI manner with delicate boiserie framing the mirror above the fireplace. To the west of the reception room was the living room, which also served as the house's library and had as its focal point an exquisite English Adams-style marble mantelpiece. To

Entrance hall, ca. 1910. (Private Collection)

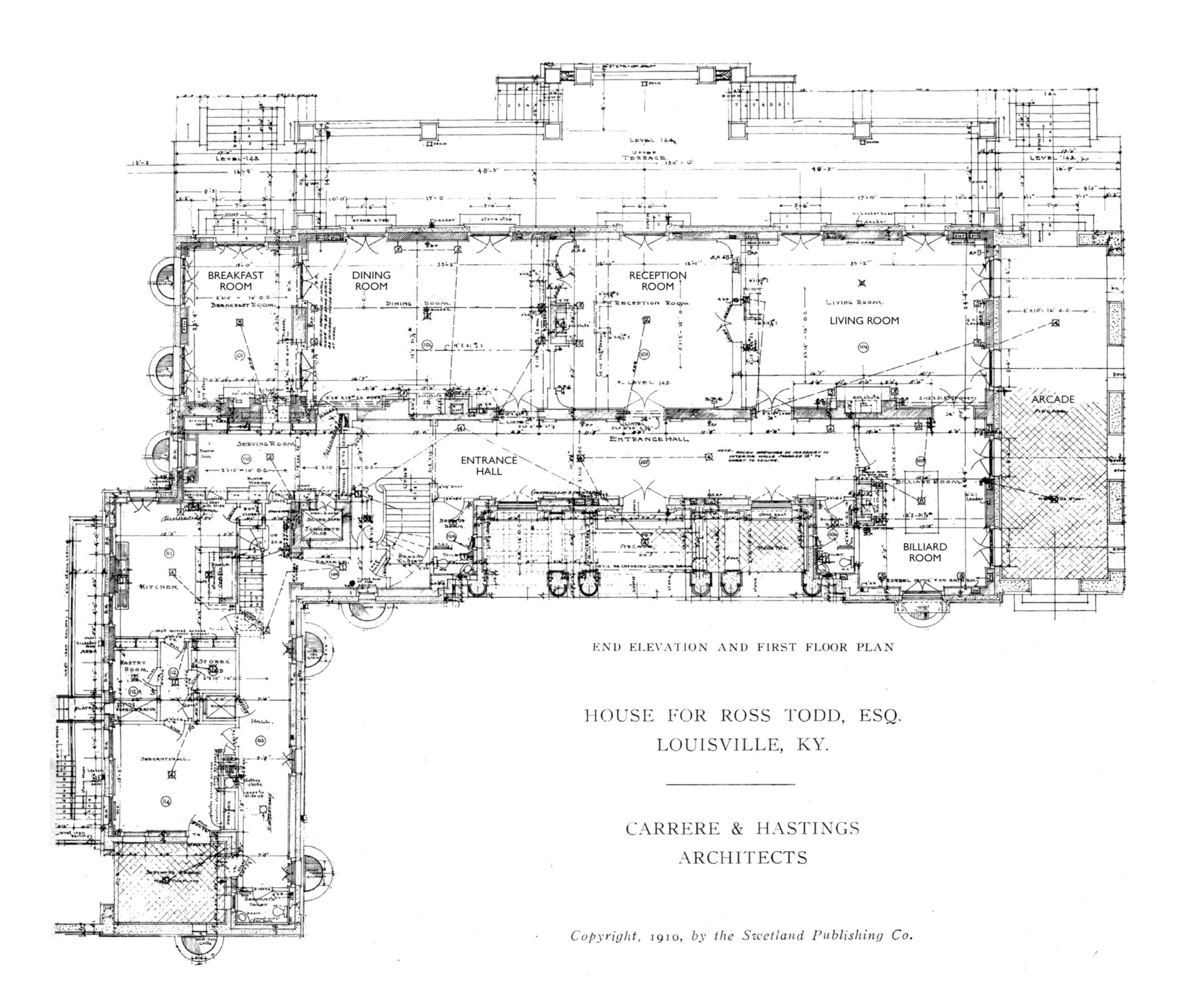

First floor plan (*The American Architect,* 1910)

Living room, ca. 1910. (Private Collection)

Billiard room, ca. 1910. (Private Collection)

Breakfast room, ca. 1910. (Private Collection)

the east of the reception room was the dining room, which also featured a striking English mantelpiece at the fireplace. Beyond the dining room was the breakfast room, a stylish space finished in the manner of palm courts that were popular in the grand residences, hotels and ocean liners of the time.† At the opposite, or west, end of the entrance hall was the oak paneled billiard room that, together with the adjacent living room, opened to an arcaded open-air arcade, or loggia. An elevated terrace stretched across the entire south side of the house.

The second floor contained a series of bedroom suites aligned along a hallway that mirrored the entrance hall below. The southeast bedroom was known as the "Presidents' Room," having hosted Warren G. Harding

Dining room, ca. 1910. (Private Collection)

† In his book, *The Tasteful Interlude: American Interiors through the Camera's Eye, 1860-1917* (New York: Praeger Publishers, 1975), page 251, historian William Seale observed in describing *Rostrevor*'s Breakfast Room that: "For most Americans who could afford what they wanted, there were two desirable styles of interior decoration: colonial or one of the French Louis styles. This barren breakfast room..., the work of a New York interior decorator secured for the Todds by the architects Carrère and Hastings...contains the most expensive kind of Louis Seize furniture then on the market. It came almost certainly from John Helmsky's shop in New York, a very small and restricted manufactory producing reproductions of many kinds. Sturdy and only slightly inaccurate, it was considered highly appropriate for this large room, with its marble floors, marbleized and trellised walls, rich damask window hangings and sheer Austrian shades, and oriental carpet...The whole room was created on the drawing boards of the decorator and Carrère and Hastings."

Staircase, ca. 1950. (Private Collection)

and Herbert C. Hoover as overnight guests.[6] The service ell contained, on the first floor, the kitchen, pantry and related functions; servants' rooms were located on the second floor. Upon completion, *Rostrevor* was published in the July 20, 1910 issue of *The American Architect*; it has since been featured in numerous newspaper articles, magazines and books.[7]

The landscaping at *Rostrevor* was relatively simple in contrast to other great estates of the day. Olmsted Brothers did execute some work for Todd in 1911 shortly after the house was completed, but that was apparently limited to specifying certain plantings for the forecourt and driveways.[8] Todd offered an explanation for this surprising absence of a formal landscape when he told a reporter in

Reception room, in use as a living room, ca. 1950. (Private Collection)

1908 that it was his "intention to do as little with the ground as possible, as he desires to leave all the natural beauty unmarred by formal and artificial walks and gardens."[9] In any event, it wasn't until years later that a formal garden was created off the west terrace, taking the form of a small, partially walled reflecting pool framed within an allée of clipped magnolia trees. The garden adopted as its eastern focal point sculptor Paul Manship's "Cycle of Life," an armillary sphere purchased by Todd in 1924 and installed atop the stairs of the west terrace.[†]

James Ross Todd was born in 1869, the son of James Todd, who emigrated to Louisville from Newry, County Down, Ireland in

Arcade, ca. 1910. (Private Collection)

† In 1964, Mr. and Mrs. Jouett Ross Todd donated "Cycle of Life" to Louisville's J. B. Speed Art Museum where it remains on prominent display.

Magnolia allée and reflecting pool, ca. 1950. Note the "Cycle of Life" armillary sphere by artist Paul Manship, atop the terrace steps, now located at Louisville's Speed Museum. (Private Collection)

1838, and the former Mary Louise McGavock of Nashville. He was educated at Princeton University, studying under Woodrow Wilson. Later in life he rose to become a major force in Louisville's financial community, serving as director of the Fidelity and Columbia Trust Company, Citizens Union National Bank and the Union Joint Stock Land Bank.[10] In 1902, he built one of Louisville's first skyscrapers, the ten-story Todd Building designed by local architects Clarke & Loomis (Loomis would serve as the supervising architect for the construction of *Rostrevor*).[11] Following his death in 1952, *Rostrevor* passed to Todd's son, Jouett Ross Todd.

Rostrevor underwent very few alterations over the years. Room uses were changed - the dining room became a living room, the breakfast room the dining room, the living room a ballroom and the billiard room a library – and certain modernizations were undertaken, including the removal of the palm court finishes in the breakfast room and the pediments above the primary doors in the entrance hall. At some point mid-century, architect Frederic Morgan was hired to create a pair of elaborate gateposts at the eastern approach to the forecourt, each topped with a stylized fox said to come from the Todd family coat of arms.

In 1960, Jouett Todd began the first of three efforts to subdivide the property. That year, he proposed replacing the house with a blend of apartments and single-family houses. The zoning board rejected his request. In 1963 he again asked for a change in zoning to allow for a high-rise apartment building, "strips of smaller apartments" and fifteen single-family houses. Again, his request was rejected. Finally, in January 1964 he entered into an agreement to sell *Rostrevor* to a group of investors who planned to save the house and subdivide the remaining land into 29 single family lots of a half-acre each.[12] The estate was subsequently thus subdivided, the west garden and the stable/carriage house demolished to allow for a roadway and Morgan's fox gates relocated closer to the forecourt. The house, along with the service ell, remains intact and in excellent condition as a private residence.

Fox atop an entrance gatepost, 2011. (Blackburn)

Entrance elevation, 2010. (Blackburn)

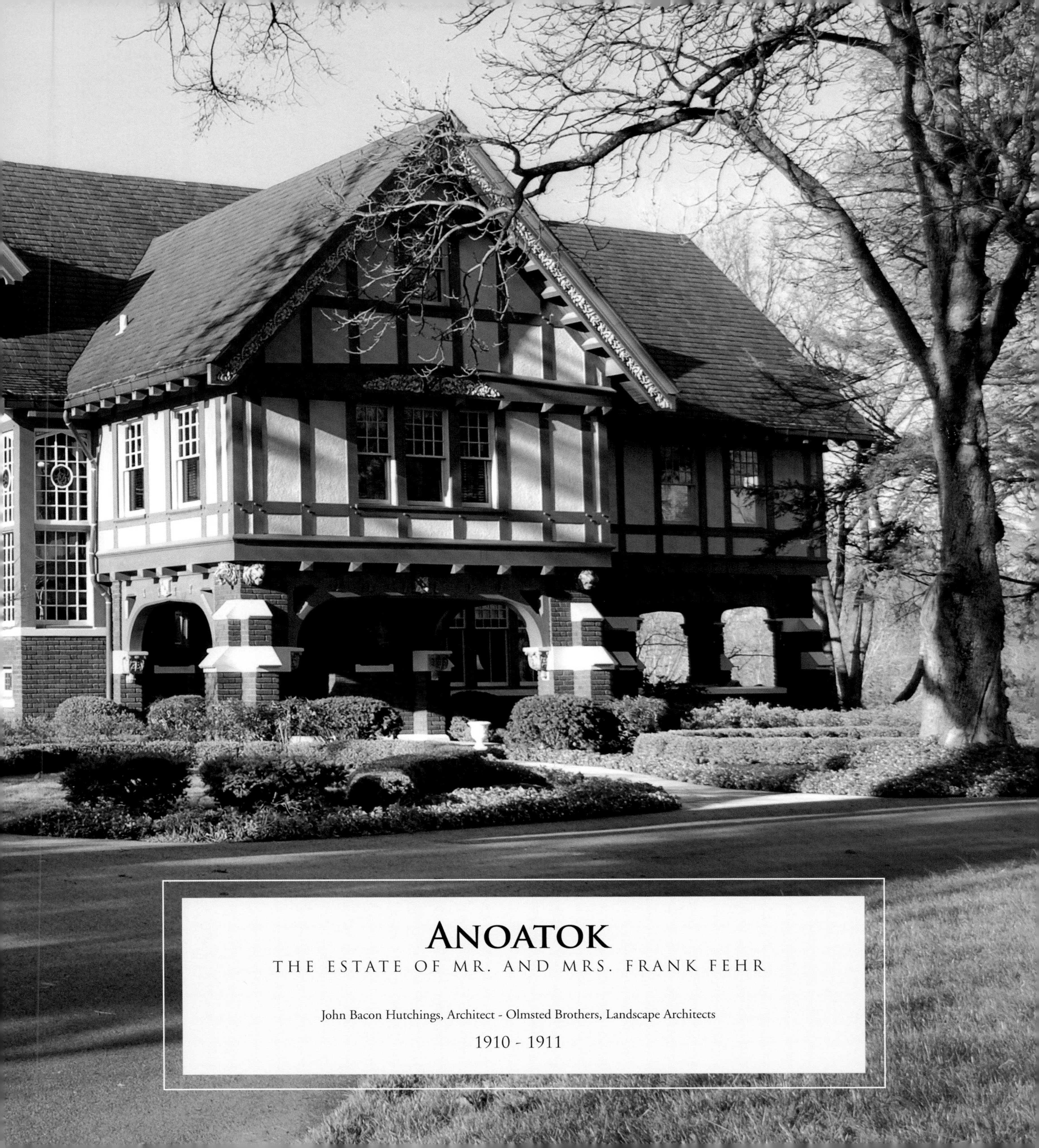
ANOATOK
THE ESTATE OF MR. AND MRS. FRANK FEHR
John Bacon Hutchings, Architect - Olmsted Brothers, Landscape Architects
1910 - 1911

In early 1905, brewer Frank Fehr acquired almost thirteen acres of land along Cherokee Drive, most likely from the Bullitt family.[1] It would appear that his plans for the property were consistent with those of other prominent Louisvillians; that is, to build a sizable country house for his family. Indeed, Fehr promptly engaged the Olmsted Brothers to plan not one but a pair of houses for the site.[2] Mirror images of each other, separated by a common motorcourt and joined by a colonnade, the scheme was soon abandoned in favor of a single structure.

By late 1909, Fehr's plans had changed. Sometime before October of that year, he had acquired the neighboring Zehnder property and hired Olmsted to plat a subdivision to be called "Braeview," joining John B. McFerran as a developer of residential enclaves surrounding Cherokee Park.[3] The entire tract as conceived in 1910 was to contain about 36 building sites – including four carved out of the north side of Fehr's original Bullitt tract – ranging from large, estate-sized lots to much smaller, suburban-scaled parcels. At the same time, Fehr engaged prominent Louisville architect John Bacon Hutchings to design a substantial residence on approximately the same site proposed for the twin houses four years earlier. The name Fehr chose for his new estate was "Anoatok," Eskimo for "the wind-loved spot."[4]

Hutchings and Olmsted worked together from the start. While the architect crafted the house and related structures, the landscape architect positioned the mansion on a knoll overlooking the park, designed the residence's terrace and service court walls and sculpted a graceful oval driveway.[5] By the end of 1911, the Olmsted firm had completed most of its work on the house and turned its attention to expanding Fehr's Braeview subdivision following their client's acquisition of lots 5 and 6 of McFerran's Alta Vista development. As enlarged, Braeview consisted of 43 building sites on 43 acres.

Frank Fehr was named after his father, a native of Germany who immigrated to the United States in 1862. Within fourteen years, the senior Fehr had moved to Louisville and established what became known as the Frank Fehr Brewing Company, a large beer-making enterprise that lasted until 1964. At the time of his father's death in 1891, the younger Fehr was vice president of the firm; in 1909, he assumed the role of president.[6] Fehr's wife was the former Pauline Hecht of Chicago, whom he married in about 1896.

The house Hutchings designed for Fehr was executed in the Tudor Revival style, perhaps owing to the style's approximation of early German half-timbered architecture. Stout in massing, the structure had a brick first floor with stone-accented buttresses, above which was a half-timbered second story that extended slightly beyond the walls below in true Elizabethan fashion. Carved lion heads and griffons served as decorative brackets, and sturdy beams with exposed pegs implied a medieval post and girt construction. Heraldic crests appeared above most major openings and roped copper downspouts accented the walls, as they similarly did at Hutchings' nearby *Edgecombe* for Senator F. M. Sackett. Elaborately carved vergeboards enlivened the front and rear gables, which in turn crowned the ponderous center bays that projected from the entry and park-side façades. A steeply pitched roof punctuated by prominent dormers contributed to the imposing silhouette of the house.

Olmsted sited the mansion in typical fashion at the edge of a ridge overlooking Cherokee Park. As was the firm's wont with its other park-side houses, the Fehr residence reposed on a high lawn terrace enclosed with low walls of native limestone capped with a brick balustrade similar to that Hutchings used in his contemporaneous house for Charles Ballard in Glenview. Service and laundry yards adjoined the house to the east; a carriage house would be built later.

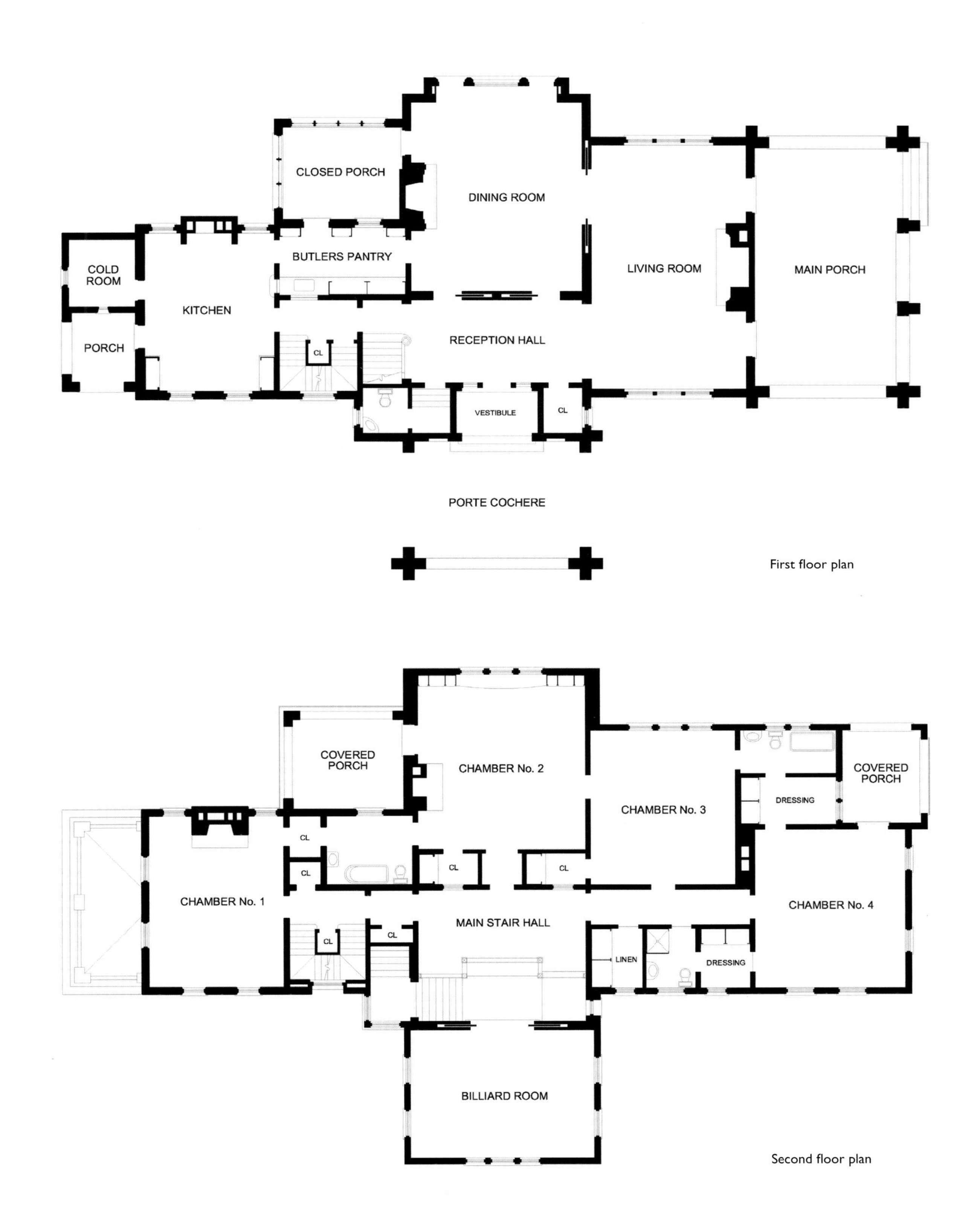

First floor plan

Second floor plan

Reception hall, 2011. (Blackburn)

Within, Hutchings likely planned a Tudor interior consistent with the architecture of the exterior. However, whatever finishes Hutchings had in mind were not realized, as the Fehrs hired the William F. Behrens Co. of Cincinnati to design and furnish the mansion's principle rooms. Behrens was a firm of national repute, whose notable work included the interiors of Louisville's grand Seelbach Hotel and the State Reception Room of the new Kentucky State Capitol in Frankfort.[7] In a departure from Hutchings' presumably more anglo-teutonic ideas, the Behrens Co. chose to work in an Italian Renaissance-inspired idiom.

One entered beneath a broad porte cochère through iron gates to the reception hall, a room distinguished by its rich oak woodwork with carved egg-and dart-banding but made especially notable by its murals. The wall paintings, executed in 1913, depicted a 15th century pastoral of two maidens and a youth in the woods near a castle. Opening from the hall at the west

Living room, 2011. (Blackburn)

was the living room or library, the focal point of which was a massive carved limestone fireplace mantel and dressed limestone chimneybreast, both executed in a manner favored by the then-popular Beaux-Arts movement in architecture and design. Behrens did away with Hutchings' suggested beamed ceiling in favor of a paneled plaster surface that implied the framed frescoes of Venetian palaces. A wide crown molding of English oak panels trimmed in a richly carved band of fruits of the forest encircled the room. Behrens designed glass-fronted oak bookcases for the walls, and specified the elaborate gilded torchères that still remain on either side of the fireplace.

Adjoining the living room to the east and reception hall to the south was the dining room, sumptuously paneled in mahogany trimmed in carved bands of leaves, flowers, acorns, pine cones and the like. Above the wall paneling were murals featuring garlands and urns of colorful flowers. A plaster ribbon of fruits of the forest framed the ceiling. Behrens installed ornate silver plated wall sconces and a tiered crystal chandelier, all of which remain in place.

Dining room, 2009. (Blackburn & Stegeman)

Interior elevation of living room, William F. Behrens Co., ca. 1911. (Private Collection)

The stairway to the second floor was one of Hutchings' most distinctive elements, and while Behrens changed the architect's proposed iron railing to an elaborate system of carved oak balusters based on Renaissance models popularized by the Beaux-Arts, the unusual tall corner windows remained as originally planned. A secondary landing found the visitor between a built-in seat on one side and the billiard room on the other. Located above the porte cochère, the billiard room was paneled in oak with traditional linenfold panels. Rather than applying the customary Tudor plaster strapwork, Behrens detailed the ceiling in a decidedly classical grid of coffers with centered rosettes. In addition to the billiard room, the second floor contained four bedrooms and two sleeping porches. Servants were housed on the third floor.

Shortly after its completion, *Anoatok* was featured as a photographic centerspread in the June 26, 1915 *Official Program of Crescent Hill Big Day*. Entitled "One of Louisville's Most Beautiful Homes – the Residence of Mr. and Mrs. Frank Fehr on Cherokee Drive in Beautiful Braeview," the article featured the Fehrs' living, dining and billiard rooms, along with photos of the west living porch and south façade.[8]

Frank Fehr passed away in 1962, his wife, Pauline, having predeceased him by 22 years. During his lifetime, Fehr continued to sell building sites in Braeview, including lot 21, a carve-out from the original Bullitt property, and lot 25, which became the location of Louisville architect Stratton Hammon's much-imitated Goldberg house of 1948.[9] The four eastern-most lots (Alta Vista lots 5 and 6) were sold shortly after Fehr acquired them to Mrs. Thomas Dudley for the construction of her elaborate new mansion, *Homewood*. Following his death, the land surrounding Fehr's Tudor country house was subdivided into eight additional parcels. The mansion and carriage house, along with many of Behrens' original furnishings, remain in excellent condition in private hands.

Park elevation, 2011. (Blackburn)

Garage, 2009. (Blackburn)

Detail of living room fireplace, 2011. (Blackburn)

Entrance elevation, undated. (University of Louisville Archives and Records Center, Louisville, KY)

EDGECOMBE

THE ESTATE OF SENATOR AND MRS. FREDERIC MOSELEY SACKETT, JR.

John Bacon Hutchings, Architect - Olmsted Brothers, Landscape Architects

1910 - 1913

Edgecombe, the country estate of Frederic M. Sackett, Jr., and his wife, Olive Speed Sackett, was perhaps Louisville's most outstanding example of the serendipitous harmonization of house and landscape that results from a shared vision of architect, landscape architect and client. The synthesis of architecture and garden, of inside and out, and of vistas both expansive and carefully controlled was unparalleled amongst the city's great country houses.

Frederic Moseley Sackett, Jr., was born in Providence, Rhode Island, in 1868, the son of a wealthy wools manufacturer. In 1890 he received his bachelors degree from Brown University and, in 1893, his law degree from Harvard. Immediately following graduation from Harvard, Sackett embarked on his legal career, first practicing in Columbus, Ohio, then moving to Cincinnati in 1897 and finally to Louisville in 1898. Not long after coming to Kentucky, Sackett married Olive Speed, a member of one of the state's most prominent families and great niece of Joshua Speed (see *Cold Spring*) and sister of William Shallcross Speed (see *Kanawha*).

Sackett continued to practice law until 1907, when his pursuit of various business interests led him to become president of the Louisville Gas Co. and the Louisville Lighting Co., president and director of Brinly Hardy Co., vice president of the Louisville Cement Co. and the North Jellico Coal Co., three-time president of the Louisville Board of Trade and director of the Louisville branch of the Federal Reserve Bank of St. Louis.

In 1924 Sackett was elected to the United States Senate, a position he held until 1930 when President Herbert Hoover appointed him Ambassador to Germany.[1] The Sacketts were active in Louisville, New York and Washington society and, while in the Senate, maintained two fully staffed residences, *Edgecombe* and a townhouse in Washington, D.C.[2]

At some point prior to October 1910, the Sacketts purchased Lot 28 of John B. McFerran's Alta Vista subdivision, a parcel of about 5.6 acres.[3] By October, Sackett had engaged Olmsted Brothers to begin planning his estate. Presumably at that time he also hired architect John Bacon Hutchings to begin designing the new residence and outbuildings.[4] The site for *Edgecombe* was remarkably similar to that of George W. Norton's *Norton Hall* nearby. Located on the park side of Alta Vista Avenue, the land was flat close to the street and then fell gently southward to Beargrass Creek, thus allowing for a moderated entry experience to the house and a breathtaking vista from the rear – a view that was further

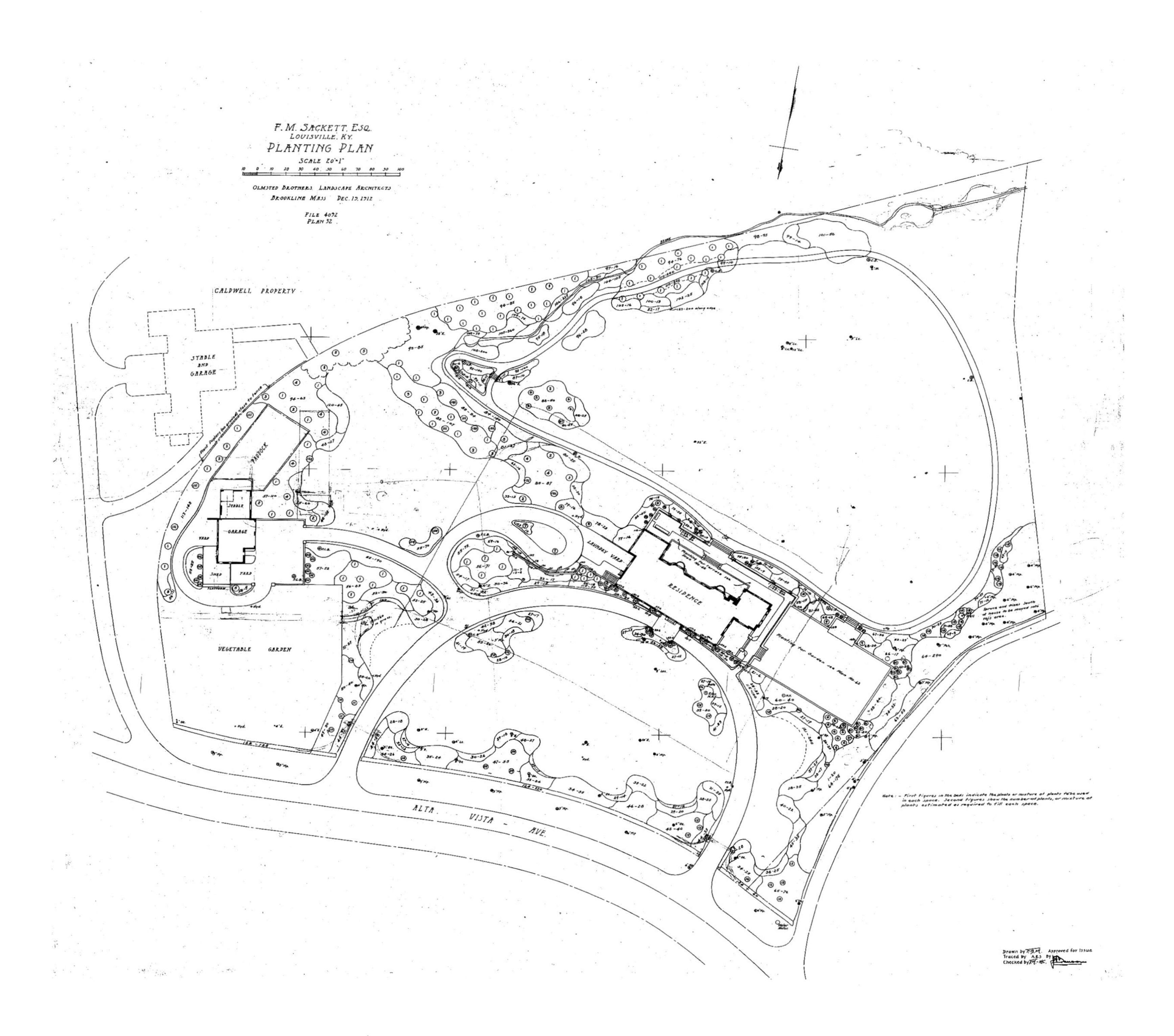

Site and planting plan, 1912. (Olmsted Brothers, Private Collection)

enhanced when Sackett acquired another two-and-a-half acres to the south in 1916. Olmsted sited the house on a north-south axis at the edge of the ridge, tucking the garage and stable group to the east abutting like structures at neighboring *Gardencourt.*

The house as designed by John Bacon Hutchings was a superb example of the English Arts and Crafts style that was then popular in certain parts of the Midwest and East Coast. The choice was particularly fortuitous in that the informal, cottage-like nature of the type was distinctly conducive to an integration of the house with the landscape. An architecture of multiple gables, green flat tile roof, warm stucco walls, roped copper downspouts, broad eaves and heavy timber beams and brackets reflected an abstraction of nature itself.

The street elevation was at first glance somewhat conventional, flat and almost banal. A broad arched porte cochère marked the entry; the second floor was distinguished by the slight projection of three gabled bays. Stout wood support beams extended beneath each projection and devolved into a sort of stringcourse that wrapped the balance of the façade. Only at the front door itself, framed in a deeply carved wide molding and balanced on either side by similarly cased windows with robust flower boxes, was there a hint of the creativity that lay beyond, for it was at the rear where the house achieved its exceptional noteworthiness.

The south, or park-side, façade of *Edgecombe* was a carefully considered work of architecture. Clearly influenced by domestic masters

Park elevation, ca. 1916. (Filson Historical Society)

Park elevation looking west, ca. 1916. (Private Collection)

of the style, such as Harrie T. Lindeberg, Howard VanDoren Shaw and Wilson Eyre – or their English progenitors, Hutchings' composition of a tri-gabled central bay flanked by two projecting, seemingly shed-roofed wings enjoyed a plasticity of form and play of light and shadow that, when combined with the structure's richness of colors, materials and textures, made this house unique among the country houses of Louisville. The contrast with the front elevation could not have been greater. A massive chimney anchored the façade, protruding from the wall rather than simply rising from the roof; twin dormers with shed roofs seemed to blend into the main roof unlike their street-side counterparts with prominent hip roofs; slender groupings of casement windows with transoms lent a delicacy that the double-hung windows facing the street

Front entrance, ca. 1916. (Filson Historical Society)

lacked; and small buttresses supported the walls of the two projecting wings, a feature absent at the front of the house. The composition of the central bay was indeed exceptional. The roped downspouts, bookended on either side by small square windows, emphasized the tripartite nature of the façade, while the second floor appeared almost to float above the bay windows that flanked the broad recess of the door to the house, itself accentuated by the flower box beneath the window above.

Within, the house was an eclectic combination of styles. The stair hall extended from front to back, affording the visitor a carefully crafted view over the park. In finish, it was a blend of Colonial Revival moldings and a more rustic iron stair rail. To the west of the

Stair hall, ca. 1916. (Filson Historical Society)

Dining room, undated. (Filson Historical Society)

hall was the expansive library, an asymmetrically shaped room with a heavily beamed ceiling, high paneled wainscoting and bookcases and wallpaper that evoked the organic designs of William Morris. To the west of the library, overlooking the estate's walled garden, was the living porch, a sun-drenched Tudor affair whose beamed ceiling rose into the gabled attic space. An inglenook led to the rear terrace.

To the east of the hall, overlooking the park, was the dining room, the most formal space in the house and an amalgam of Colonial Revival egg-and-dart moldings, reeded pilasters and columned mantelpiece; Tudor archways; and simplified recessed paneled wainscoting. Beyond the dining room, occupying the opposite projecting wing from the living porch, was the breakfast room. The Italian tile floor, elliptical archways with Colonial keystones and Tudor vaulted ceiling with plaster strapwork made this room a particularly lively space.

Library, ca. 1916. (Filson Historical Society)

Study, ca. 1916. (Filson Historical Society)

The second floor, reached by a stairway that bore a noticeable resemblance to that designed by Hutchings for Mrs. Morris Belknap at *The Midlands*, contained, at the center and overlooking the park, Sackett's private office, as well as additional bedroom suites, a sleeping porch and servants' quarters.

The Olmsted firm's work on the property began in 1910 and continued until 1938.[5] Perhaps their most dramatic achievement was the ever-broadening progression of spaces and vistas that began within the privacy of the house, moved out to the uppermost, intimate terrace, expanded further at the second, lower terrace and then opened fully at the level of the great lawn. The view southward was carefully composed and the slope purposely graded to control the viewer's experience, just as the firm did at *Norton Hall*.

At the west end of the house was a walled formal garden, enclosed on three sides and open to the park through a stoutly columned pergola. An artistic blend of clipped boxwoods, manicured turf and English wildflowers, this remarkably private space featured a reflecting pool as well as a fountain embedded in the north wall and, when combined with the south lawn, demonstrated the Olmsted firm's dexterity at designing environments both seemingly natural and unquestionably man-made.

Olmsted's exceptional work at *Edgecombe* would not have been possible without the cooperation of both the client and the architect. Orientation, siting and architectural compatibility were essential to the development of a cohesive whole. In virtually no other Louisville estate would such an integration be achieved. Justifiably appreciated, the house and gardens were published on at least three separate occasions.[6]

Frederic Sackett died unexpectedly in 1941. Seven years later, Olive Sackett passed away, leaving an estate valued at almost $3.4 million.[7] As the couple had no children, *Edgecombe* was sold to another family. By the late 1950s, the estate had become difficult to manage and the owners sold the property to a developer who also acquired the neighboring McFerran estate. Shortly thereafter, both houses, their outbuildings and gardens included, were razed, replaced by new houses on new streets.

Formal garden, ca. 1916. (Filson Historical Society)

Entrance elevation, 2011. (Blackburn)

COLD SPRING

THE ESTATE OF MR. AND MRS. SAMUEL C. HENNING

(ORIGINALLY BUILT FOR JOSHUA AND FANNY SPEED, 1867)

Townsend & Fleming, Renovation and Landscape Architects

1911 - 1912

Joshua Fry Speed was born in 1814 at *Farmington*, the Speed family seat on the outskirts of Louisville. In 1834, he moved to Springfield, Illinois, where, in 1837, he met a young lawyer – also from Kentucky – named Abraham Lincoln. Lincoln, newly arrived to the city, needed a place to stay and Speed, who operated a small store, offered to share his room above the shop. Thus began a strong and close friendship that would last until the fateful night at Ford's Theatre in 1865.

In 1841, Speed returned to Louisville to establish himself as a farmer. That same year, Lincoln visited the family for several weeks at *Farmington.*[1] A year later, Speed married Fanny Henning and, in 1851, formed a real estate firm with his brother-in-law, James W. Henning. During the Civil War, Speed supported the Union cause and carried confidential information between Kentucky and Washington, D.C. Although he reputedly declined Lincoln's offer of a cabinet position, his brother James Speed accepted and served as Lincoln's Attorney General.

In 1867, Joshua and Fanny Speed built a new home on an expanse of land that abutted Beargrass Creek on the edge of what would later become Cherokee Park.[2] T-shaped in plan, it was a tall three-story structure with long shuttered windows, simple gabled roofs and a broad wrought iron porch extending across the west façade. Most likely, the property included a large working farm. The Speeds named it "Cold Spring."

Joshua Speed lived until 1882, and Fanny until 1902; the couple had no children. At some point following Fanny's death, *Cold Spring* passed to her nephew, Samuel Cowan Henning, and his wife, Julia Duke Henning.

Samuel Henning was a broker whose business operated under the name of S.C. Henning & Co.[3] Julia Duke Blackburn Henning was the daughter of Basil Wilson Duke, a Confederate lieutenant, attorney and historian who helped found Louisville's Filson Historical Society. In 1911, the same year Samuel reincorporated his firm as Henning, Chambers & Co.,[4] the Hennings engaged Townsend & Fleming of Buffalo, New York, to radically transform *Cold Spring* into a sumptuous Italian villa. The scheme, while only partially realized, was certainly one of the most ambitious of the time and stands today as one of but two remaining examples in Louisville of Bryant Fleming's integrated work as both building and landscape architect.[†]

Townsend & Fleming came to Louisville in about 1911 to work on the first of many projects the firm would ultimately complete in the estate areas surrounding the city. Over the next 23 years, Townsend & Fleming or, after the firm dissolved, Bryant Fleming, would complete projects for no fewer than eight prominent clients in the Louisville area.

Cold Spring as planned by Townsend & Fleming was to be doubled in size from the simple T-shaped house of Joshua Speed into an H-shaped villa with its principal orientation shifted from the west entry façade to a new north-south axis focused on an elaborate formal garden. On the exterior, the roofs were to be changed from gable to hip, with broad bracketed eaves extending around the entire perimeter. Second floor windows were to be shortened to eliminate their Victorian appearance, and stone pedimented hoods drawn directly from the Italian Renaissance would have surmounted the first floor windows and French doors.

The undisputed focal point of the house was to be the dazzling salon that linked the two legs of the plan's H form. Finished in classical pilasters, heavy moldings, mullioned mirror panels above the wainscot and oak parquet floors, this elegant room was to open on the north to a covered loggia and on the south to a classically finished enclosed corridor that in turn would lead to the parterre gardens beyond. Both

† The other is *Rockledge*, built at approximately the same time for George Babcock in Glenview.

South courtyard, 2011. (Blackburn)

South garden, 2011. (Blackburn)

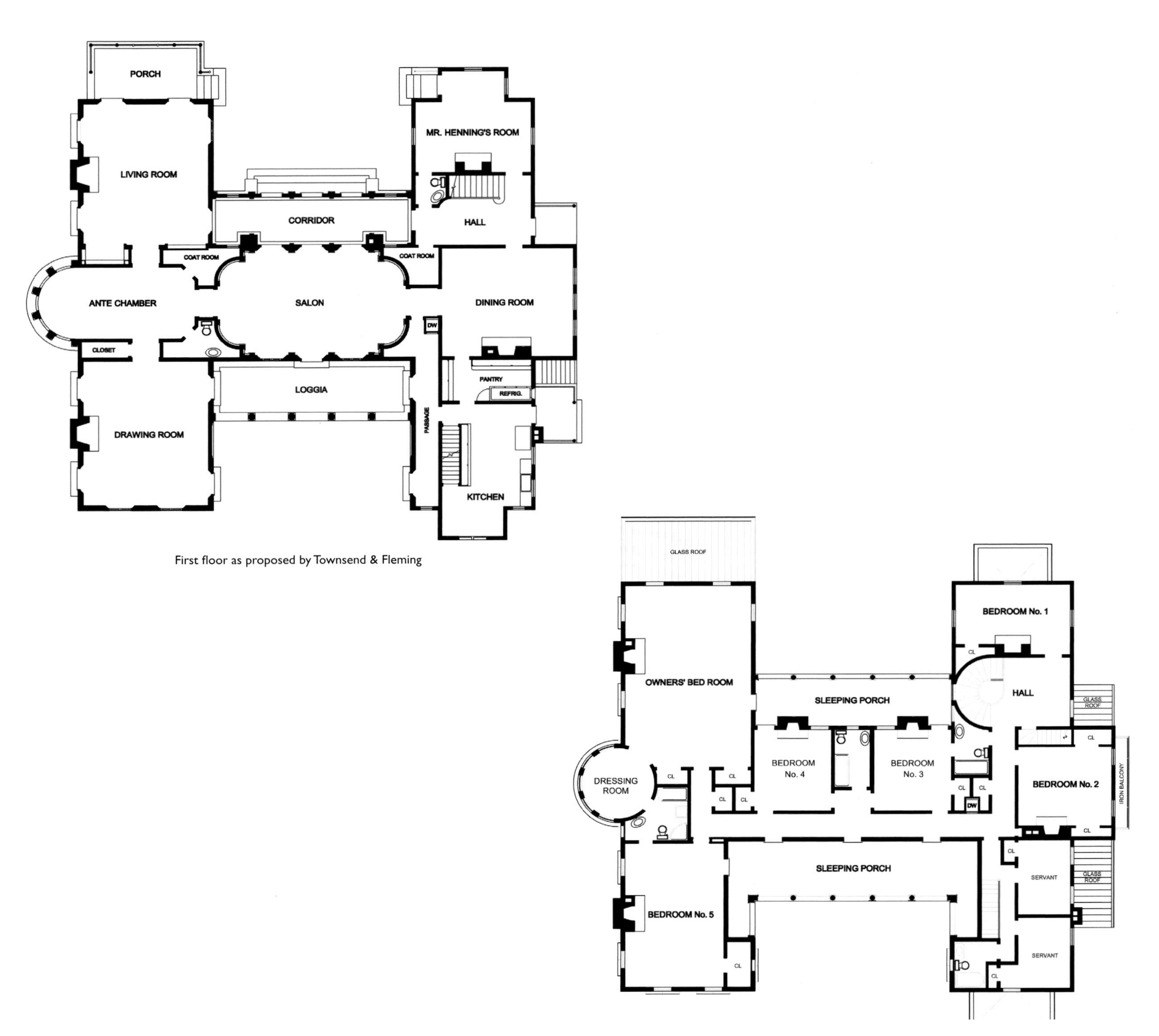

First floor as proposed by Townsend & Fleming

Second floor as proposed by Townsend & Fleming

Entrance hall looking toward salon corridor, 2002.
(stephenphotography.com)

Library, 2002. (stephenphotography.com)

Salon, 2002. (stephenphotography.com)

the north and south facades of this architectural hyphen featured arcades drawn from the Italian Renaissance with colonnaded sleeping porches above. When devising the new plan, Townsend & Fleming carefully integrated the comparatively modest farmhouse house with the imposing addition. The hall, room for Mr. Henning, dining room and kitchen area of the Speed house were retained, and linked almost seamlessly in axial relationships with the loggias and salon of the addition. While the original rooms retained a certain degree of simplicity in their finish, the new rooms reflected a Beaux-Arts formality and opulence commensurate with the obviously grand intentions behind the renovation.[5]

The Hennings' expansion plans were ultimately scaled back in scope, but still retained the key design elements of the original scheme. Employing the Louisville firm D.X. Murphy as contractor and local architect,[6] the salon was built, but in a less lavishly rendered rectangular shape with a fireplace at one end, beside which was a door leading to an elegantly paneled library in the location intended by Townsend & Fleming for the ante chamber and drawing room. An open porch replaced the living room and the north loggia and sleeping porch were omitted. The formal gardens and reflecting pool, however, were executed substantially in accordance with the architects' intentions.[7]

Samuel Henning died in 1913, and his widow continued to live in the house until approximately 1941. Five years later, the estate was sold to Mr. and Mrs. Walter Girdler, Jr., he the head of the Louisville *Herald-Post* newspaper and owner of the Girdler Corporation (which would subsequently become part of Chemetron Corporation). Employing a British designer based in New York, the Girdlers redecorated the interiors, giving them substantially the appearance they have today. [8]

Cold Spring, which consisted of approximately 34 acres at the time the Hennings embarked on their ambitious plans,[9] remains intact today, after several subdivisions, on 7 acres. [10] The house Joshua Speed built and Samuel Henning expanded still overlooks Bryant Fleming's immaculately maintained gardens; Mrs. Henning's French Provincial carriage house continues to serve as a garage. The estate remains in private hands.

View toward Mr. Henning's room, 2009. (Blackburn)

Entrance elevation, 1927. (Caufield & Shook Collection, University of Louisville Archives and Records Center, Louisville, KY)

Barnard Hall

The Estate of Mr. and Mrs. Louis Seelbach

McDonald & Dodd, Architects - Olmsted Brothers, Landscape Architects

1912 - 1914

The new residence of Louis Seelbach, which is being built by McDonald & Dodd in Cherokee Drive, will be a departure from the better class of suburban homes built around Louisville in recent years, which have tended rather to novelties in architecture instead of following well-established precedents.

Mr. Seelbach's house will be the pure Southern colonial style with a magnificent setting, overlooking the valley and Cherokee Park. On that side there will be a high, stately, two-story porch. On the opposite side, in a court, will be the entrance. At each of the narrow ends of the house will be large enclosed porches, screened in summer and glassed in winter. Doors from both of the broad sides will enter a spacious colonial hall 40 x 20 feet. At one end will be the large living room and at the other a spacious dining room opening on a screened dining porch.

The second story will have six bedrooms with four bathrooms. The exterior of the house will be faced with red vitrified brick set with wide white mortar joints. All the trimmings of the house ... will be white stone. The roof will be light-shaded green tile. The residence will be fireproof.[1]

The Courier-Journal made a noble attempt in its 1912 description of hotelier Louis Seelbach's new mansion overlooking Cherokee Park. The house, while certainly not the largest of the park-side estates, was unquestionably one of the most imposing – and stylistically contradictory. An intriguing amalgam of two great architectural revivals, embellished with the exuberance of the Beaux-Arts, the house was unique in that it offered the visitor two distinct facades: one Greek and the other Georgian. From that perspective, the Seelbach estate occupied a singular place among the great country houses of Louisville.

Louis Seelbach was born in Rhenish, Bavaria, Germany in 1852 and emigrated to the United States at age 17, taking a position as a bellhop at Louisville's Galt House Hotel. Five years later, he set out on his own and opened a restaurant and café; by 1886, he and his brother, Otto, had expanded their business with Seelbach's European Hotel. In 1903, with Louisville booming, the brothers were ready for their grandest venture, and began construction on what would immediately become Kentucky's most elegant hotel. The Seelbach opened in 1905 to great fanfare and was so successful that the brothers expanded it two years later, almost doubling the number of rooms. The opulent salons, restaurants and bars drew the wealthy, the famous and the infamous, including author F. Scott Fitzgerald, who featured the hotel (under the pseudonym "Muhlbach") in his classic book, *The Great Gatsby*.[2] An important fixture in Louisville even before launching his celebrated hotel, Seelbach was a member of the Board of Park Commissioners that oversaw the implementation of the Olmsted Park system throughout the city.[3]

For their new estate Seelbach and his wife, Marie Durbeck Seelbach, purchased almost 10 acres from John B. McFerran, acquiring lot 7 in the far northeastern corner of the Alta Vista subdivision.[4] A relatively narrow parcel, it nevertheless afforded magnificent views to the southwest over Beals Branch Creek into the heart of Cherokee Park. Seelbach engaged the Louisville firm of McDonald & Dodd as his architects and, following the course of his neighbors, Olmsted Brothers as landscape architects.

Seelbach's design team began work in 1911. Apparently, Olmsted originally positioned the house perpendicular to Alta Vista Road with the entrance to the northwest. This scheme allowed for an elevated lawn terrace and adjacent arbor and formal garden in a manner very similar to

Park elevation, 1927. (Caufield & Shook Collection, University of Louisville Archives and Records Center, Louisville, KY)

Norton Hall. However, Mrs. Seelbach seemed to have insisted on siting the house at ninety degrees to the Olmsted plan so that the rear fronted the roadway and ultimately the park.[5] The result was an unusual dichotomy: the customarily private side of the residence now became the public front. The driveway arced to the north and entered a secluded motorcourt at the highest point on the site; the mansion and carriage house were placed at the edge of this crest, making way for the desired vistas.

The house was constructed of a deep red vitrified brick in Flemish bond, surmounted by a green tile roof concealed behind a classical balustrade that in turn rested on a heavy Georgian cornice supported by a sculptural ribbon of modillions. Stylized quoins – chamfered at their edges – rose at the corners above a brick water table, and a brick stringcourse wrapped the walls beneath the second floor windows. Splayed Federal jack arches in limestone served as lintels above the double

Detail, park-side portico, 2011. (Blackburn)

Rear elevation, carriage house and stables, 2009. (Blackburn)

sash windows, and panels carved with garlands in bas-relief decorated the central bays of both facades. Despite these consistencies, the east and west elevations were otherwise dramatically different.

The east, or entry, façade was essentially an exercise in a robust Georgian – and more pointedly Federal – revival architecture. The consistencies just described were fundamentally of this style, and augmented by the prominent center gable, projecting canopy and dark-painted window shutters. The Pompeian Doric (half-fluted) columns at the canopy and at either porch might have been considered eccentric, as might the Greek Revival lintels over the tripartite windows (themselves divided by engaged Tuscan Doric columns) at either wing. Such anomalies were not unusual in an era of Beaux-Arts eclecticism.

The west façade of the house, by contrast, was stylistically almost a different structure. A monumental portico of six colossal fluted Corinthian columns (the capitals for which were derived from the ancient Tower of the Winds in Athens) transformed the comparatively delicate Georgian residence that faced the motorcourt into a grand Greek Revival mansion that overlooked the park. On this western side of the house, such classic Georgian features as the elegant swan-neck pediment above the front door now became eccentricities subsumed within the Grecian frontispiece. Such a dramatic architectural dichotomy was certainly unusual, and lent the Seelbach house a surprising visual complexity.

Within, the plan of the house was quite straightforward. One entered past a broad and richly detailed stairway into an elegant and expansive living hall, which was finished elaborately in a blend of Georgian and Beaux-Arts moldings, overdoors and light fixtures. To the north, past an ornately detailed mantle and chimneybreast, was the living room, a more masculine space with carved paneling interspersed with rich wallpaper, and an English strapwork plaster ceiling. Beyond the living room was a glassed-in porch that served as a veranda. At the south end of the living hall was the dining room, which was more restrained in finish than either the living hall or living room; it in turn opened to a screened dining porch. The butlers pantry, kitchen and service porch extended eastward from this end of the house.

Tucked off the living hall, between the living room and the entrance hall, was an intimate library. The most Germanic in feel of the rooms, the library featured oak box paneling that extended to door height and leaded glass bookcase doors that recalled the work of turn of the century Viennese architects. Simple moldings and details identified this as a quiet and private space.

McDonald & Dodd were clearly quite pleased with the Seelbach commission, and included it – along with a similar residence for Hunter Raine in Memphis, Tennessee – in the first exhibition of the American Institute of Architects in Louisville of 1912.[6]

Olmsted Brothers worked on the Seelbach estate for two years, from 1911 through 1913. Although the scope of the project was significantly more modest than the firm's earlier commissions for the Norton family, certain similarities were inevitable. As with *Norton Hall* and *Gardencourt*, Olmsted designed an arrival forecourt; similarly, the landscape architects placed the house on an elevated lawn terrace, here bounded by an elegant classical stone balustrade that echoed the wood balustrade atop the residence. Instead of a formal garden, a boxwood-lined brick walk extended southward from the dining porch to a pair of classical pavilions connected by a columned pergola – a composition reminiscent of the pavilion group designed at Gardencourt. The east pavilion served as the entry to an elaborately enclosed tennis court, and the west pavilion assumed the role of a belvedere.[7]

Dining room, ca. 1915. (Private Collection)

Library, ca. 1915. (Private Collection)

Living room, ca. 1915. (Private Collection)

Louis Seelbach died in his suite at the Seelbach Hotel in 1925. Shortly after his death, his Cherokee Park estate was sold to James B. Brown, owner of the *Herald-Post* newspaper and chairman of the National Bank of Kentucky. Following Brown's bankruptcy in 1930, the house sat vacant until it was occupied by A. Gilmore Ouerbacker, the son of prominent coffee and wholesale grocery merchant Samuel Ouerbacker, while his own nearby estate, was being remodeled.[8] In about 1944, the property was donated to the Southern Baptist Seminary by Mrs. George G. Neela and Mrs. Ben S. Clarkson in memory of their parents, Mr. and Mrs. I.P. Barnard, at which point it was christened "Barnard Hall" and used as women's housing for the Seminary's music school.[9] From 1974 until 1982, the mansion served as the residence of the dean of the University of Louisville Medical School until it was sold to a developer who subdivided what remained of the original 9.5 acres.[10] Today, the house is in private hands and in excellent condition, albeit minus its rooftop balustrade and with several alterations made by the Seminary still intact. The tennis court and garden pavilions are gone, but the carriage house remains, still in service as a garage and guest cottage.

Homewood

THE ESTATE OF MRS. THOMAS UNDERWOOD DUDLEY

Gray and Wischmeyer, Architects

1913 - 1915

In 1800, Charles Carroll of Carrollton (Maryland), a signer of the Declaration of Independence and one of the wealthiest men in America, purchased a 130-acre tract of land just north of Baltimore as a wedding present for his son and new daughter-in-law, Charles Carroll, Jr., and Harriet Chew Carroll. As he had for his daughter, Carroll Sr. funded the construction of a new house on the property – ultimately with some reticence as the price tag grew to more than $40,000. Likely designed by Charles Jr. acting as a gentleman architect (there is no known architect ascribed to the project), the estate was christened *Homewood.*

The grand Federal style house was organized in a five-part plan that reflected the well-known works of Italian Renaissance architect Andrea Palladio, with the proportions altered to make the three primary blocks of the residence appear to be only one story in height (a full second floor was concealed behind dormers in the central structure). The front portico featured Corinthian columns, an order that connoted a higher status than the comparatively sober Doric order more typical of the era while also reflecting the owner's ability to afford the considerable expense of skilled woodcarvers. The delicate swags on either side of the pediment window were hallmarks of Adamsesque details that graced this and other houses of the Federal era. Exceptionally large windows with expansive – and therefore expensive – glass panes lent an unusual grandeur to the residence.

In plan, *Homewood* consisted of a wide central hall with two large rooms arranged to either side – the dining and parlor on one, the drawing room and guest chamber on the other. A cross-axial hall led through each hyphen (or connector) to the kitchen and pantry at one end and the master bedchamber at the opposite. Within the two hyphens were a housekeeping room and office; children's and additional guest rooms occupied the second level.

In 1838, Charles Carroll III sold the estate to dry goods merchant Samuel Wyman, whose heirs in turn donated the property in 1902 to Johns Hopkins University as the center of its new campus (named after, and architecturally influenced by, *Homewood*) where it remains as a magnificently restored house museum.[1]

Thomas Underwood Dudley, the Episcopal Bishop of Kentucky, in 1881 took as his third wife – following the deaths of his previous spouses – Mary Elizabeth Aldrich of New York. The daughter of Elizabeth Wyman Aldrich and Herman D. Aldrich, the co-founder of a large commission dry goods company, Mrs. Dudley was also the granddaughter of Samuel Wyman, the second owner of *Homewood.*[2] As a young woman, Mary Aldrich often visited her family at their famous country estate, and clearly grew quite fond of the house for, in 1913, nine years after the death of Bishop Dudley, she set out to build an extraordinary virtual replica of the homestead in Louisville's fashionable new neighborhood surrounding Cherokee Park.[3]

Mary Dudley acquired approximately seven acres of Frank Fehr's newly-platted Braeview subdivision, extending along the west side of Alta Vista Avenue southward from present-day Lexington Road, as the site for her new residence.[4] For her architects, Mrs. Dudley hired George Herbert Gray and Herman Wischmeyer of Louisville. Well versed in grand traditional architecture, Gray and Wischmeyer undertook this unusual project with vigor, artfully adapting the original *Homewood* to the needs of a household changed by a century of time, yet remaining exactingly faithful to the Baltimore model. It was the last of the great country houses built at the far north end of Cherokee Park.

From Lexington Road, the house Mrs. Dudley also dubbed

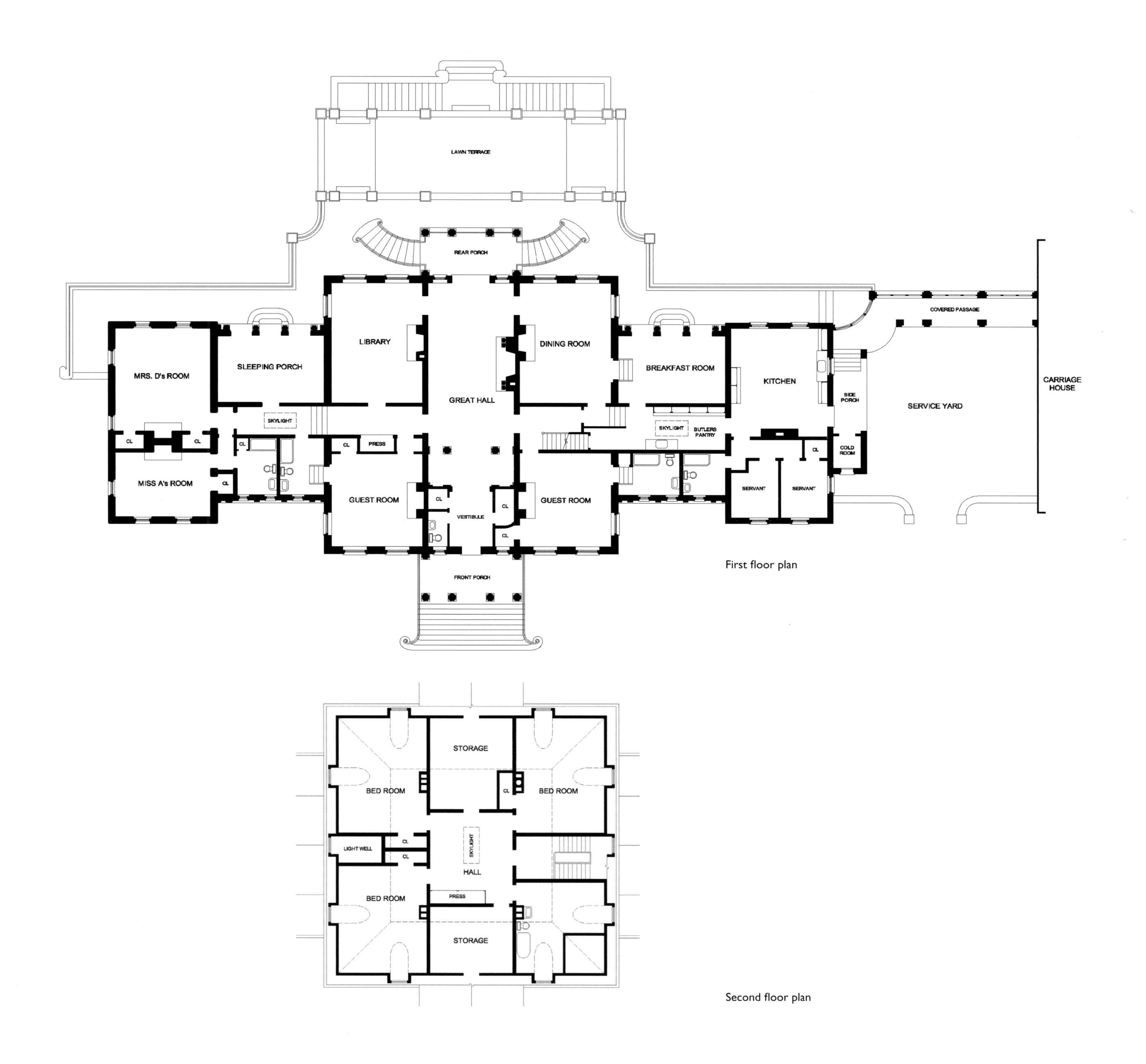

First floor plan

Second floor plan

Park elevation, undated. (Image used by permission of Archives and Special Collection, The Southern Baptist Theological Seminary)

Homewood was virtually identical to her grandparents' estate. The only noticeable difference was in the hyphens, where a triptych of windows between brick pilasters supplanted the single door and flanking Palladian windows of the original.

The architects took more license with the rear, or park-side, south elevation of the house. Whereas the Carroll house had a flat roofed porch extending out from a gabled frontispiece, Gray and Wischmeyer simply reproduced the fully gabled portico of the front. And as they did on the north facade, the firm altered the fenestration of the hyphens, this time creating elegant colonnades infilled with delicately mullioned French doors.

Perhaps the most notable departure from the Baltimore original was the extravagant set of terraces and stairs that cascaded from the rear of the house down the slope toward the park. The Carroll house was sited on a flat expanse of land, unlike the Dudley mansion, which sat at the edge of a gently rolling hill. The architects did not attempt to

Great hall, 2009. The consoles, candelabra and mirrors were originally in Norton Hall. (John Nation)

Great hall, showing original mantel, undated. (Image used by permission of Archives and Special Collections, The Southern Baptist Theological Seminary)

address the problem of extending the brick of the house down the extra distance to the ground, instead placing the brick structure atop a heavy contrasting plinth of Kentucky limestone, which in turn pushed outward into the great terrace and stair grouping. To the west of the house a columned trellis extended past the service court to a three story-carriage house and garage, itself an architectural departure from the house with a high pitched roof and extended eaves. These three elements – the plinth and terraces, trellis and garage – together with the more French-inspired colonnades of the hyphens reflected the influence of the fashionable Beaux-Arts movement on an otherwise solidly American Federal design of the house. Interestingly, no known gardens were ever planned for the estate.

Within, the plan was very close to that of Carroll's *Homewood*. Again, the main block consisted of a grand axial hall flanked by four rooms. However, in Louisville, one entered a narrow vestibule beneath a coffered barrel-vaulted ceiling and passed between a pair of slender Corinthian columns – all neoclassical devices of the Beaux-Arts not seen in the Baltimore original – before entering the great hall. The delicately pilastered door casings and leading in the doors to the south portico were clearly derived from the Baltimore precedent, as was the dining room mantle derivative of that in Carroll's own dining room.

A transverse hall extended east and west through the hyphens to the kitchen and master bedroom wings, mirror images of those at the Carroll house. In a bow to contemporary living, the hyphens were widened to accommodate the modern convenience of indoor bathrooms. Gray and Wischmeyer relocated the stair to the second floor from a concealed location off the main hall in Baltimore to a similarly discrete placement in the west transverse hall in Louisville. Bed and storage rooms occupied the second level.

Door to dining room from great hall, 2009. (John Nation)

When nearing completion in 1915, the house garnered much praise, as evidenced from an effusive article in *The Louisville Evening Post*:

> THE HOUSE IS ONE OF THE LARGEST AND MOST PERFECT HOMES IN JEFFERSON COUNTY, AND IT ADDS ANOTHER TO THE MANY BEAUTIFUL HOUSES THAT HAVE

BEEN BUILT IN THE ATTRACTIVE REGIONS AROUND LOUISVILLE IN THE LAST FEW YEARS, PARTICULARLY AROUND CHEROKEE PARK AND ON THE RIVER ROAD.[5]

Mrs. Dudley passed away in 1919, and in 1920 the property was sold to Col. Patrick Henry Callahan, a prominent industrialist and owner of the Louisville Varnish Company. Callahan died in 1940, leaving the house to his wife, Julia Callahan, and daughter, Edith Callahan.[6] In 1943, with the financial help of auto dealer V.V. Cooke, the Southern Baptist Theological Seminary acquired the property for use as the Seminary's School of Church Music.[7] Renamed Cooke Hall, the house was altered to accommodate classrooms, practice rooms, offices and a small dormitory for female students. When the Seminary acquired the neighboring Seelbach mansion a year or so later, the dormitory function was moved across the street to *Barnard Hall.* With the exception of changes to the bathrooms, kitchen and servants' quarters, the house fortunately escaped irreversible modifications.[8] In 1960, following the sale of *Norton Hall* (which had served as the Seminary president's residence since 1950) to the Presbyterian Theological Seminary, *Homewood* was renovated by architects Nevin & Morgan as the new home of the Southern Seminary's chief executive. It is in that capacity that Mrs. Dudley's homage to her ancestors continues to this day.

Dining room, 2009. (John Nation)

Library, 2009. (John Nation)

Entry court, ca. 1940. (Private Collection)

THE ESTATE OF MRS. ERNEST ALLIS

Lewis Colt Albro, Architect

1914

The Italian villa architect Lewis Colt Albro designed for Mrs. Ernest Allis was located at the southern-most edge of the arc of estate houses overlooking Cherokee Park, at the place where the urban grid met country life in a section known as "Douglass Park" – an area "desired and inhabited by people of great refinement and taste."[1] To the east marched the country houses of David Wilson and Richard W. Knott, culminating in the grand Tudor estate of Colonel Andrew Cowan. At the north were strung the J.D. Stewart and William Grant estates (to be joined eight years later by the imposing Marion and E. Leland Taylor duplex mansion) and to the west were the Samuel Henning and Richard Montfort estates. Beyond Mrs. Allis' tree-lined southwest borders were the rapidly developing subdivisions of Louisville's Highlands neighborhood.

Penelope Winston Allis, known as Lady, was the widow of Ernest Allis, the sixth of twelve children of Edward Phelps Allis, the founder of the Allis Company of Milwaukee, later known after its 1901 merger with the Fraser and Chalmers Company as the Allis-Chalmers Manufacturing Company. She was also the maternal granddaughter of William and Penelope Prather, who settled in Louisville in about 1794 – a relationship she shared with Sadie Witty, whose own house, *Casa Mia*, would be constructed nearby in the 1920s.[2]

How Lady Allis came to select Lewis Colt Albro of New York as her architect is a matter of conjecture – he received but one other known commission in Kentucky, the Tidewater Georgian residence of Dr. M. E. Johnston in Lexington[3] – and does not appear to have had any prior relationship with the Allis family, either in Louisville or Milwaukee. Nevertheless, it is quite likely that the commission was originally given to the partnership of Albro & Lindeberg before that firm disbanded in 1914.

The house as completed by 1914 was placed toward the rear of the site, allowing for a broad sweeping lawn descending toward Douglass Boulevard (which served as the de-facto southern point of entry to Cherokee Park) from the entry forecourt. Nominally Italian in design, the house drew heavily on Albro's preference for the formality and symmetry inherent in the Colonial Revival style he typically favored. Architect Lionel Moses, writing in *The Art World* in 1917, approvingly described the exterior:

> MRS. ERNEST ALLIS'S HOUSE AT LOUISVILLE, KY., IS AN EXAMPLE OF AN ITALIAN VILLA HAVING THE SAME ATMOSPHERE AS MANY OF THOSE WHICH WE COME ACROSS

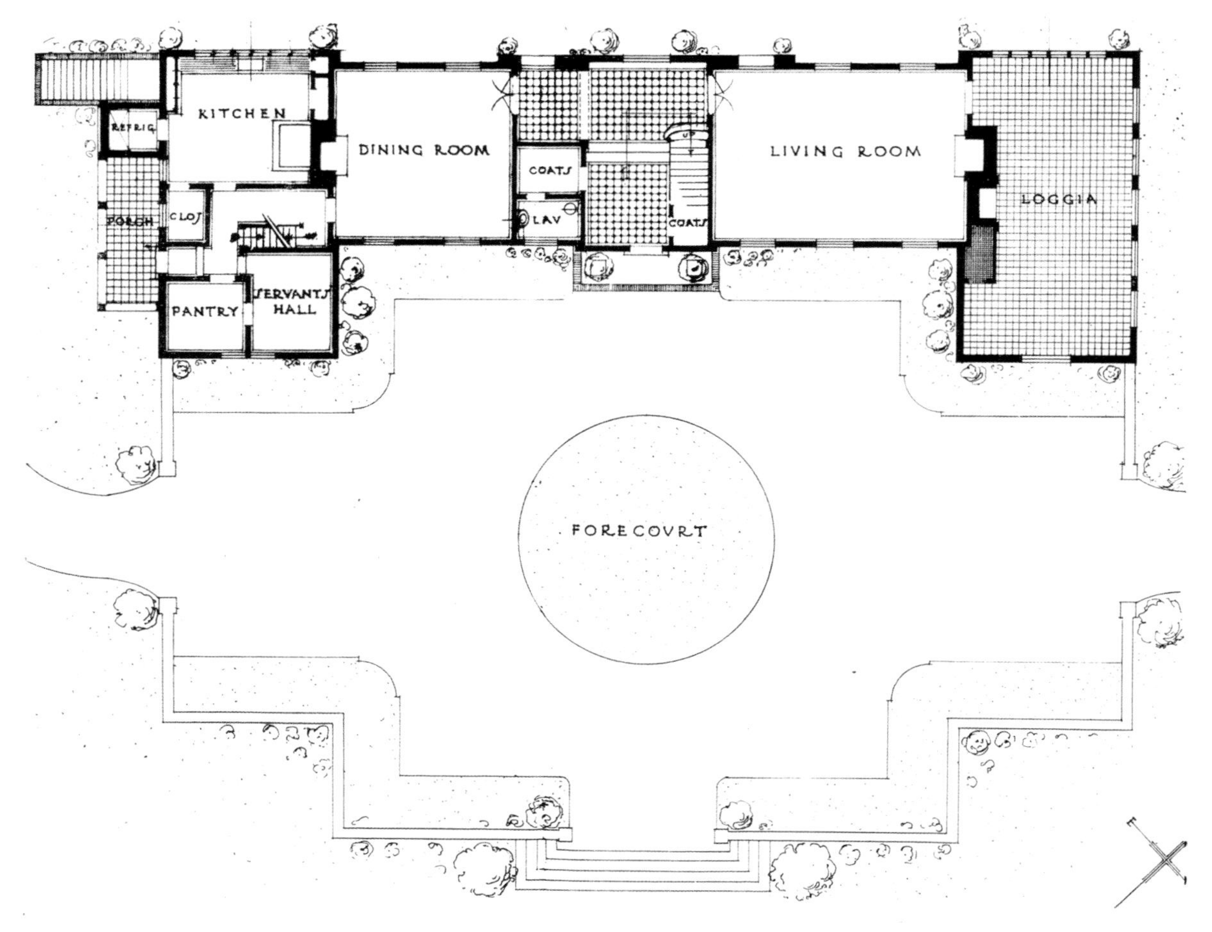

HOUSE OF MRS. ERNEST ALLIS, LOUISVILLE, KY.

MR. LEWIS COLT ALBRO, *ARCHITECT*

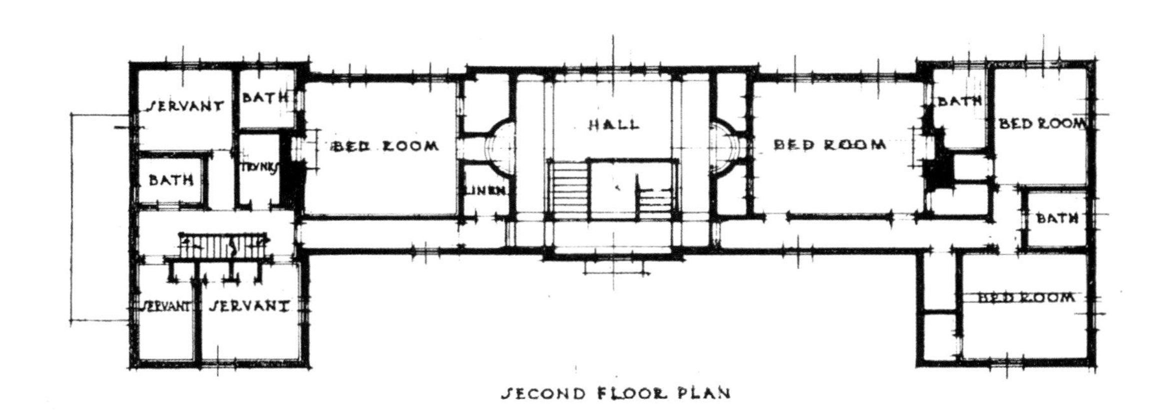

First and second floor plans, (*The American Architect*, 1915)

IN THEIR NATIVE CLIME AND ATTRACTS ATTENTION BY REASON OF ITS SIMPLE STRAIGHTFORWARDNESS AND EVENLY BALANCED COMPOSITION. WHEN ONE HAS SAID THIS IT WOULD SEEM AS THOUGH HE WERE FINISHED BUT A FURTHER ANALYSIS REVEALS OTHER QUALITIES WHICH MAKE THE DESIGN SO EMINENTLY SATISFACTORY. WE NOTE THE LARGE WALL SURFACES, THIS BEING A REQUISITE OF GOOD ARCHITECTURE SOMETIMES IGNORED IN ORDER TO OBTAIN A MAXIMUM OF WINDOW SPACE. WE ALSO NOTE THE "LONG LOW EFFECT" SO MUCH TO BE DESIRED, AND THE PRACTICALLY UNBROKEN TILE ROOF, PIERCED ONLY BY TWO CHIMNEYS AND TWO SMALL WINDOWS. THE FEATURE OF THE ELEVATION IS THE ENTRANCE DOOR WHICH IS WELL PROPORTIONED AND QUITE PROPERLY ORNAMENTED.[4]

The house was constructed of tile block covered in a buff stucco with a reddish-brown tile roof; the windows and shutters were painted a complementary blue-green.[5] Encircling the structure was a wide stringcourse, which served the dual purpose of relieving the planar wall surface and highlighting the division of the first and second floors. Mullioned casement windows with transoms flanked the front door, a classically framed affair surmounted by a broad bracketed cornice, all set beneath a dramatic scroll-framed window. On either side of the door were wrought iron light fixtures of a style so often used by Albro's former employer, the celebrated New York architecture firm of McKim, Mead & White.

The first floor plan was simple and straightforward, being one room deep to allow for maximum light and cross ventilation. On either side of the central stair hall were the living and dining rooms; extending from

Entrance hall. (*The American Architect*, 1915)

Living room, ca. 1940. (Private Collection)

the former was an enclosed sunroom, or loggia, and from the latter the kitchen and related service functions. The second floor consisted of two primary family bedrooms, two smaller family bedrooms and three servant rooms tucked, along with the trunk room, discretely above the kitchen wing. The doors to the primary bedrooms were set within distinctive semi-circular alcoves, a feature that, along with a high coved ceiling and stairway open on three sides, transformed an otherwise ordinary space into a richly detailed living hall. A separate garage with quarters above was located at the rear of the property.

House & Garden described the house in its December 1915 issue as "frankly an American adaptation" of its European antecedents, and perhaps nowhere is that observation more evident than in the interiors.[6] The millwork details throughout the house reflected Albro's admiration

Second floor living hall, ca. 1940. (Private Collection)

for the Colonial Revival. The hall stairway, in form and with its turned balusters and boxed steps, was clearly more derivative of American Colonial precedents than of traditional Italian villa design, as were the pilasters, wall and ceiling moldings and fireplaces that graced the home's primary rooms. The two notable exceptions were the living room and loggia mantles, which came closest to acknowledging some degree of Mediterranean influence. The hall woodwork, according to the same article, was painted white and the walls a light grey; the floor was of green and white marble.

The house was a critical success as evidenced by the coverage it received for several years following its construction. In addition to *The Art World* and *House & Garden*, the estate was featured in *The American Architect*, *Architecture*, *The Architectural Review*, *The American House* and the Louisville *Herald-Post.*[7]

Lady Allis passed away in 1918, and her daughter and son-in-law sold the estate to Mina Breaux Ballard, the widow of Charles T. Ballard (see "Bushy Park/Melcombe"), that same year. Mrs. Ballard made several alterations to the house, the most notable of which was replacing the loggia fireplace with an additional set of French doors to the living room, at which time she also reduced the height of the living room fireplace mantle and added bookcases to the second floor living hall. Mina Ballard died in 1933, and in 1936, her family sold the house to Marvin Davidson Beard and his wife, Eleanor Robertson Beard (Mrs. Beard would become nationally famous for her Eleanor Beard Studio, a maker of hand-quilted comforters and other linens). The Beards replaced a portion of the existing formal gardens with a swimming pool and added a pair of stucco and iron gates at the rear entrance to the property. Further, Mrs. Beard followed Mrs. Ballard's lead and once again changed the living room fireplace wall, this time filling in the French doors to the left of the fireplace, and paneling the entire surface – including replacing the mantle - in a Georgian-styled hand-carved butternut.[8]

The Beards lived at the estate until Eleanor died in 1951, at which time her family sold the property to Congregation Adath Jeshurun. In 1965, following the adjacent construction of the J. J. Gittleman Education Center, the house was razed. Today, Mrs. Beard's gates, remnants of the low walls and steps that led from the forecourt to the lawn and the urns that served as sentries to these steps remain as reminders of one of Louisville's most distinctive and appreciated country houses.

Park elevation. (*The American Architect*, 1915)

Swimming pool at rear of house, ca. 1940. (Private Collection)

Entrance elevation, ca. 2011. (Blackburn)

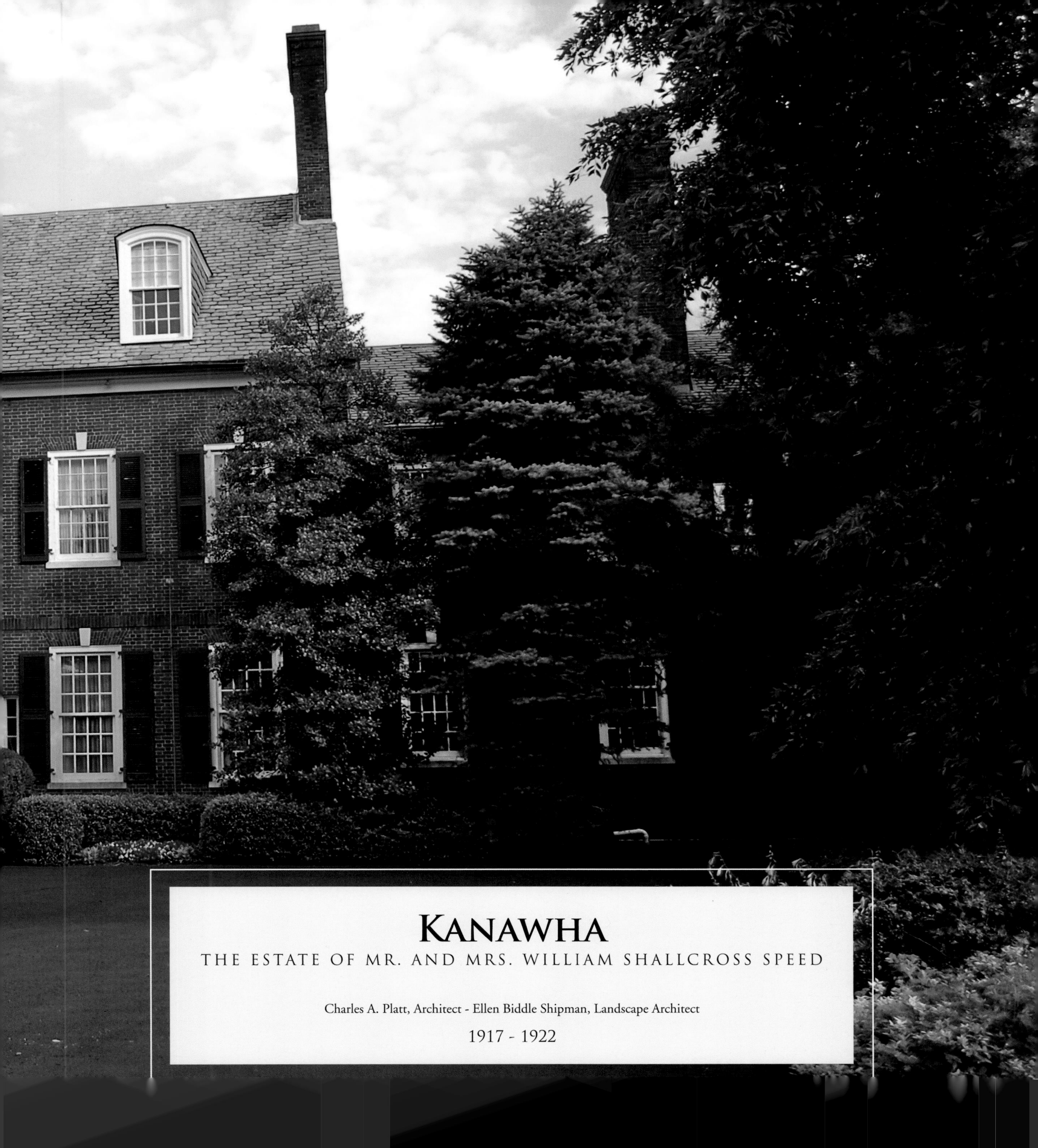

Kanawha

THE ESTATE OF MR. AND MRS. WILLIAM SHALLCROSS SPEED

Charles A. Platt, Architect - Ellen Biddle Shipman, Landscape Architect

1917 - 1922

Akers' carriage house, 2009. (Blackburn)

The history of William Shallcross Speed's grand Colonial Revival estate actually began in the year 1850 when the Rev. James Craik purchased 30 acres abutting Workhouse (now Lexington) Road and built a sturdy brick Italianate villa, which he named *Kanawha* after his former home on the Kanawha River in Charleston, West Virginia.[1] Craik, the son of George Washington's secretary and grandson of Washington's family physician, initially practiced law in Charleston but soon became an Episcopal priest before moving to Louisville in about 1844. There, he directed the Christ Church congregation until his death in 1882.[2]

Mrs. Craik died in 1896. Following her death, John M. and Maria B. Atherton, who had purchased the neighboring Charles Speed[†] estate,

† *The Poplars* was for a number of years the estate of Charles' father, James Speed, who served as United States Attorney General under President Lincoln; he was also the brother of Joshua Speed, the close friend of Lincoln who built *Cold Spring* on the southern end of Cherokee Park.

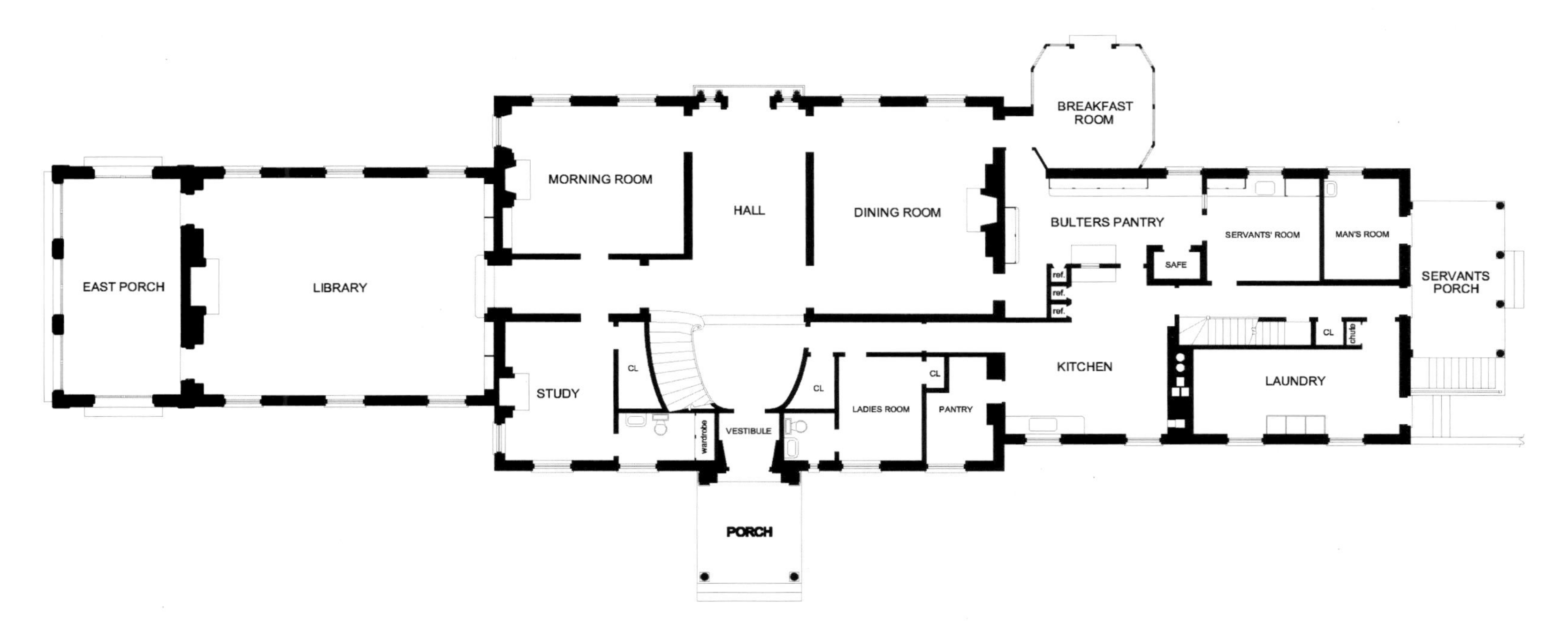

First floor plan. (Drawn from the 1921 originals held at the Avery Library, Columbia University)

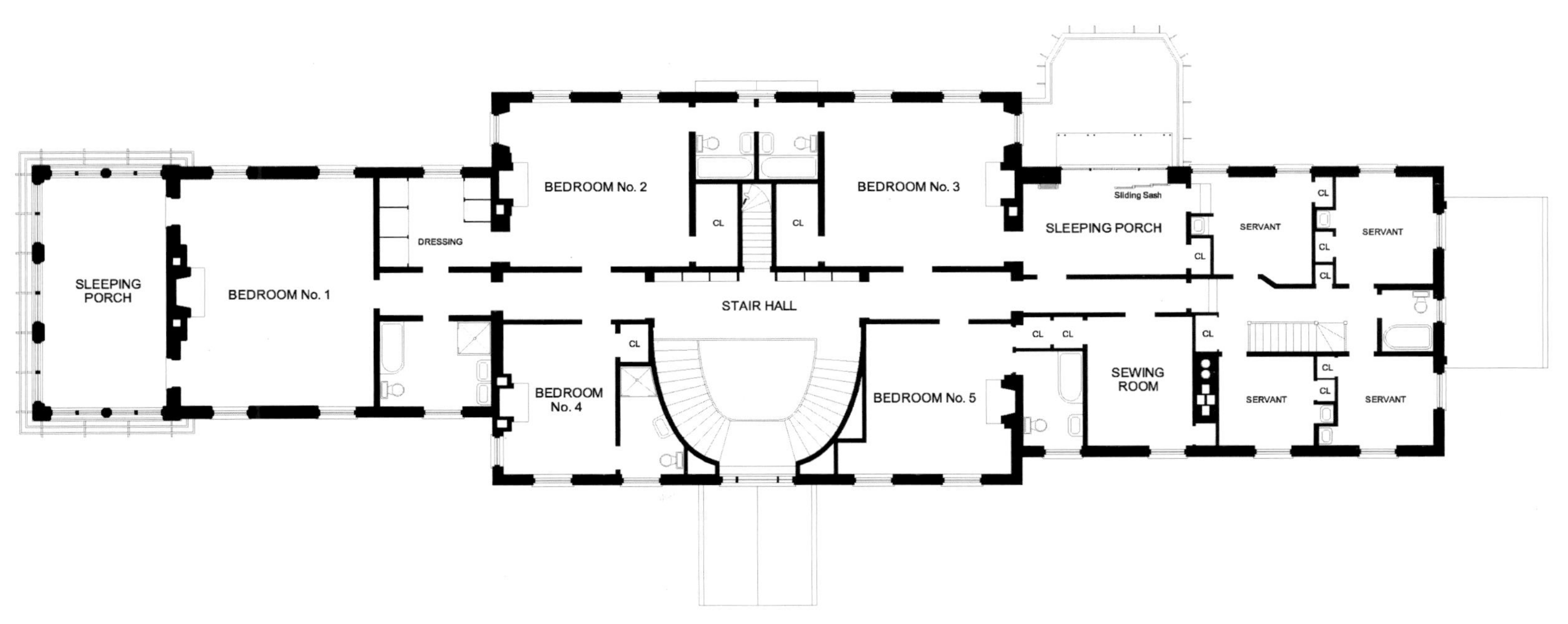

Second floor plan. (Drawn from the 1921 originals held at the Avery Library, Columbia University)

The Poplars, in 1893, bought *Kanawha* from the Craiks' heirs.[3] In 1908, 24 acres[4] of the original Craik property, including the house, were sold to Matthew L. Akers, general agent for the Chesapeake & Ohio Railway, vice president & secretary of the Louisville and Jeffersonville Bridge Co. and president of the Louisville Soap Company.[5] It was under Akers that *Kanawha* began to assume its present form.

Shortly after acquiring the property, Akers engaged Louisville architect John Bacon Hutchings to design a completely new house, carriage house and gardens.[6] The carriage house, completed in 1911 and in use by 1912, was constructed in a unique blend of the Romanesque, Byzantine, Tudor, Colonial Revival and Arts & Crafts styles.[7] It appears that Akers demolished the Craik house and laid out a long axial driveway from Lexington Road to a new rectangular forecourt in anticipation of the grand new mansion that was to come.[8]

Hall, 2010. (John Nation)

Hall from stair, 2010. (John Nation)

Akers never built his new mansion, instead selling the property in 1913 and ultimately moving to a suite in the Seelbach Hotel where he lived until his death in 1926.[9] By 1916, William Shallcross Speed and his wife, Virginia Speed, had purchased *Kanawha* and engaged Louisville architects Loomis & Hartman to design a sleeping porch for the carriage house.[10] Late that same year or early in 1917, the Speeds hired New York architect Charles A. Platt to design a new country house on the site Akers had selected for his own.

Charles Adams Platt (1861-1933) began his artistic career as an etcher and then turned to landscape painting. His interests evolved into landscape design, the result of a trip to Italy with his brother that produced America's first photographic book on the gardens of that country, the enormously influential *Italian Gardens* of 1894. His work

Dining room, 2010. (John Nation)

Detail, dining room mantel, 2010. (John Nation)

on formal gardens led him into architectural design, a pursuit he adeptly mastered despite his lack of a formal education (unlike many of his counterparts, he did not attend the École des Beaux-Arts). By the time he encountered the Speed family, he had become "the most important country house designer of his time ... the inventor of new models for the house and garden, and a fundamental influence on the succeeding generation of architects."[11]

Library, 2010. (John Nation)

The house Platt designed for the Speeds bore no resemblance to Akers' exotic carriage house. Instead, the architect and his clients chose to work in a taut, restrained Colonial Revival idiom that drew from the architecture of the mid-Atlantic states and New England in lieu of southern models. Platt's precedent for *Kanawha* was likely his own design for James A. McCrea in Woodmere, New York, of 1909.[12] Like McCrea, the Speed house consisted of a tall, noble central block balanced on either side by long, comparatively low wings. The high-pitch slate roof and elegant slender chimneys were likewise shared traits, as were the carefully placed downspouts that emphasized the center entry bay of each residence. For the unusually fragile and deceptively grand front porch, Platt appears to have borrowed from his house for Meredith Hare, *Pidgeon Hill*, in Huntington, Long Island, which he designed just before *Kanawha*.[13]

An elegant simplicity and delicate detailing distinguished *Kanawha's* exterior. On the entry façade, the afore-mentioned porch sheltered a slender paired door above which was a blind fan light, itself concealing the stair landing behind. A thinly wrought Palladian window rose above the porch, while a narrow string course, louvered shutters and limestone keystones and sills at the windows provided relief to the otherwise planar walls rendered in Flemish bond. A highly unusual feature of the center block was the string of electric lights inserted beneath the roof cornice, a nod to the country's fascination with the possibilities of this relatively new technology.

Rear elevation, 1922. (Caufield & Shook Collection, University of Louisville Archives and Records Center, Louisville, KY)

The rear elevation of the house was virtually identical to the front, with two notable exceptions. The first was the octagonal breakfast room, delicately executed in wrought iron, above which was an equally intricate iron balcony with copper-roofed trellage that opened from one of the residence's two sleeping porches. Such a feature was not unusual in Platt's work, and was preceded by his 1915 *Manor House* for John T. Pratt in Glen Cove, New York.[14] The other distinguishing element of this south façade was the shallow and relatively plain pedimented surround that framed a pair of French doors leading from the first floor center hall.

Noted architectural theorist and landscape architect Charles Jencks, writing in his introduction to Keith N. Morgan's work, *Charles A. Platt, the Artist as Architect*, described Platt's architectural aesthetic as "aristocratic;" the words aptly define the subtle elegance of *Kanawha*:

> Aristocratic taste can be defined as a series of paradoxes: as a taste for the monumental without ostentation, for the dignified without solemnity,

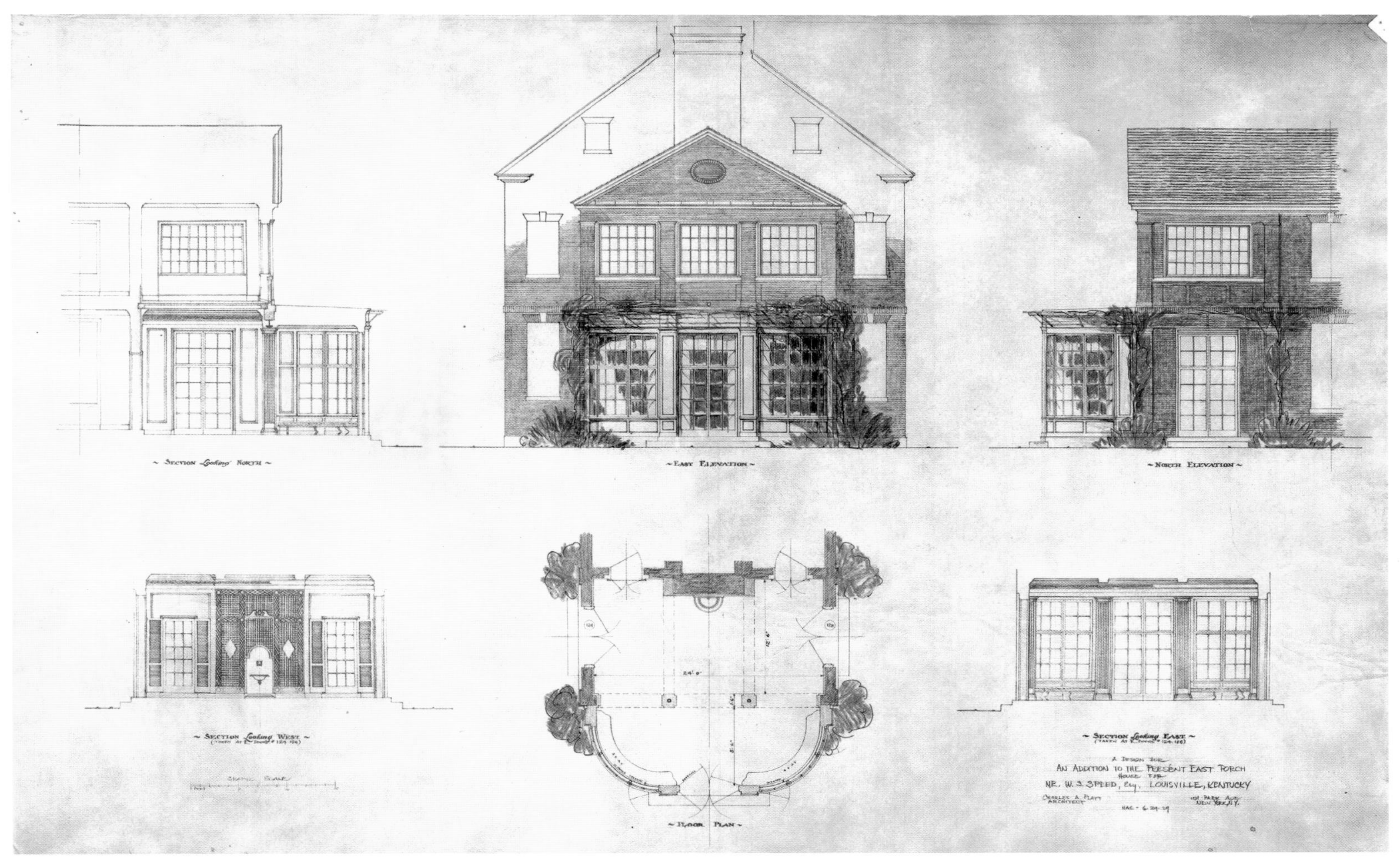

Proposed east porch addition (unbuilt), Charles A. Platt, architect, 1929. (Private Collection)

FOR THE UNDERSTATED WITHOUT RETICENCE, FOR THE SENSIBLE AND RATIONAL WITHOUT DOGMATIC RIGOR.[15]

In plan, the Speed house was simple and straightforward. One entered a small vestibule above which a semicircular stair with wrought iron railing (similar to the stair Platt designed for the Clifford Brokaw residence, *The Elms*, in Glen Cove, New York[16]) rose to the second floor. The vestibule opened to a stair hall, from which one rose two steps into a wide center hall that led to the south terrace beyond. To the east, a hall led past a morning room to the south and a gentleman's study at the north to the imposing library. The library, measuring over 25 by 32 feet, was set three steps lower than the first floor of the house; the resulting soaring ceiling height gave the room an extraordinary grandeur. Beyond the fireplace was the east porch, designed to be enclosed on three sides by tall, delicately mullioned French doors. To the west of the center hall was the dining room, with a richly modeled cornice of modillions and Greek key frieze; a door to the south of the fireplace allowed passage to the iron and glass octagonal breakfast room. The kitchen and related service functions extended to the west.

Proposed east gardens (unbuilt), Ellen Biddle Shipman, landscape architect, undated. (Private Collection)

On the second floor were the master bedroom with adjacent sleeping porch, four additional primary bedrooms, a second sleeping porch and servants' quarters. The third floor was designed to contain a playroom, two servant's rooms and storage.

Perhaps Platt's greatest contribution to American country house design was his insistence on the integration of house and garden. The architect described his philosophy in a 1931 interview:

> THE ESSENTIAL TRUTH IN COUNTRY HOUSE ARCHITECTURE...IS THAT HOUSE AND GARDENS TOGETHER FORM ONE SINGLE DESIGN. THEY CANNOT BE SEPARATED. THEY MUST BE TAKEN AS A WHOLE. THAT PRINCIPLE HAS BEEN IMPRESSED UPON ME FROM THE FIRST, MAINLY, I SUPPOSE, THROUGH MY BEGINNING PROFESSIONAL WORK AS A LANDSCAPE PAINTER.[17]

Platt apparently assigned *Kanawha's* gardens to his frequent collaborator and neighbor in Cornish, New Hampshire, landscape architect Ellen Biddle Shipman. Her drawings first appeared in late 1917 and consisted of three distinct landscape elements. The first was a wide lawn that extended southward from the brick terrace at the rear of the house. The second was a formal garden that was to have framed the western boundary of the lawn. The third and most elaborate element consisted of the flower and rose gardens, planned for a site 130 feet to the east of the residence where the gardens of the earlier Craik house had been. Shipman's concept called for an axial "oleander walk" extending from the east porch to a classical teahouse at the east side of a new flower garden. At the north corners of this garden were to have been two octagonal pavilions: a tool house and a playhouse. To the south of the flower garden the landscape architect designed a separate rose garden, laid out in an Italian Renaissance manner of geometric parterres, overlooking an existing tennis court.

Of the three landscapes Shipman conceived, only the south lawn was constructed. She continued to design alternative schemes for the east gardens and tennis court area through at least 1923, but none was ever executed. The only garden structure – a brick gardener's "cabin" with attendant green house designed by Platt – was built on a site between the mansion and the carriage house.

William Shallcross Speed (1873-1955) was a member of one of Kentucky's most distinguished families and the son of James Breckinridge Speed, after whom Louisville's J.B. Speed Museum was named, and a cousin of Joshua Fry Speed (see *Cold Spring*). Speed's sister, Olive, lived nearby with her husband, Senator Frederic Sackett, at *Edgecombe*. William Speed succeeded his father as head of the Louisville Cement Company and, in 1925, endowed the Speed Scientific School; together with his wife, the former Virginia Perrin, he founded the Louisville Collegiate School for girls.[18]

Virginia Speed passed away in 1968. Following her death, *Kanawha* was sold to a developer who divided the estate into 31 home sites.[19] The house remains in excellent condition on 1.6 acres (although an earlier fire in the library destroyed much of that room's original detailing) and Platt's entry gates and the former driveway now serve as a roadway for the new houses. Although the gardener's cabin and greenhouse are gone, Akers' lavish carriage house survives as a private residence.

Detail from "Sketch Plan for Treatment of Tennis Court Area," Ellen Biddle Shipman, undated. (Private Collection)

Entrance, east residence, ca. 1925. (Courtesy Four Courts at Cherokee Park)

FOUR COURTS

TWIN HOUSES FOR MRS. MARION E. TAYLOR & MR. E. LELAND TAYLOR

E. T. Hutchings, Architect - Olmsted Brothers, Landscape Architects

1922 - 1924

Marion Elliott Taylor was born in Greenwood, Louisiana, in 1853, and moved to Louisville from Natchez, Mississippi in 1884. Shortly after arriving, Taylor joined with John J. Wright to form the Wright & Taylor distillery, producers of Old Charter whiskey. In time, Taylor would come to own the entire firm, the success of which helped propel him to prominence as president and director of the Louisville Board of Trade. His ventures also led him into commercial real estate, including the eponymous Marion E. Taylor Building and the Francis Building, named after his wife, Francis Maize Taylor.[1]

Following Marion Taylor's death in 1921, and clearly not wanting to live alone in her Italianate townhouse in downtown Louisville, Francis Taylor engaged architect E.T. Hutchings to design one of his most unusual residences, a duplex mansion near Cherokee Park for her and her nephew, Edward Leland Taylor.

Four Courts, as the estate would be called, was conceived as two discreet houses within one large envelope that appeared to be a single, grand residence. The site Taylor selected consisted of a twelve-acre parcel at the south end of Cherokee Park, separated from the park by the Middleton estate, from whom Taylor purchased her land. The Olmsted Brothers, working with Hutchings, located the house at the at the highest point of the property – at the far south end – leaving an expansive front lawn that sloped toward the park to the north.

The house as viewed in plan was U-shaped, a result of the combination of the two L-shaped residences within. The building took the form of an impressive formal Italian Renaissance main block behind which extended two decidedly subsidiary service wings. The primary, north façade of the house was distinguished by a row of two story engaged colossal Ionic columns flanked on either side by slightly projecting wings with wrought iron balconies. French doors with either glass fanlights or blind arches above led to a wide stone terrace. A broad frieze, surmounted by a dentil cornice, stretched beneath a classical balustrade that concealed the third floor servants' quarters. Each residence was approached through its own enclosed motor court. Originally designed with columned porte cochères, the front doors were instead each framed by a shallow Ionic portico above which extended an elaborate glass and iron fan-shaped marquise canopy. Hutchings initially envisioned a more ornamented exterior, calling in his 1922 drawings for sculpted panels above the ground floor windows and within the blind arches of the French doors, as well as for heavy moldings with keystones around each opening, none of which was ultimately built.

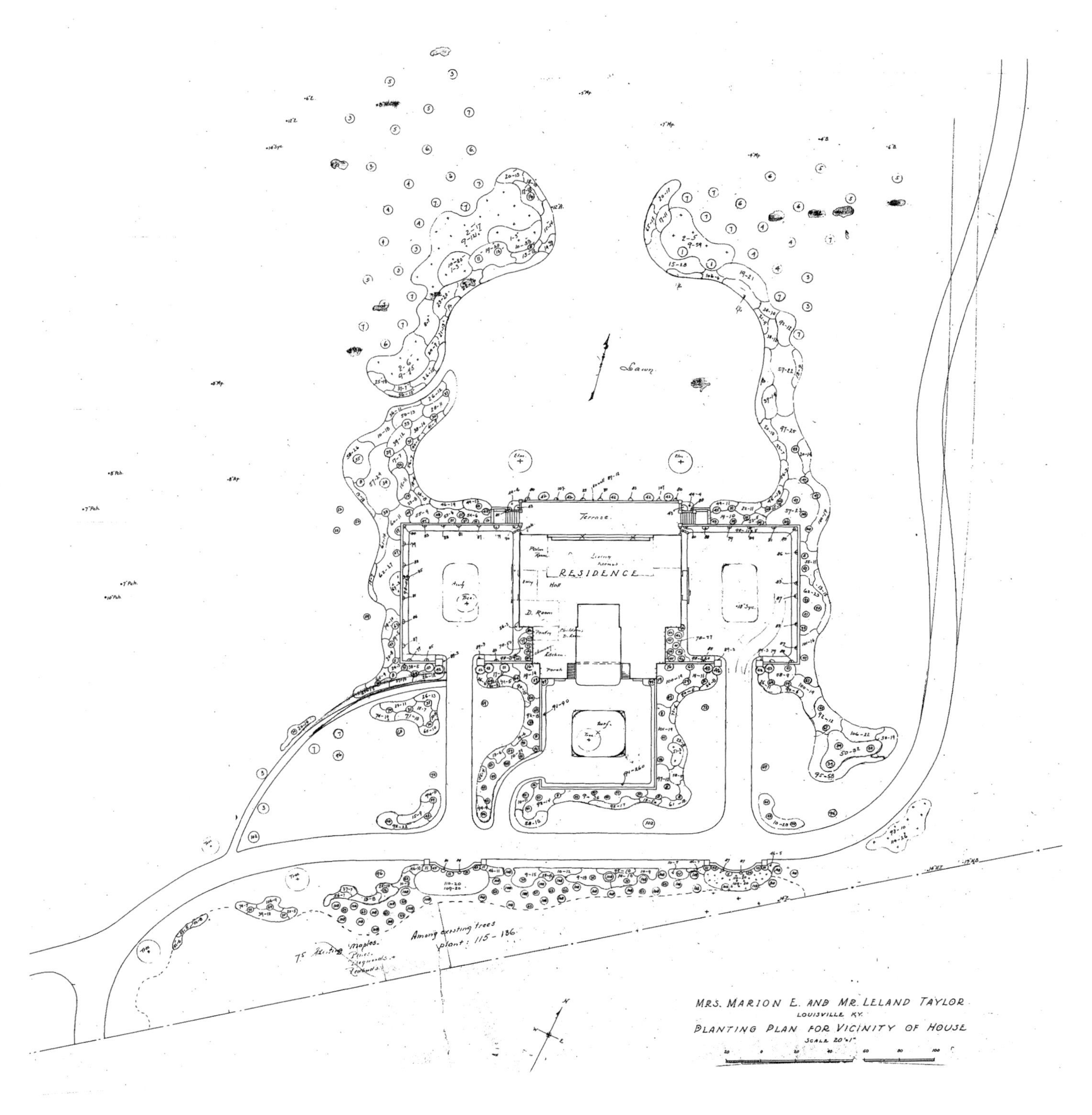

Site and planting plan, undated. (National Park Service, Frederick Law Olmsted National Historic Site)

While the main block of the house was unquestionably elegant in its classical composition and detailing, the service wings were designed in a markedly less formal manner, including the use of wide bracketed eaves in place of the sculpted balustrade, which denoted their subservient status. Hutchings even intended these wings to be finished in Roman brick, rather than the thick stucco used elsewhere on the building.

Within, each residence was laid out in mirror image of the other with an identical entry hall, palm room, living room, dining room and kitchen with attendant service functions. The second floor consisted of three primary bedroom suites, three small servants' rooms and a sewing room. The interior finishes were distinctly Mediterranean in flavor, combining elements of both Italian and Spanish Colonial influences. Surprisingly, they were devoid of architectural detail, lacking the moldings so customary in this era. At the end of each barrel-vaulted main hall was a curving stairway, perhaps the grandest architectural flourish in the house. Originally a single door at the second floor stair hall connected the two residences; later alterations would provide a set of paneled doors linking the living rooms.

Encircling the combined house were four courts: the east and west entry motor courts, a shared service court and the elevated stone terrace facing the park. Olmsted Brothers cut the entrance drive into the east hillside of the

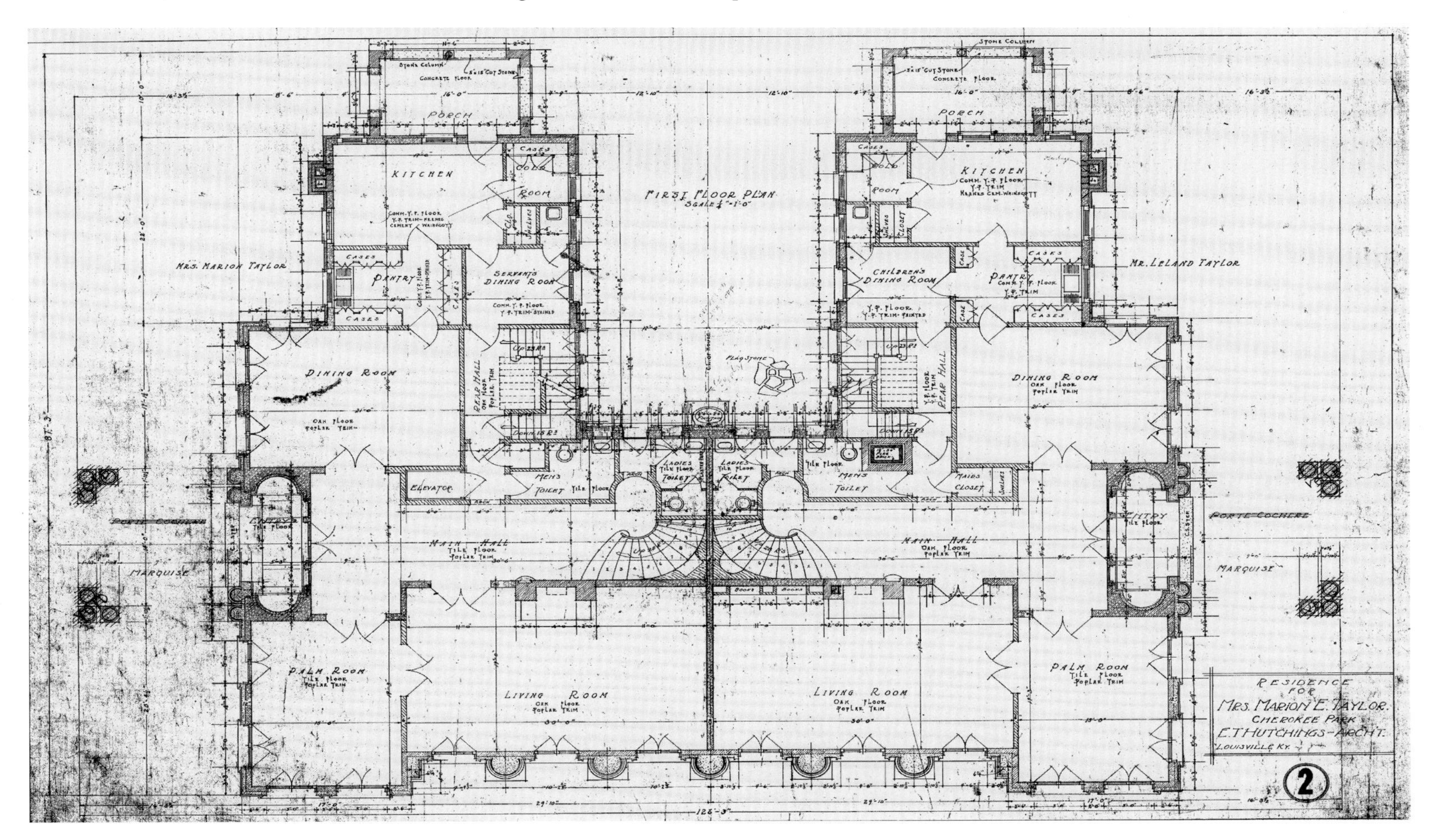

Preliminary first floor plan, E.T. Hutchings, architect, undated. (National Park Service, Frederick Law Olmsted National Historic Site)

Main hall, ca. 1948. (Courtesy Four Courts at Cherokee Park)

property, sweeping the visitor over a small stone bridge and then up the rise, all the while providing a picturesque oblique view of the impressive north façade of the house. At the summit, one could enter any of the three enclosed courts or proceed to the stylish garage and stable located at the southwest corner of the estate.

Olmsted, in exploring options for the expansive north hillside, originally proposed a pair of elaborate rectilinear Italian formal flower gardens complete with small belvedere structures overlooking the park. Each of these gardens was to have extended northward from the east and west corners of the house, and would have bracketed, together with parallel rows of trees, a broad sloping lawn.[2] Ultimately, this concept was replaced with a more modest armature of dense landscaping that still enclosed a wide greensward and directed the view toward Cherokee Park. A pair of elm trees stood as sentries at either end of the elevated terrace.

Garage, ca. 1948. (Private Collection)

Architect E.T. Hutchings was clearly quite pleased with his work for the Taylors. In the 1931 "Exhibition by Architects of Louisville, Kentucky" at the J.B. Speed Memorial Museum in Louisville, Hutchings included the house among the 14 projects he displayed, along with the Attilla Cox residence, *Malvern House*.[3]

Francis Taylor lived until 1935. E. Leland Taylor, who earned his law degree from the University of Virginia, served as Mayor of Louisville from 1945 until dying suddenly in 1948. Following Leland Taylor's death, *Four Courts* was sold and became the Louisville Hebrew Home for the Aged. In 1959, the Home added a 25-bed wing at the south end of the house; in the early 1980s, the house was demolished and a new 48-bed facility built on the site.[4] The estate is now the Four Courts at Cherokee Park, a senior living and care center. The original drive and bridge, garage building and stone terrace that formed the fourth court remain as reminders of Francis and Leland Taylors' unique and magnificent vision of a shared country house.

Park elevation, ca. 1948. (Private Collection)

Entrance motorcourt, 1929. (*Herald-Post* Collection, University of Louisville Archives and Records Center, Louisville, KY)

CASA MIA

THE ESTATE OF MR. & MRS. ALEXANDER PINKNEY WITTY

Walker & Gillette, Architects - Olmsted Brothers, Landscape Architects

1927 - 1929

Alexander Pinkney Witty was born in north central Mississippi in 1868, the son of a prominent planter whose plantation had been devastated in the Civil War. Not long after he was born, Witty's father died from wounds received in the war and Witty, his sister and mother moved to New Orleans, presumably to live with his mother's family.[1] From this point until about 1895, when he moved to Louisville to marry Sarah (Sadie) Zanone, the details of Witty's life are unknown. However, by the time of his death in 1931, he had risen to prominence as president of the W. J. Hughes & Sons lumber company, one of the South's largest makers of windows and other wood products for the building industry. He would leave behind his wife and only child, a daughter, as well as his beloved country house of less than three years, *Casa Mia*.

Sometime prior to 1922, Witty purchased Lot 15 in John McFerran's Olmsted-platted Alta Vista subdivision. Occupying the far northeast corner of the development, adjacent to Ross Todd's *Rostrevor* and Andrew Cowan's *Ayrstead* estates, the site consisted of approximately seven-and-a-half acres that rolled from its view-commanding apex down to the south and east to Beargrass Creek. Following in the stead of nearby neighbor Frank Fehr, Witty chose to subdivide his purchase, engaging Olmsted Brothers in 1926 to create a plat plan of five sites. He retained the largest lot for himself, a one-and-a-half acre parcel that included the highest point of Lot 15. He then engaged the prominent architecture firm, Walker & Gillette of New York City, to design his new home.

Walker & Gillette counted among its clients a veritable blue book of East Coast names. Its practice included commercial, multi-family and single-family structures, as well as large country estates. The firm frequently worked hand-in-hand with Olmsted Brothers, who may well have introduced the architects to Witty. This collaboration of architect and landscape architect produced one of Louisville's most distinctive estate houses, an unusual and distinctly non-indigenous Mediterranean villa.

By the mid-1920s, the Mediterranean style had become quite fashionable, especially in the resort areas of the country. Led by the work of Addison Mizner and others in Palm Beach and elsewhere in Florida, and a corresponding movement in the Los Angeles area, this hybrid of Italian and Spanish Colonial influences was certainly well-known among the nation's wealthy and socially prominent. Although originally intended for warmer climates, the style occasionally followed its aficionados north. Prior to meeting Witty, Walker & Gillette and

Entrance to motorcourt, undated. (Private Collection)

Olmsted had accommodated at least two such clients. *Black Point*, a magnificent ocean front villa constructed in 1916 in Southampton, New York, for Henry Huddleston Rogers,[2] as well as the equally grand suburban Cleveland residence of Henry Payne Bingham[3], clearly demonstrated the firms' facility in working in this idiom.

Casa Mia (literally, "My House") was sited at the crest of the property to allow for light, views and, perhaps most importantly, cooling cross breezes. Completed in early 1929, the house was organized around a walled rectangular courtyard, the two story main house occupying one end, a single floor service wing enclosing the north side and a wall to the south concealing a pergola, which in turn overlooked the formal gardens. The rear, or northeast façade, looked out over an elevated lawn terrace with steps descending to a pathway that meandered through the sloping grounds. The house was built of stuccoed tile block walls surmounted by a low-pitched red tile roof. The façade was sparing in detail and taut in feel, the simplicity relieved by a rusticated Renaissance entry portal with iron balcony above, mannered second floor bathroom window surrounds, molded corner quoins and elaborate wooden service wing gates and window grilles that recalled hacienda architecture. The house was protected from the street by planted berms that rose against the courtyard walls on either side of the entry gateposts.

One entered the house through double doors into an intimate hall

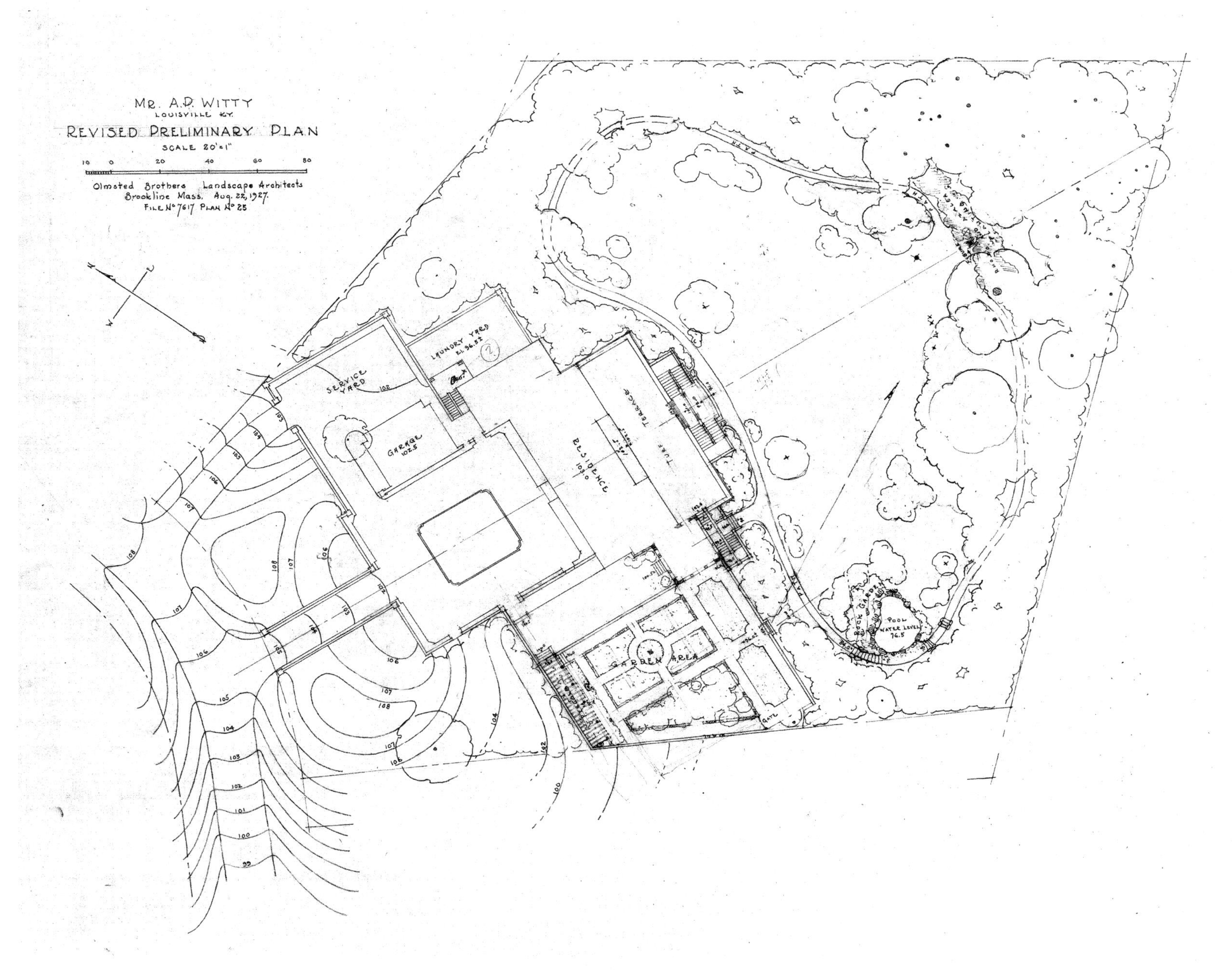

Site plan, Olmsted Brothers, 1927. (National Park Service, Frederick Law Olmsted National Historic Site)

Hall, 1929. (Private Collection)

that contained a curving stone stair with a highly stylized roped wrought iron rail. From the stair hall one passed through a high archway to the groin vaulted hall, which in turn opened to a recessed loggia that overlooked the gardens at the rear of the house. At the south end of the hall was the living room, which led to the outdoor living porch, a three sided veranda distinguished by sparsely detailed Palladian arches. At the north end of the hall was the generously scaled dining room. Beyond were the kitchen and other service areas of the house, including a stair that led down to the basement, where the laundry room and two rooms for male servants were located. To either side of the stair hall

Stair hall, 1929. (Private Collection)

were separate dressing rooms for men and women. The north wing of the house, concealed behind the courtyard wall, held an outdoor porch and three-car garage. Upstairs were four primary bedroom suites, three with fireplaces, as well as three servants' rooms. The attic was used for trunk storage.

The Wittys took a great interest in finishing the interior the house, traveling to Italy with their decorator to purchase not only furnishings but, reputedly, also the elaborate wood living room and dining room ceilings, carved wood and stone mantel pieces (that of the living room bearing an incised "W") and light fixtures.[4] Hexagonal red tile floors in the hallways, wide-planked herringbone oak floors in the living and dining rooms and plastered walls combined to complete the authentic Mediterranean feel of the residence. Whether the Wittys' interest in this decidedly non-regional style was due to prevailing fashion or Sadie Witty's Italian ancestry through her father, John Zanone , the end result was a well-executed exercise in an architectural form unusual in Kentucky.

The gardens as planned by Olmsted were only partially executed by the time of Witty's death. The firm planned a traditional formal parterre garden to the south with manicured lawns and boxwood-framed flowerbeds. Additionally, two elaborate sets of stairs were to have led from the rear lawn terrace to an informal path that was to wind down the hill past a rock garden with pond to a "figure" (a sculpture of some sort) nestled in a rhododendron and azalea garden and then back up to the house.[5] If they had been completed, the pair of complementary gardens would have joined a similar set Olmsted created nearby for Senator F. M. Sackett's *Edgecombe* as among the most imaginative landscapes of the Cherokee Park estate houses.

Shortly after it was built, *Casa Mia* was published by the Louisville *Herald-Post* in an extensive photo essay under its "Beautiful Homes of Louisville" feature. Entitled simply, "'Casa Mia' – The home of Mr. and Mrs. Alexander P. Witty, Cherokee Park," the striking interior and exterior images by photographer John T. Berry would certainly have caught the attention of Louisvillians more accustomed to Colonial Revival than Mediterranean architecture.[6]

After her husband passed away in 1931, Sadie Witty invited her

Living room, 1929. (*Herald-Post* Collection, University of Louisville Archives and Records Center, Louisville, KY)

daughter and son-in-law, Mr. and Mrs. Saunders Jones, and their two children to join her at *Casa Mia.* In 1950, following Mrs. Witty's death, the family sold the property to new owners who, preferring to reside in Florida, rarely visited the house. In time, the estate fell prey to vandals and in 1970 was set fire on three separate occasions by suspected arsonists.[7] Shortly thereafter, the house and gardens were demolished and a new house constructed on the site. Sadly, nothing remains of Alexander and Sadie Witty's *Casa Mia.*

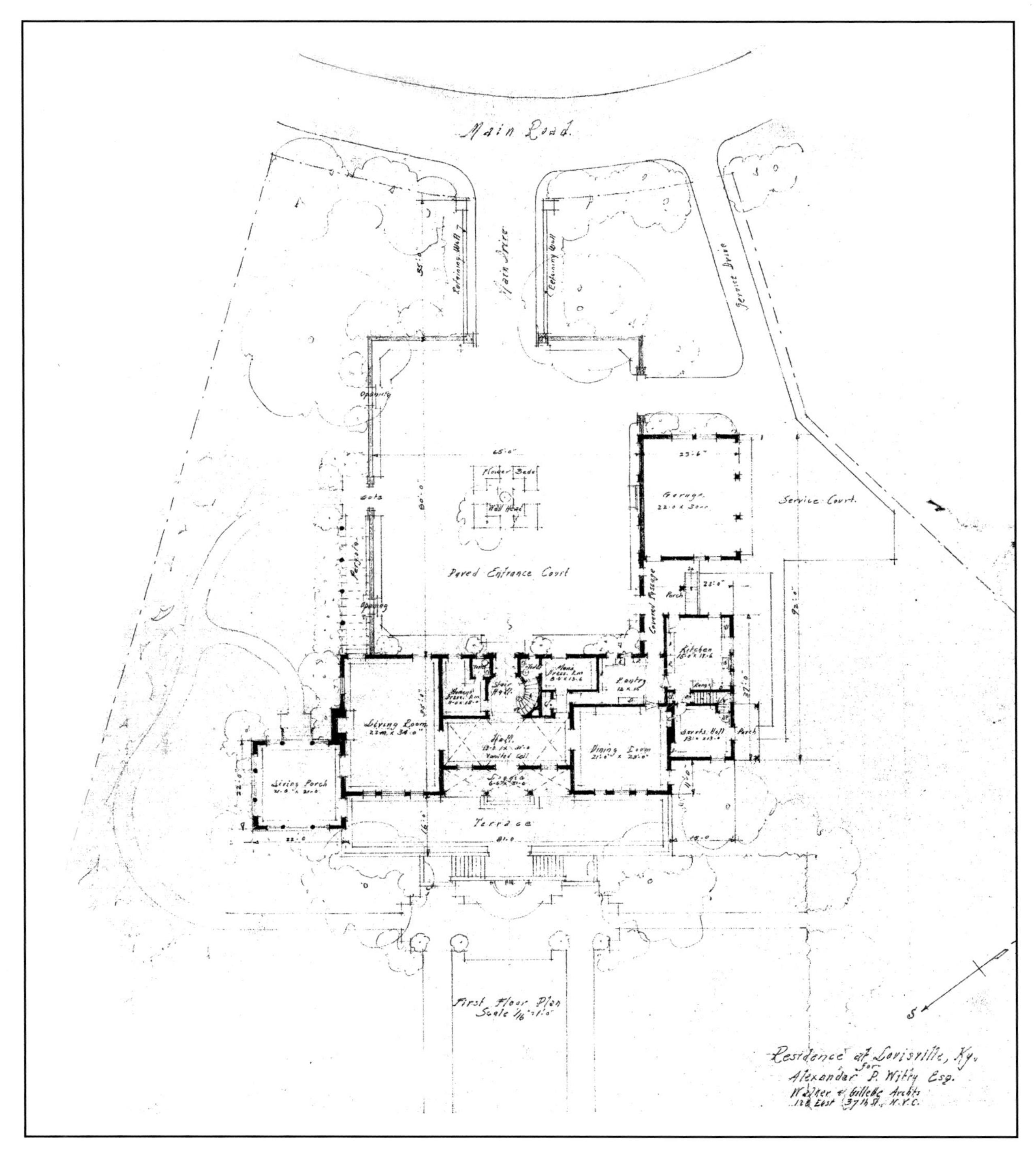

First floor plan, Walker & Gillette, architects, 1927. (National Park Service, Frederick Law Olmsted National Historic Site)

Entrance elevation, ca. 1940. (Private Collection)

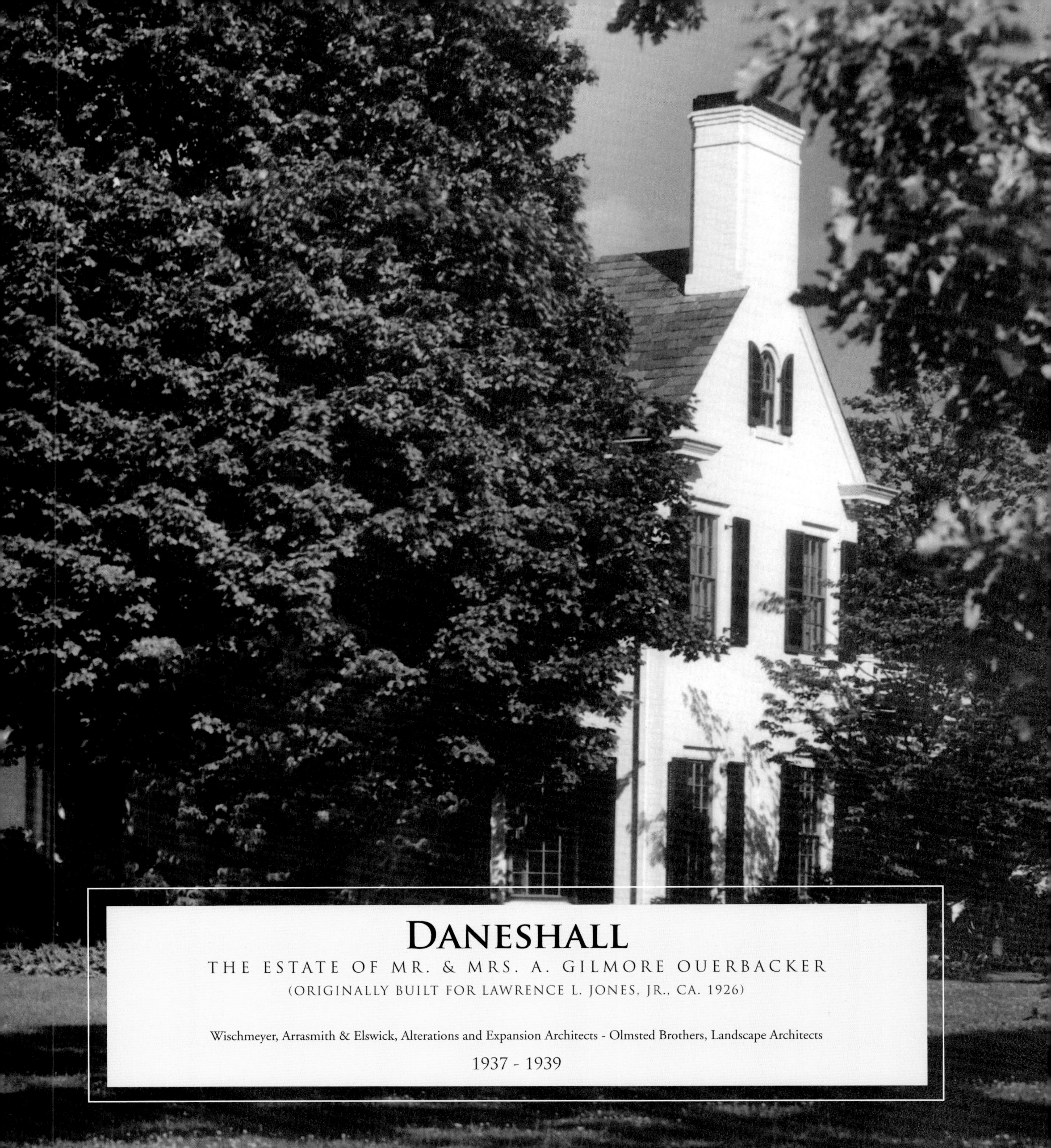

DANESHALL

THE ESTATE OF MR. & MRS. A. GILMORE OUERBACKER

(ORIGINALLY BUILT FOR LAWRENCE L. JONES, JR., CA. 1926)

Wischmeyer, Arrasmith & Elswick, Alterations and Expansion Architects - Olmsted Brothers, Landscape Architects

1937 - 1939

Aerial photo of the estate with the new subdivision, Cherokee Gardens, in the upper left, 1940.
(National Park Service, Frederick Law Olmsted National Historic Site)

Daneshall, the elegantly patrician estate of A. Gilmore and Emma Yawkey Ouerbacker, was the last of the great country houses to be built in the vicinity of Cherokee Park. Undertaken following an almost decade-long hiatus after the 1929 construction of Alexander Witty's *Casa Mia*, the project was actually a remodeling and expansion of an existing house, similar to Samuel Henning's undertaking a quarter century earlier at *Cold Spring*.

The story of *Daneshall* began in 1923, when distiller Lawrence L. Jones and his wife, Mamie, acquired *The Poplars*, the 58-acre estate of John M. and Maria Atherton abutting Alta Vista Road.[1] Two years later, Mr. and Mrs. Jones deeded a five-acre parcel at the western end of the property to their only son, Lawrence L. Jones, Jr.[2] Shortly thereafter, the younger Jones constructed a relatively modest six-columned Colonial Revival house loosely based on the popular Potomac façade of George

To the west of the hall, one entered the richly paneled library, the focal point of which was an elaborately carved antique fireplace mantel and chimney breast crafted, like the rest of the room, of mellow butternut.[9] Adjoining the library was the sunroom, a comparatively simple salon with cool terrazzo floors.

Staircase, ca. 1940. (Private Collection)

The living room, which extended southward from the library, was the largest of the formal rooms, measuring a spacious 20 by 32 feet. The ceiling was unusually high, the floor being lowered two steps down from the rest of the house. The walls were finished in painted paneling, and a broad bow window provided a view across the south lawn to the anticipated formal garden beyond. A crystal chandelier punctuated the center of the room and indirect lighting – a relatively new invention – illuminated the family's artwork.

Below the living room, in the lower level, was an informal entertainment room finished in a sleek moderne style that evoked images of the fashionable transatlantic liners of the time. The ceiling, lighting, curved wall corners, streamlined fireplace and art deco bar (with paintings of two Great Danes) all recalled the ocean liner aesthetic. Large glass block windows were deceptively illuminated from deep light wells concealed beneath grates set within the terraces above.

The second floor featured a lavish two-bedroom master suite with sitting room and four additional bedrooms, all decorated in individual styles. The third floor contained additional servants' quarters, storage and a playroom.

Shortly after its completion, the interiors of the house were published in an enthusiastic article in the *Bulletin of the Women's Club of Louisville*[10]; it was featured again – following subdivision – in *The Courier-Journal* almost 30 years later.[11]

Olmsted's work on the estate was relatively limited compared to their earlier projects in the area, likely owing to the fact that the house already existed (albeit in smaller form). The firm began by platting the new driveway that arced gracefully from new brick gateposts – designed by the firm – to a circle at the east end of the great portico, eliminating

Living room, ca. 1940. (Private Collection)

Library, ca. 1940. (Private Collection)

Dining room, ca. 1940. (Private Collection)

Bedroom, ca. 1940. (Private Collection)

Lower level entertainment room, ca. 1940. (Private Collection)

the former westerly approach that led directly to the front of the house. Low, custom-designed lampposts provided discrete illumination at the edges of the gravel surface.

At the rear of the house, the landscape architects took advantage of the garage court wall to create an arbor that extended from a stone terrace between the living room and service wing southward to a proposed set of formal gardens, a design element that recalled Olmsted's work years earlier at *Norton Hall* and *Gardencourt*. The formal flower garden intended for the south end of the property also incorporated the courtyard wall, where Olmsted designed an arched recess with a fountain to serve as a terminus for the garden's east-west axis, not unlike the firm's work at Frederick Sackett's *Edgecombe* of 1912. While the garden as a whole was never completed, a "lilac path" was built along the boundary abutting Seneca Park and a formal rose garden was constructed at the south end of the arbor incorporating the arched recess in the garage court wall. Olmsted's work for the Ouerbackers, which continued until 1940, also included a pond abutting Beals Branch creek, kennels, a birdhouse and rose poles for the rose garden.

Gilmore and Emma Ouerbacker divorced not long after the completion of *Daneshall*, and Emma continued to live at the estate until her death in December 1963. In early 1964, the property was sold to Louisville attorney S.J. Stallings, who announced plans to sell the mansion and subdivide the grounds.[12] Today, the house and garage survive as two separate private residences surrounded by 19 additional homes. Olmsted's gates are gone – the driveway relocated to accommodate the new building sites – as are the formal gardens, greenhouses, kennels and pond. From completion to subdivision, the Ouerbackers' great country retreat lasted a scant 25 years.

Lincliff from the air, 2010. (Nation)

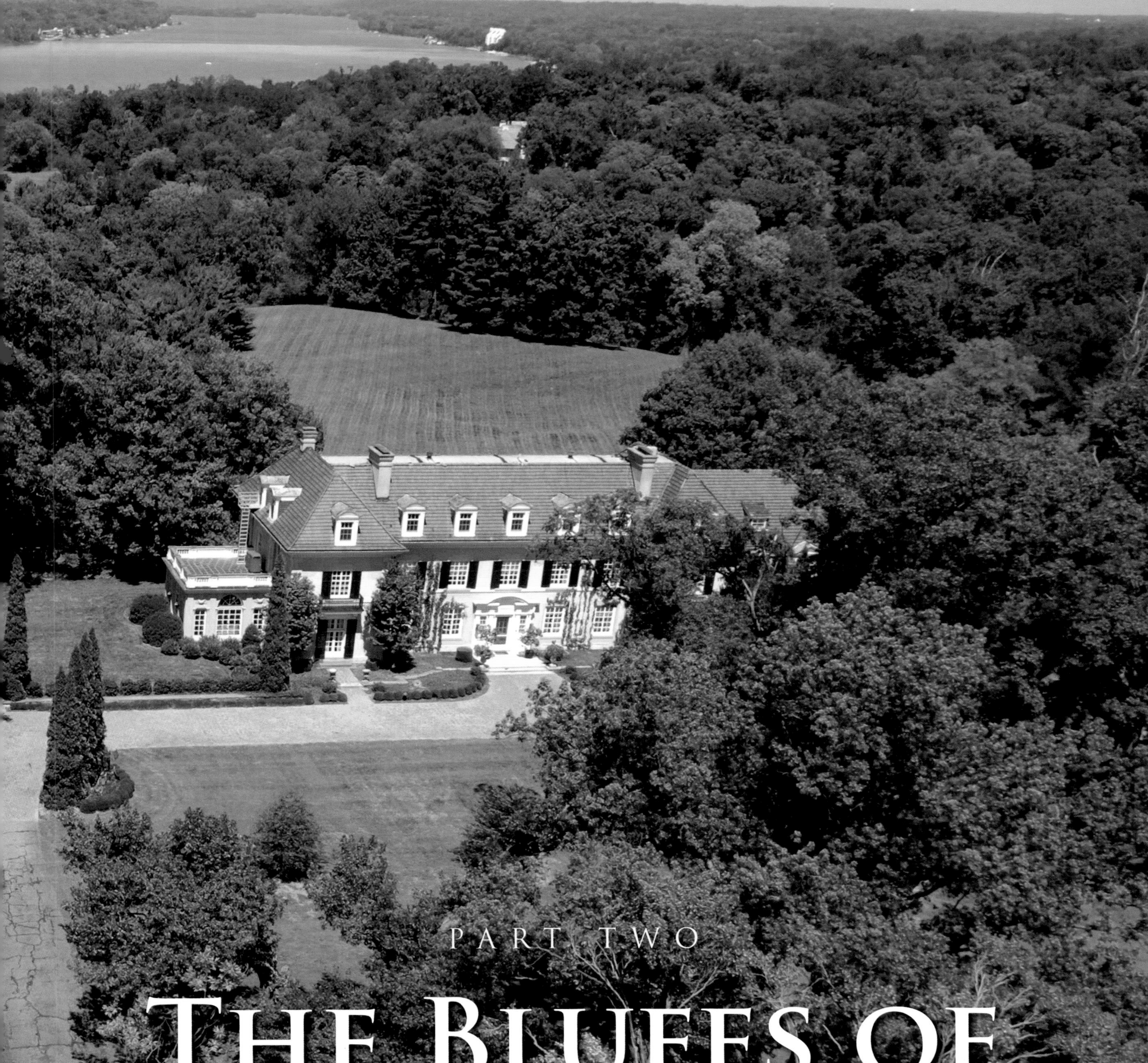

PART TWO

THE BLUFFS OF THE OHIO RIVER

Lansdowne shortly after completion, 1909.
(Rogers Clark Ballard Thruston Photo Collection, Filson Historical Society)

LANSDOWNE

THE ESTATE OF MR. & MRS. S. THRUSTON BALLARD

William J. Dodd, Architect

1899, BURNED 1906

REBUILT

McDonald and Dodd, Architects

1907 - 1908

LANSDOWNE

Far from the turmoils of the town
Where restless passion strives,
Here, near to Nature's heart, our friends
Have fixed their pleasant lives.

On this high hill shall rise a home,
Clear cut against the sky;
To cheer the hearts of happy guests,
And charm the passer-by.

Upon this Rock, they build their House;
And – till long life shall cease –
Without, be waters, wood, and sky;
Within, love, friendship – peace.

GEO. M. DAVIE, "LAYING OF THE CORNER STONE AT LANSDOWNE," MAY 20, 1899

In 1897, S. Thruston Ballard and his wife, Sunshine, purchased 109 acres in Glenview.[1] Their acquisition extended from the banks of the Ohio River westward over the high bluff as far as Fincastle Hill, site of the exclusive Fincastle Club, and from Glenview Avenue at the south to Lime Kiln Road at the north. In terms of sheer acreage, it was among the largest of Louisville's country estates of the era. The Ballards gave this vast property the name "Lansdowne," after the early homestead of the Thruston family at Gloucester Point, Virginia.[2]

Samuel Thruston Ballard was born in Louisville in 1855, the son of Andrew Jackson Ballard and Frances Thruston, she the daughter of Charles W. Thruston, a successful manufacturer and merchant. Ballard's maternal grandmother, Mary Elizabeth Churchill, was a member of the family after which Louisville's celebrated Churchill Downs racetrack was named and also a descendant of American Revolutionary War General George Rogers Clark and his more famous brother, William Clark of the Lewis and Clark expedition. Ballard graduated from Cornell University in 1878 and, in 1883, married Sunshine Harris of Louisville, the daughter of Theodore Harding Harris, founder of the Louisville National Bank. The couple had four children together, only one of whom, Mary Harris Ballard, survived to adulthood, marrying Dr. David Cummins Morton.[3]

In 1880 Ballard and his younger brother, Charles Thruston Ballard, formed the Ballard and Ballard Company, which became one of the country's largest and most successful flour manufacturers, and ultimately a part of the Pillsbury Corporation. Ballard also served as Vice President of the Louisville National Bank and a director of the United States Trust Company. President Woodrow Wilson appointed Ballard to the National Industrial Commission in 1913; later that same year he was elected Lt. Governor of Kentucky.[4]

From the outset, *Lansdowne* was intended to be a grand country mansion. The Ballards selected prominent Louisville architect William J. Dodd to design an impressive and sumptuously fitted house, and he complied with a lavish Colonial Revival residence placed at the bluff's edge with a commanding view over the alluvial plain – now known as Ballard Meadow – out to the Ohio River. Constructed entirely of wood on a limestone foundation and painted a crisp white, the house was distinguished by a great pedimented portico of colossal Ionic columns, a bold entablature with richly rendered modillions and an elegant crescent shaped screened porch overlooking a raised formal garden to the west. This garden was particularly well-crafted. Enclosed within a classical balustrade and planted with clipped hedges and colorful flowers that framed gravel paths and a rectangular reflecting pool, it was elevated so as to catch breezes from three sides while offering breathtaking views

The original house, before the fire, 1902. (Rogers Clark Ballard Thruston Photo Collection, Filson Historical Society)

Aerial view of the estate, 1938. Lime Kiln Lane, the eastern edge of the property, is at the bottom of the photo. (National Park Service, Frederick Law Olmsted National Historic Site)

over the landscape and the river. The far corners of the garden were crowned with exuberant tea houses in the form of classical tempiettos – influenced, no doubt, by the highly impactful neoclassical architecture that emanated from the World's Columbian Exhibition six years earlier in Chicago.

Reputedly requiring eighteen months to construct, the house when completed was said to be the "handsomest and most expensive home in the county of Jefferson, and with the exception of the Third Street residence of Mr. Ed Ferguson [also by W.J. Dodd], the most expensive in either city or county," with woodwork that was "unquestionably the finest in the county" if not the state.[5] Considered to be of "the latest and most modern architecture," it was "one of the most richly appointed country homes in Kentucky."[6] One entered into a large reception hall facing a grand stairway to the second floor. To the west was a large ballroom that opened to the semicircular porch, and to the east were double parlors; service functions extended into the eastern wing of the house. On the second floor were bedroom suites, each with its own bath – an extravagant feature for a house of the time. Built using metal lath, patent wall plaster and a slate roof to retard the chances of fire, *Lansdowne* cost an estimated $40,000 to build.[7]

Despite the use of metal lath and slate, *Lansdowne* caught fire early in the morning on Sunday, March 3, 1906. It was a rainy night, and the Ballards had dined with the Alex P. Humpreys at neighboring Fincastle Hill, returning late in the evening after the storm had ended. The fire started at about 1:00 AM in the third floor trunk room and, over the next four hours, moved slowly downward while the family and neighbors franticly removed furnishings and artwork. By 5:00 AM, all that was left of the Ballards' grand neoclassical mansion were the stone foundations, three brick chimneys and the formal garden. The loss was estimated at between $75,000 and $100,000; the cause remained unknown.[8] To the journalists who covered the sensational event, Ballard pronounced, "I shall rebuild immediately."[9]

The Ballards again turned to William Dodd, who was now partnered with Kenneth McDonald, to construct *Lansdowne* anew. This time, however, the house would be truly fireproof. Atop the reinforced foundations of the first house rose a new residence constructed almost entirely of noncombustible materials. The walls were of limestone,

Entrance hall with living room beyond, 1948. (Private Collection)

brick and hollow tile; the floors – including the grand stairway – of steel reinforced concrete. The roof structure was composed of steel beams supporting concrete slabs on top of which rested a red Mediterranean tile roof. The great Corinthian columns of the portico were monolithic pieces of stone, as were the columns of the new sun porch. Only the interior finishes and certain elements of the exterior cornice and roof balustrades were of wood. Ballard was determined: this house would not burn again.

The new *Lansdowne* was a virtual replica of the old, but as rendered in massive blocks of stone lost the delicacy and stylistic faithfulness of its Colonial Revival predecessor. On the exterior, the monumental portico now supported a ballustraded terrace and the screened porch was reshaped into a rectangular sunroom. The grand double entry doors with overarching fanlight were reproduced from the original, as were the Palladian windows to either side. The general arrangement of fenestration remained unchanged, as did the configuration of main house and service

Entrance hall with door to reception room at right of fireplace, 1913. (Rogers Clark Ballard Thruston Photo Collection, Filson Historical Society)

wing. Within, the disposition of rooms echoed that of the earlier house. One entered into a great hall facing a grand stairway that rose to a landing – illuminated by an extraordinary stained glass Palladian window – and then split to either side as it completed its journey to the second floor. To the left, or west, of the great hall, was the living room that opened, through a semicircular bay, to the marble-paved sunroom, which in turn looked out over the formal garden that had survived the fire. To the right, or east, of the great hall, at the front of the house, was the comparatively intimate reception or morning room, and at the rear of the house, across a secondary hall from the morning room, was the formal dining room, which enjoyed an expansive view across Ballard Meadow to the river. Behind the grand stairway and adjoining the dining room was the oak paneled billiard room, a gentleman's retreat with a wide bowed bay looking to the river. The interior finishes were richly molded and executed in a heavy style that reflected the grandeur of neoclassical forms as reinterpreted by the fashionable school of the Beaux-Arts. No expense was spared fitting out the new residence: even silver plated light fixtures were incorporated into the furnishings.

The formal garden, after removal of the tea houses, 1911. (Rogers Clark Ballard Thruston Photo Collection, Filson Historical Society)

The Ballards took advantage of the rebuilding project to make additional improvements to the estate. The driveway, which originated at a relatively simple limestone and iron gate, now arrived at a new great walled forecourt, entered through grand stone gateposts. To the east of the forecourt a sprawling lawn was constructed, framed on two sides by a rose pergola made of stone that served the additional purpose of shielding the garages from view. A service road traveled from the forecourt to the garages and then continued onward to various service buildings, *Lansdowne* now having become a true gentleman's farm complete with dairy barn, chicken coop and orchards. Gamekeeper's, cook's and gardener's cottages, along with a large greenhouse, completed the list of structures dotting the estate. Down in Ballard Meadow were Ballard Pond, a small figure eight-shaped man-made lake, and the "Bishop's Study," a curious one-room Polynesian-styled cabin decorated inside with paneling and painted scenes, including one of St. Stefan's Cathedral in Vienna. A dock at the river provided a perfect mooring spot for the Ballard's motor launch, the *Sunshine*.

The new *Lansdowne* was completed in late 1908, and immediately caught the attention of Louisville's ever-curious press. In a lavishly illustrated article entitled, "A Beautiful Home on the River Road," *The Courier-Journal* presented the newly built estate to a public enthralled with the seemingly endless collection of elegant country houses rising along River Road and around Cherokee Park.[10] A number of years and numerous such admiring articles later, *Lansdowne* was dubbed "the geographical center" of Glenview.[11]

The Ballards, while fortunate in their business and social lives, were less so personally. Their first son, Theodore Harris, died shortly after birth. Their second, Samuel Thruston, Jr., passed away at the age of three. Their youngest, Rogers Clark, died in 1909 at the age of eleven and, in his memory, the family donated land at the northeast corner of the *Lansdowne* bluff for the construction of a new school. Named the Rogers Clark Ballard School, the stone structure was completed and opened in 1914.[12]

In 1924, the Ballards constructed a large addition to their residence. Measuring twenty-four feet by forty-five feet, the new library and music room extended out toward the river from the living room. Featuring a stone Tudor Revival fireplace at one end, a sizeable pipe organ at the other, walls paneled in dark oak and a high ceiling finished in richly patterned strapwork, the vaguely Elizabethan space was the new showpiece of the house as well as a more informal equivalent of a modern day family room.

Library and music room, **1948.** (Private Collection)

Only known photo of the rear (river-side) of the residence, from the 1971 film, *Asylum of Satan,* produced by J. Patrick Kelly, III, and directed by William B. Girdler.

Samuel Thruston Ballard died in 1926, and his widow continued to live at *Lansdowne* until her own death in 1938. The estate fell to their grandson and future Senator, Thruston Ballard Morton who, preferring not to live at the house, divided the property into three parts, selling the mansion and forty-two acres to one party, the farm operations to another and the orchards to yet a third. The house and gardens remained intact, albeit in somewhat declining condition, for another 38 years until 1976, when the estate was sold to developers who, following an auction of its fittings, demolished the mansion and subdivided the bluff into nine home sites.[13] Today, all that is left of the once-proud *Lansdowne* are the main and farm-side gates, walled forecourt and rose pergola.

One of two tea houses at the corners of the formal garden, 1902. The tea houses were removed not long after the house was rebuilt following the fire. (Rogers Clark Ballard Thruston Photo Collection, Filson Historical Society)

The library at *Robinswood*, 2001. (stephenphotography.com)

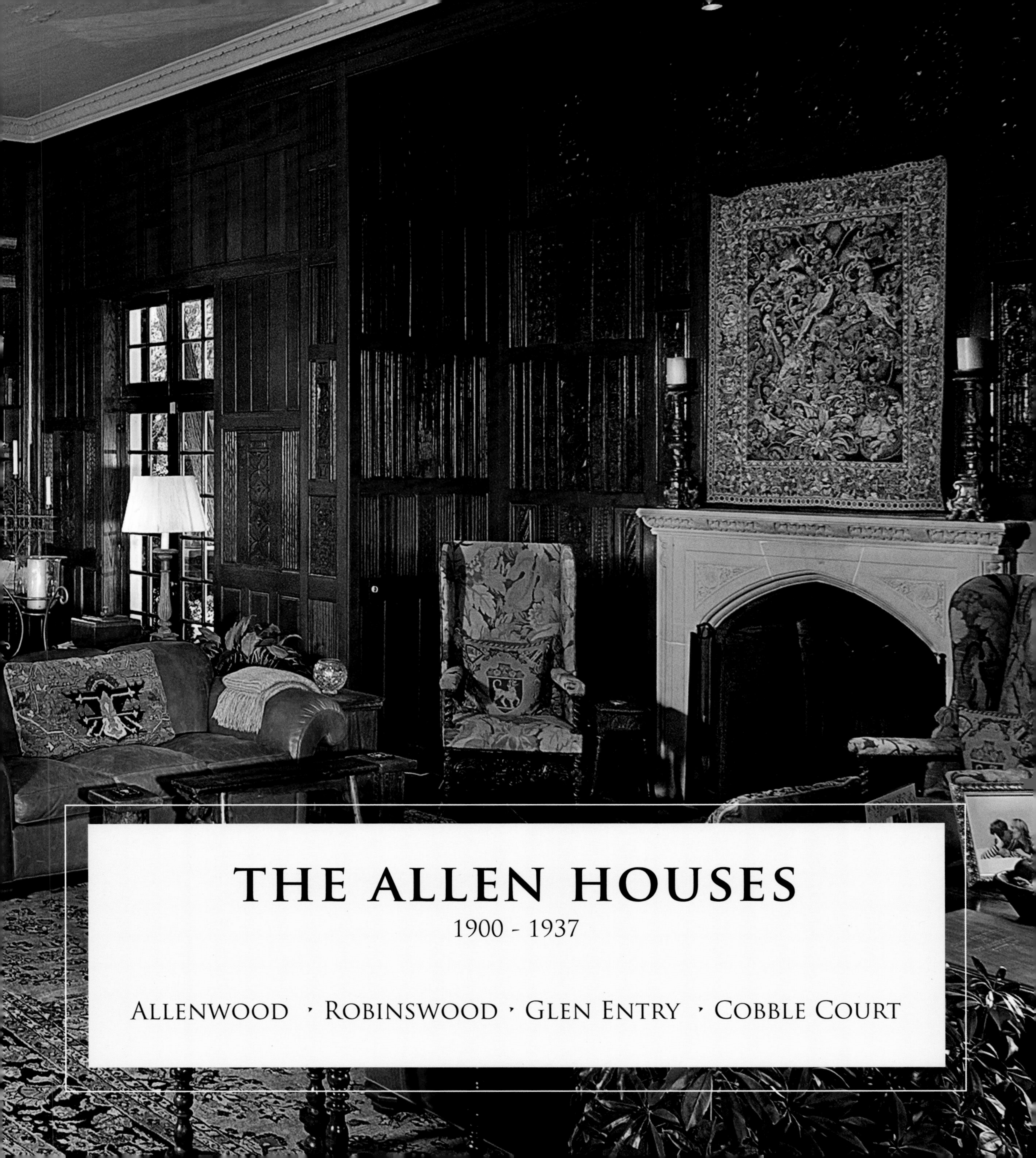
THE ALLEN HOUSES
1900 - 1937
ALLENWOOD · ROBINSWOOD · GLEN ENTRY · COBBLE COURT

Major Charles James Fox Allen was born in Pittsfield, Massachusetts, in 1834. In 1855, he graduated from Yale University and subsequently from Harvard's School of Law, after which he moved to Louisiana to practice as an attorney. In 1861, at the outbreak of the Civil War, Allen entered the Union army as a captain in the paymaster's department and was stationed in Louisville, where he met Caroline Belknap, the daughter of William Burke Belknap, founder of W.B. Belknap and Company. Captain Allen and Carrie Belknap were married in 1864; a year later, following the end of the war, Major Allen (his rank elevated) joined W. B. Belknap at his rapidly growing hardware firm. By the time he retired in 1900, Major Allen was vice president and a major shareholder of the company – as well as a widower, Caroline having died in 1897.[1]

Shortly after his wife's death, Major Allen decided to build a family retreat a short train ride away from his townhouse in downtown Louisville. The site he selected consisted of about 46 acres in suburban Glenview, on a bluff just west of the exclusive summer gathering place for the city's well-to-do, the Fincastle Club. There he would construct a "cottage" he and his three youngest children, Lafon, Charles and Arthur, could enjoy in casual comfort. It was the start of a building dynasty of sorts, as the property would ultimately host a total of four Allen family residences, beginning with the Major's own substantial house, "Allenwood."

ALLENWOOD - ELEVEN HEARTHS

FOR MAJOR CHARLES JAMES FOX ALLEN

John Bacon Hutchings, Architect

1900 - 1901

In 1900, Major Allen hired Louisville architect John Bacon Hutchings to build a "man's house" for him and his sons.[2] Hutchings complied, designing a stout cottage in the fashionable Shingle Style. Reaching its peak of popularity in the late 1880s, the Shingle Style evolved on the East Coast and had been employed to great effect by such notable firms as Peabody & Sterns and McKim, Mead & White. Allenwood could almost have sprung from the pages of a pattern book of the era, so faithfully did it reflect the examples of this architectural type.

The house was asymmetrical – if only slightly so – with a heavy limestone first floor supporting a shingled second. The stone coursing and shingle layering were distinctly horizontal, which helped elongate and visually lighten the structure as well as prevent it from appearing too massive. A thin belt band wrapped the house beneath the second floor windows to relieve the potential monotony of the shingled wall surface. In a juxtaposition of design elements favored by Shingle Style architects, neoclassical dentil moldings and Ionic porches with classical balustrades stood in contrast to the half timbered Tudor wall surface and Elizabethan paneled vergeboards of the prominent cross gable that rose above the entrance.

Upon completion, *Allenwood* was evidently considered to be such a fine example of this distinctly American architectural idiom that it was paired with another, although not as fine, example – the J. H. Caperton residence by Louisville architect J.J. Gaffney – in the 1903 edition of *Art Work of Louisville.*[3]

Within, the plan of the house reflected the openness characteristic of the Shingle Style. One entered a large living hall into which the stairway descended from the second floor, reaching into the space almost like a freestanding piece of furniture. Opposite the stair was a richly paneled fireplace. The living hall, which extended the full depth of the house, was divided into two spaces by a pair of fluted Doric columns, since removed, that were mirrored on the walls by fluted pilasters. To the east of the living hall was the living room or library, with a distinctive oak mantelpiece inscribed with the family's allegiances:

> Their House Was Built in the Year of Our Lord 1901
> Of the Independence of the United States of America
> One Hundred and Twenty-Fifth
> Of Yale College Two Hundredth[4]

Entrance elevation. The balustrated terraces to either side of the entry portico were removed in 1929. (*Art Work of Louisville*, Part 8, 1903)

Living hall. (*Antiques in Kentucky*, 1974)

The paneled dining room was located to the west of the living hall, overlooking the river, and a small study was tucked behind the stair at the front of the house. The kitchen was placed in the basement – a dumbwaiter brought food up to the first floor warming kitchen – as was a gymnasium for use by Allen's sons.

Allenwood sat at a distance back from the bluff's edge, with a clear view to the Ohio River over a wide, rolling lawn. To the east, extending from the covered porch outside the library, was a garden with rose pergola and a small round reflecting pool. A separate carriage house was located to the southwest of the house.

Major Allen died in 1911, the large shingled cottage passing to his middle son, Charles Willis. Born in 1877 Charles, like his father, was educated at Yale, and in 1902 took as his wife Emily M. Lindsay of West Newton, Massachusetts.[5] At the time of his retirement in 1935, he was General Manager of the Belknap Hardware and Manufacturing Company. The Charles Allens lived at *Allenwood* for over forty years, eventually renaming the estate *Eleven Hearths*, after the number of fireplaces in the house.[6] In 1957, the Major's grandson, Charles Willis, Jr., and his wife, the former Alberta Wood, took up residence in *Eleven Hearths*, and moved the kitchen to the first floor and constructed a swimming pool in the basement. The residence remains on 31 acres, well kept and, alone among the four houses built on the Major's property, still in the Allen family.

ROBINSWOOD

FOR MR. AND MRS. ARTHUR D. ALLEN

John Bacon Hutchings, Architect
1911 - 1912

Cowles & Colean, Expansion Architects
1929

Shortly after Major Allen passed away, his youngest son, Arthur D. Allen, began construction of a new country house at the south end of the *Allenwood* estate.[7] Christened "Robinswood," it preceded by a few months brother Lafon Allen's late 1911 groundbreaking for *Glen Entry* at the northeast corner of the property.

Robinswood, designed by John Bacon Hutchings – he and his son, E.T., were the preferred architects of the Allen family – was a somewhat curious house architecturally. In some ways Georgian in style, as evidenced by the brick walls in Flemish bond with pronounced string course, decidedly colonial fenestration and pedimented Tuscan Doric entry porch, it was in other ways indebted to the Arts and Crafts movement. Its asymmetrical composition, extended eaves and half-timbered gables lent the residence a romantic informality that tempered any pretense of grandeur: this was clearly a house in the country.

In plan, the house consisted of a large living hall with fireplace that opened, at the north end, to a screened porch, and at the south end, to a small formal parlor at the front of the house and the dining room at the rear. At the back of the living hall, partly concealed by an archway, was the main stair to the second floor. The living hall was partially paneled in dark wood, with a ceiling supported by heavy beams. The dining room was similarly finished, with a high paneled wainscot along the walls, a beamed ceiling and an elaborate, hand-carved mantel supported at either end by pairs of Ionic columns. Upstairs were bedrooms and the customary sleeping porches; servants' quarters and service functions occupied the south wing of the residence.

As early as 1914, the Allens sought to expand *Robinswood* with the addition of a library. They first hired Bryant Fleming, the Buffalo, New York, architect and landscape designer who had already worked on several Louisville estates, to design a freestanding pavilion within a new set of gardens. By 1917, and after additional sketches for a "dipping pool" and new terraces, the project was abandoned. Instead, in 1929 the Allens engaged the Chicago firm of Cowles & Colean to expand the existing house. The result dramatically altered the appearance of the residence and simultaneously elevated its status from casual country house to grand country estate.

The architects replaced the screened porch at the north of the

Entrance elevation, 2010. The addition by Cowles & Colean is at the left. (Blackburn)

Entrance elevation, prior to the addition and renovations by Cowles & Colean, undated. (Private Collection)

residence with an extraordinary room that was longer than the house was deep and with a ceiling substantially higher than that of the adjacent living hall. At either end, the new library was illuminated by enormous floor to ceiling windows, each divided by heavy mullions which in turn held delicate leaded glass panes. A limestone mantel, carved with the Allen family monograms, occupied a broad recess in the north wall. Most dramatically, the entire room was paneled in disassembled dower chests Mr. and Mrs. Allen had acquired in France, the earliest dating to 1612. The carved panels were interspersed, where necessary, with new matching oak inserts to ensure complete coverage of the walls.

Above the grand library, Cowles & Colean constructed a new master bedroom suite, which was decorated in the subtly condensed classicism that was a hallmark of residential American art deco. The sitting room was distinctively finished in a grid of veneer square panels – both walls and ceiling – that may well have been influenced by fellow Chicago architect David Adler's contemporaneous work in Lake Forest, Illinois, and produced by Mrs. Allen's father's wood factory.†

Dining room, 2010. (Blackburn)

† The dining room of Adler's William E. Clow, Jr., house of 1927 was finished in a similar treatment.

On the exterior, the architects used the addition as an opportunity to transform the house into an imposing Georgian manor of at least implied symmetry. The eaves were trimmed back substantially, and the gables – intended by Cowles & Colean to be replaced with hip roofs – lost their half-timbering in favor of traditional weatherboarding. The pediment above the front porch was removed and replaced with an iron railing, behind which a new pair of French doors eliminated the ornamental brick and stone fan motif that had decorated the wall. The brick string course of the original house gave way to a limestone version that belted the addition at the approximate level of the library ceiling; brick jack arches with triple section keystones mimicked those found above windows elsewhere on the structure. Mindful of details, the architects included subtle corner pilasters on the library wing, and even dressed the new chimneys in molded limestone caps. When completed, virtually all the windows were fitted with louvered shutters.

Arthur Dwight Allen was born in 1879 and, following his graduation from Yale, worked at Belknap Hardware along with his brother, Charles, rising to the position of treasurer before leaving Belknap to become secretary-controller of the Fidelity Trust Company. He was married to Jane Potter Mengel of Louisville, the daughter of Charles C. Mengel, founder of the C.C. Mengel & Brothers Co., the country's largest manufacturer of wooden boxes; Arthur would retire in 1924 as president of the Mengel business.[8] The couple – both known in their later years as accomplished painters – had four children, one of which, Jane, assumed ownership of *Robinswood* in 1953.

Today, *Robinswood* has been significantly expanded with the addition to the south of a new kitchen, conservatory, family room and attached garages. Within, the wall between the living hall and the stair has been opened to expose the stair, which now features a wrought iron railing. The Allens' extraordinary library remains untouched, as grand and impressive today as it was when the room was completed.

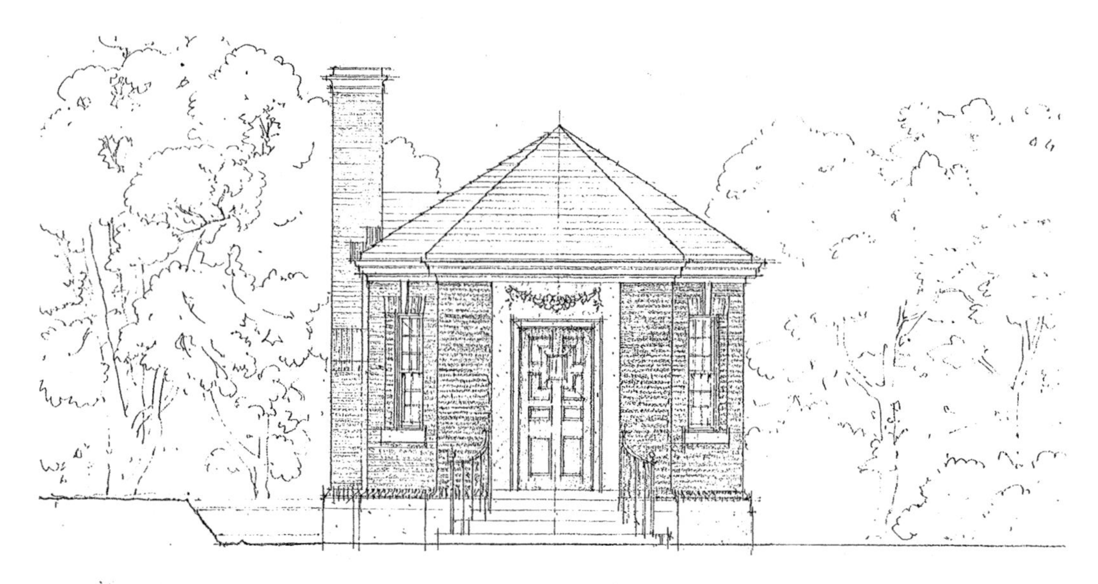

Front elevation, proposed library pavilion (unbuilt), Townsend & Fleming, 1914. (Private Collection)

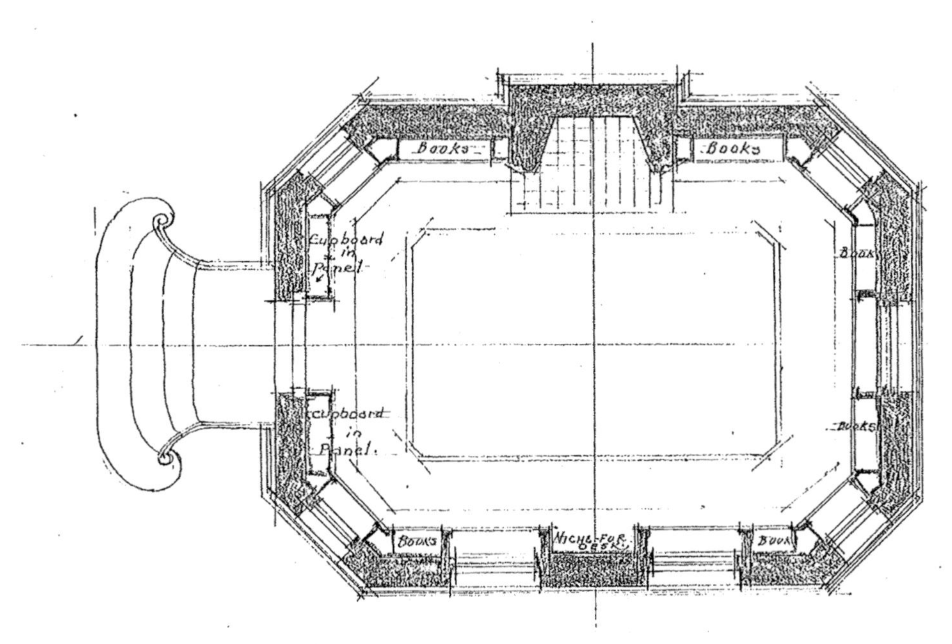

Plan, proposed library pavilion (unbuilt), Townsend & Fleming, 1914. (Private Collection)

Master bedroom sitting room, ca. 1930. (Cowles Archive, Ryerson and Burnham Libraries, Art Institute of Chicago)

GLEN ENTRY

FOR JUDGE AND MRS. LAFON ALLEN

John Bacon Hutchings with E. T. Hutchings, Architects†

1911 - 1912

Entrance elevation, 2011. (Blackburn)

† The design of Glen Entry is attributed to John Bacon Hutchings, and likely his son, E.T., due to the architects' close connection to the Allen family. No concrete proof is presently available.

The third house to be built on a portion of Major Allen's *Allenwood* estate was "Glen Entry" for Lafon Allen, the eldest of the Major's three sons. Like his siblings, Lafon Allen, who was born in 1871, graduated from Yale, but instead of pursuing a career at Belknap, earned his law degree at the University of Louisville and became a lawyer. In 1878, he took as his wife Emma Hunter Powell of Cleveland, Ohio. From 1922 until 1934, he served as a circuit court judge, a title that was thereafter appended to his name.

Glen Entry was built on the far northeastern corner of the *Allenwood* river bluff, occupying a promontory that overlooked the river as well as the valley through which Glenview Avenue traveled below. Likely designed by the Allens' preferred architects, John Bacon and E.T. Hutchings, the house was rendered in a romantic, almost storybook interpretation of the Tudor Revival style. Meandering across the hilltop as though it had been incrementally expanded over the years, the house featured varied roof and eave lines, tall chimneys topped with chimney pots and lavishly half-timbered stucco walls set atop a limestone foundation. Splayed vergeboards accentuated the steep gables and leaded glass windows were grouped within heavy wood framing. At the entrance court, a slender tourelle sprouted from the left side of the main gable, at the center of which was a broad balcony. An exaggerated gable supported by massive brackets sheltered the front door.

Glen Entry was certainly the most imposing of the three bluff-top Allen houses, an impression that was enhanced by the fact that the residence was entered, in essence, at the basement level, which presented the visitor with a three story façade at the arrival court. The inspiration for this arrangement, as well as for the main stair that climbed first to the formal level and then upward to the private, bedroom level of the house, could very well have been drawn from *Rockledge*, the neighboring estate of George Babcock that was under construction as *Glen Entry* was being designed.

Judge Allen broke ground for his new house in late 1911.[9] Upon completion, the property included a small formal garden and grass tennis court, as well as a stone icehouse tucked into the hillside off the driveway. Stone gateposts, perhaps a later addition, marked the entry to the estate at the base of the bluff.

Judge Allen died in 1952, his wife, Emma Hunter Powell Allen, in 1957. Following Mrs. Allen's death, Caroline Allen Kannapel and her husband, Jack, moved to *Glen Entry* from their home, *Cobble Court*, at the foot of the *Allenwood* knoll. At first, the Kannapels' inclination was to replace the house with a new residence but, deeming such an effort impractical, chose to remodel the place. Their alterations included expanding windows to enhance the view of the river, changing various interior walls to rework certain rooms and extending the driveway to the top of the bluff.[10] Over time, additional changes and additions were made, yet none diminished the poetic spirit of the Hutchings' large Shakespearean cottage.

Glen Entry, no longer in the Allen family, today remains a private residence in excellent condition.

COBBLE COURT

FOR MR. AND MRS. GARNETT COOK

Nevin-Morgan & Kolbrook, Architects - Olmsted Brothers, Landscape Architects

1937 - 1938

Entrance elevation, 2011. (Blackburn)

In 1937, Judge and Mrs. Lafon Allen presented their daughter, Caroline, with a lovely wedding gift: in honor of her marriage to Mr. Garnett Cook, the Allens would build the young couple a new house on a site carved from their estate, *Glen Entry.*

The Allens hired the prestigious Louisville architectural firm of Nevin-Morgan & Kolbrook to design the Cook residence on a site that was arguably challenging. Located on a narrow piece of land between Glenview Avenue and the drive to *Glen Entry*, the parcel was virtually all hillside. The architects responded by taking their cue from the Allens' large Elizabethan cottage, designing a Tudor Revival house – although this time in brick – that had its main living level on the second floor and bedroom level on the third. As with *Glen Entry*, the Cook house was entered on the ground floor from a stair that arose from an enclosed motorcourt. The motorcourt was paved in cobblestones, providing the house with its name, "Cobble Court." Judge and Mrs. Allen engaged Olmsted Brothers to design the landscape for the relatively shady site as well as for the walled rectangular garden that extended southward from the living room.[†]

Following the death of Caroline's mother in 1957, the Cooks moved up the bluff to *Glen Entry*, selling *Cobble Court* to Caroline's cousin, Arthur Allen, Jr. In 1966, a paneled library and new master bedroom suite were added to the house, again to the designs of architect Frederic Morgan. Today, *Cobble Court* remains in superb condition as a private residence, its garage-top weathervane, depicting a cook carrying a covered plate, providing a whimsical reference to the original occupants.

Entrance elevation, ca. 1910. (University of Louisville Archives and Records Center, Louisville, Ky)

Rio Vista

THE ESTATE OF MR. & MRS. JOHN H. CAPERTON

McDonald & Dodd, Architects

1909 - 1910

Earlier *Rio Vista* by J.J. Gaffney, architect, burned 1907. (*Artwork of Louisville*, Part 8, 1903)

Perhaps one of the most distinctively eclectic residences constructed during Louisville's golden era of the country house was *Rio Vista*, the highly mannered home of John Hays and Virginia Standiford Caperton.

John Hays Caperton was born in Louisville in 1858, the son of John and Mary Guthrie Caperton. The senior Caperton, a native of Virginia, came to Kentucky after "the adventures and undertakings which attracted young men at that time" had taken him first to Texas for land speculation and then to California to join the Gold Rush. From San Francisco, where he served as deputy sheriff, Caperton settled in Louisville where he married Mary Guthrie, who in turn gave birth to four children, including John Hays.

The junior Caperton entered the real estate business in Louisville at a young age and over time acquired a substantial portfolio of properties, which he operated under the Caperton Realty Company. In 1892, he married Virginia Standiford, the daughter of Elisha David Standiford, former president of the Louisville and Nashville Railroad and the man after whom Louisville's largest airport would in time be named. The couple had one child, a son named Hugh John Caperton, born in 1893.[1]

At some point, presumably not long after the arrival of Hugh John, the Capertons acquired a summer house on the high bluff overlooking the Ohio River. Named "Rio Vista" – River View in Spanish – the house was destroyed by fire a few short years later. Undaunted, the family hired Louisville architect J. J. Gaffney to design a replacement residence, which was completed by early 1900 when it was featured in *The Courier-Journal*.[2]

The new *Rio Vista* was a robust hybrid of the Shingle, Queen Anne and Colonial Revival styles. A true summer cottage (versus full-time residence), the house rested on a limestone block foundation, which in turn supported a broad recessed front porch above which was a ponderous and weighty shingled second floor. A modified Palladian window filled the face of a large dormer, which projected from the tall gable-on-hip shingled roof. The recessed porch extended outward to the west as a Doric colonnade that further enclosed a tall porte cochère. A wide Ionic front porch that projected beyond flanking classical balustrades enlivened the main façade, as did the exuberantly mullioned and fanlighted windows above the front door. The fretwork of the dormer fly rafters – almost Gothic in appearance – completed the lace-like ornamentation that served as a counterpoint to the heavy massing of the stone, brick and wood shingle house.

In 1902, the Capertons hired Olmsted Brothers to plan the grounds of the new estate. The firm revised walkways, specified plantings and designed a rose garden.[3]

A year later, the completed house was photographed for *Art Work of Louisville* and in 1907 for *The Courier-Journal Illustrated Magazine.*[4] And, unfortunately, shortly after the 1907 article appeared, *Rio Vista* again burned to the ground.

Following this second fire, John and Virginia Caperton set out to build a third iteration of their bluff-top country house, a mansion that would reflect their prominent social status within the community. Not only was Caperton maturing in his real estate endeavors, but by 1901 both his father and mother had died, leaving him a "considerable estate" which, when combined with his wife's already substantial resources, enabled the family to embark on the ambitious building project.[5]

To design their new *Rio Vista,* the Capertons hired one of Louisville's most prominent architectural firms, McDonald & Dodd. This was the second of five suburban estates Kenneth McDonald and William Dodd would construct before parting ways, the others being *Lansdowne* for Samuel T. Ballard, *Lincliff* for William Belknap, *Ladless Hill Farm* for Alfred Brandeis and *Barnard Hall* for Louis Seelbach. It would also be among their most imaginative.

First and foremost, the house was to be fireproof. Just as Thruston Ballard's *Lansdowne* was rebuilt in stone, brick, steel and concrete with a tile roof after the first house burned in 1906, so was *Rio Vista* constructed of stuccoed masonry walls, cut stone and a red tile roof (one can presume a steel and concrete structure as well). The long and comparatively narrow house stretched along the bluff on an east-west axis that afforded commanding views out to the river and simultaneously presented an imposing façade to visitors. In a manner that anticipated Gray and Wischmeyer's 1915 estate of Mrs. Thomas Dudley, *Homewood,* the garage and stable building, although separate from the house, was connected to the main structure by a walled motorcourt that visually elongated the entire composition.

Stylistically, the house was a vibrant blend of Mission Revival, Prairie, Colonial Revival and Beaux-Arts influences. Especially noteworthy was the horizontality implied by the strong molded stringcourse that belted the planar walls of the house and garage and the broad uniform eave line of the roofs – gestures that likely stemmed from William Dodd's early training under Chicago's Prairie School architects. Another distinctive grouping of elements was the central triad of projecting porte cochère (with a balustrade derivative of the Vienna Secessionist movement), deeply recessed arched opening leading to the porte cochère balcony rooftop and robust upward-thrusting mission style parapet. Also unusual were the dormers, with their flared and arched fronts, and the roofed gateway to the garage courtyard that suggested far eastern counterparts.

Within, the house was architecturally more homogenous, deriving its inspiration and particular details from the richly plastic forms of the Colonial Revival as then espoused by such well-known and published firms as McKim, Mead & White of New York. Composite crown and ceiling moldings, pilastered door surrounds, paneled walls and marble fireplace hearths with chimneybreasts of fluted Ionic pilasters lent the residence an aura of fashionable and genteel elegance. Of particular note was the sun room, a bright and airy space with three exposures at the west end of the first floor. Furnished with potted palms and rattan tables and chairs, the room offered views to the front lawn, the terraced garden and the Ohio River.

The main entrance to the estate was through a limestone gatehouse with red tile roof located on River Road. The drive passed southward through the flat alluvial plain directly toward the bluff, and then turned westward before crossing the Interurban tracks and climbing in an eastward direction up the hill. Once at the top of the bluff, the drive proceeded to the south before making a U turn to head directly northward on axis to the front of the house. The mansion itself rested on a limestone platform that served to the north as an elevated lawn terrace. The north elevation of the residence was framed by a pair of arbors that functioned as belvederes for the vistas beyond. At the south end, a series of terraces stepped down the side of the bluff, at least one containing a formal garden. The designer of the gardens is unknown, Olmsted having only worked on the previous house in 1902.

Hall, ca. 1912. (*Catalogue of the First Exhibition*, Louisville Chapter, American Institute of Architects, 1912; reprinted by the Central Kentucky Chapter of the AIA, 2008)

Entrance gate, originally located on River Road, in its new location in Louisville's Mockingbird Gardens, 2009. (Blackburn)

Rear elevation, undated. (Filson Historical Society)

The new incarnation of *Rio Vista* was completed by September 1910, when it was presented to the city in a lavish photo essay in *The Courier-Journal*.[6] The estate consisted of over 61 acres, 22 of which were located in the alluvial plain at the base of the bluff. McDonald & Dodd considered this one of their most notable works, including it in the First Exhibit of the Louisville Chapter of the American Institute Architects in 1912.[7]

Virginia Caperton passed away in 1914, leaving her husband to preside by himself over *Rio Vista*. In 1922, two years into Prohibition, the estate again made the newspapers, but this time for a different reason:

> RIO VISTA ... WAS THE SCENE OF A BOLD HOLDUP BY A DESPERATE GANG OF CRIMINALS LAST MARCH, WHEN MORE THAN 100 CASES OF LIQUORS FROM MR. CAPERTON'S PRIVATE STOCK WERE STOLEN... THE BANDIT GANG PUT THE BURGLAR ALARM AT THE CAPERTON PLACE OUT OF COMMISSION AND ATTACKED AND OVERPOWERED THE AGED NIGHTWATCHMAN. TRUCKS WERE USED TO HAUL THE PRIZED LIQUORS AWAY.[8]

John Caperton died in Havana in 1923 while on a six week cruise through the West Indies. The house and his estate – valued at $1.5 million – passed to the Caperton's son, Hugh, and his wife, Dorothy Bonnie Caperton.[9] A favorite of the local press, *Rio Vista* was once more the subject of a feature article, this time in the *Herald-Post* in 1928.[10] In 1944, Hugh Caperton died, and about 10 years later, Dorothy Caperton, who had never been too fond of the house, sold the estate to a developer, who demolished the mansion and subdivided the bluff-top property.[11] In 1957, Louisville architect Stratton Hammon constructed a new house for American Barge Lines executive Armin Willig using *Rio Vista's* foundations.[12] A portion of the garden terrace walls survives, as does the River Road gatehouse, which was relocated in the late 1980s to a park within the new Mockingbird Gardens subdivision several miles away.

Entrance elevation, 1967. (© *The Courier-Journal*)

WINKWORTH - BOXHILL

THE ESTATE OF MR. W.E. CHESS

Joseph E. Chandler, Architect† - Olmsted Brothers and Townsend & Fleming, Landscape Architects††

CA. 1904 - 1905

† Attributed. Please see endnote #2.
†† Olmsted contributed through preliminary design work. However, the gardens as executed are strongly attributed to Townsend & Fleming. Please see text and endnote #7.

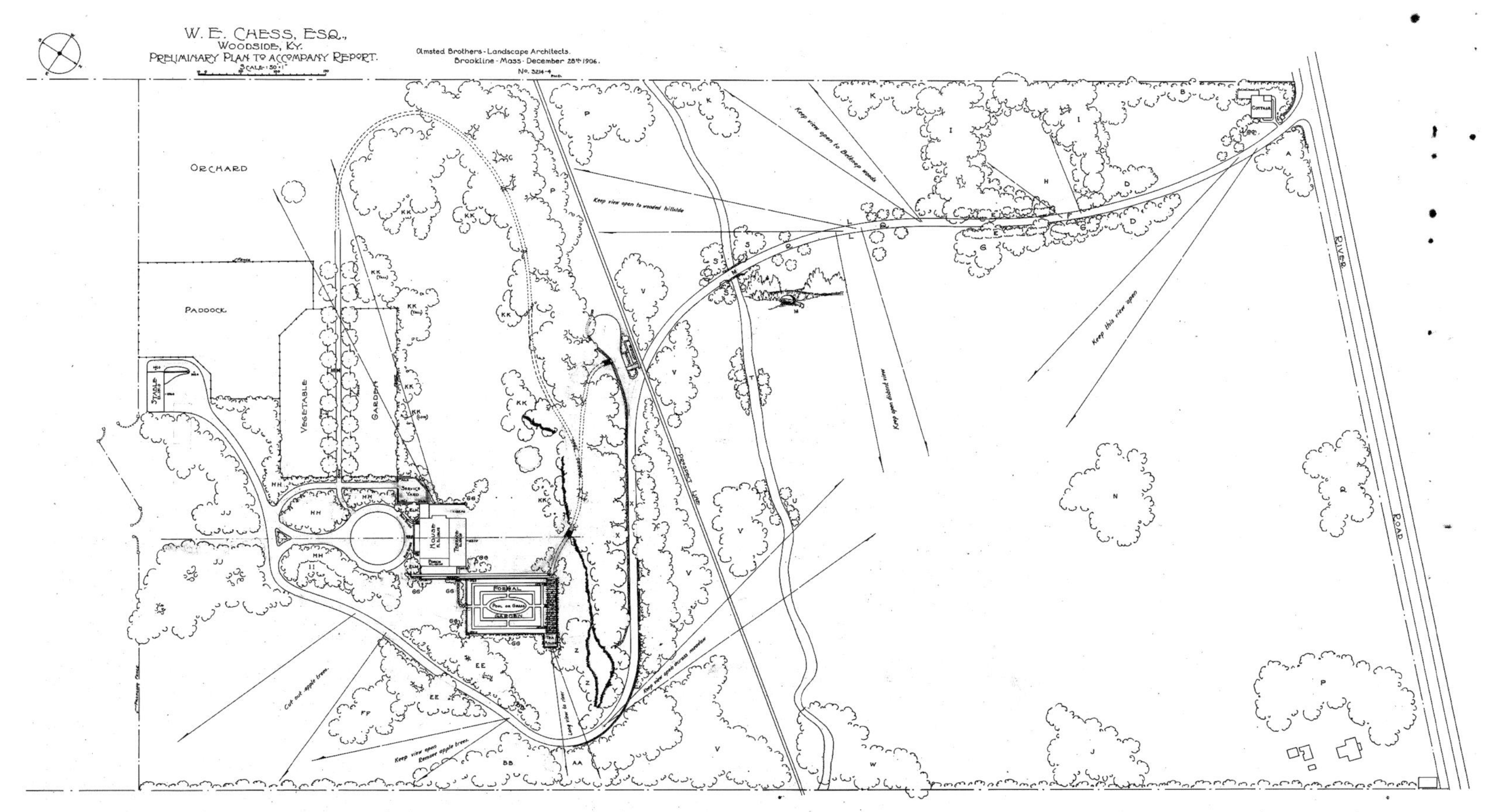

Detail, proposed landscape plan, Olmsted Brothers, 1906. (National Park Service, Frederick Law Olmsted National Historic Site)

The precise details surrounding the beginning of *Winkworth*, the aristocratic country estate of William Edward Chess, are elusive, but suffice it to say that by 1903 or 1904, the widower co-founder of the Chess & Wymond Cooperage Company had acquired almost 76 acres of choice bluff-top land just to the east of what would soon become William R. Belknap's *Lincliff*.[1] The property took the shape of a chamfered rectangle, with about one-third located in the alluvial plain abutting River Road, another third consisting of a former apple orchard atop the bluff and the last portion falling off to a creek valley to the southeast. The ridge of the bluff offered a commanding site for Chess' new country house.

The designs of the house, entrance gates and driveway bridge over the Muddy Fork of Beargrass Creek have been attributed to Boston architect and historian Joseph Everett Chandler, but the supportive documentation is unfortunately anecdotal and circumstantial.[2] What is certain is that, by 1906 when the Olmsted Brothers surveyed the "existing conditions" of the estate, the house, formal gardens and long driveway carved into the limestone bluff had been built.[3]

At the top of the bluff, *Winkworth* was approached on axis down a wide and impressive divided driveway, or mall, that opened to a formal forecourt at the foot of the mansion's imposing limestone portico. The residence was a grand five-bay Federal Revival structure built of red brick set in Flemish bond with limestone details. The design of the aforementioned portico broke with classical architectural canon, as the great stone columns were paired at either end rather than more equidistantly disposed. In a manner just as unconventional, the architect positioned the three center second floor windows so as to clear the portico's heavy entablature.[4] A modillioned cornice surrounded the eaves and graced the pediment of the portico, and a balustrade of alternating panels and classical turned balusters crowned the main house, the west kitchen wing and the east porch.

In plan, the residence was quite straightforward. One entered beneath the stair as it rose in a U, curving up the east wall, across the entry door and then up along the west wall to the second floor. Directly ahead,

Living room, 2002. (stephenphotography.com)

Dining room, 1978. (© *The Courier-Journal*)

and opening through French doors to a terrace that in turn offered a view to the river, were the living and dining rooms, the former measuring a substantial 35 feet by 22 feet and occupying the northeast corner, the latter measuring 26 feet by 22 feet and located in the northwest corner. An intimate study was tucked behind the stairway, to the right of the portico, and a butlers pantry connected the dining room to the single-story kitchen wing that projected to the west. The three public rooms all featured fireplaces; the living and dining room walls were decorated with box moldings and the twelve-foot ceilings with oval plaster reliefs and a modillioned crown. Upstairs were four large bedroom suites, three with fireplaces, as well as access to the third floor servants' quarters.

The original landscaping surrounding the house consisted of the grand bifurcated driveway and a terraced formal garden, constructed atop chamfered earthen berms, that extended from the east porch.[5] However, for reasons unknown, Chess engaged the Olmsted Brothers in late 1906 to revisit *Winkworth's* landscaping, and the designers responded with a plan that proposed significant alterations to both the approach drive and the formal garden.

Using the existing space occupied by the front mall, Olmsted suggested replacing the bifurcated roadway with a single drive that opened into a wide circle in front of the house, replacing the broad paved forecourt. The landscape architects then recommended that the existing formal garden be removed and a new garden built away from the house to the northeast. This new garden would be rectangular in shape, with an oval pool or planting in the center, and a pergola at the far end; a teahouse belvedere was to offer a controlled vista through a trimmed landscape to the river.[6] Perhaps not surprisingly, this garden bore a striking resemblance in design and placement to a similar garden the firm created a few years earlier for George Norton's *Norton Hall* at Cherokee Park.

Apparently Olmsted's plans were not implemented, but they appear to have been adopted – at least in part – by a successor landscape architect whose designs were indeed constructed. The designer of choice was clearly the Buffalo, New York, firm of Townsend & Fleming, which likely executed the work prior to the onset of World War I.[7] Townsend & Fleming had received several notable commissions in Louisville, beginning in 1911 with houses and gardens for Samuel Henning at *Cold Spring* and George Babcock at *Rockledge*, followed by extravagant gardens for Robert Carrier in 1913 and a forecourt and gardens for Louis Wymond's river front *Shore Acres* in 1914 – the last three within a quarter mile radius of *Winkworth*.

Sketch of proposed flower garden (unbuilt), Olmsted Brothers, 1906. (National Park Service, Frederick Law Olmsted National Historic Site)

For Chess, the firm designed three major landscape elements. First, the bifurcated driveway was extended to a distance equal to an almost imperial length of approximately 450 feet. The landscape architects retained the paved forecourt, but narrowed the width of the mall. Second, at the far end of the mall, where the main drive turned to approach the house, the firm created a set of terraced gardens that recalled those built for Robert Carrier nearby. Constructed using the designer's signature blend of coarse stone, dressed classical elements and red brick, and laid out – like Carrier – using simple geometries that paired formal structure with shapes that followed the contours of the hill, this garden served both as a terminus to the view from the house as well as an elaborate entry to a badminton court that overlooked the shallow valley below.

The third landscape element created by Townsend & Fleming was a rectangular, sunken garden on the site proposed for the formal garden by Olmsted. The garden as built featured a pergola as recommended by the Boston firm, and similarly a pool in the center. Unlike Olmsted's classical approach, Townsend & Fleming's design was intended to offer a more naturalistic environment within a subtly formal structure, as observed by writer A. Carter Goodloe in the October 1917 issue of *House & Garden:*

> The Buffalo landscape artist who designed this garden must have offered up a prayer of fervent thanksgiving at the perfect setting he found ready to his hand. This garden, situated at only a moment's walk from the house, is yet completely detached from any architectural impositions. ... I know of no other garden about Louisville that strikes a deeper note of simplicity and informality, of tranquility and privacy. ... The simple, natural beauty of the plan of this garden coupled with the apparent irregularity of the planting...are really enchanting. Here nothing is forced, nothing distracts the eye... The pool in the center has entirely the effect of nature with its concrete contours softened and almost concealed by masses of creeping Japanese juniper.[8]

William Chess founded the Chess & Wymond Company, the "largest cooperage concern in the world," in 1887. He was also involved in the oil business – a company that later became Standard Oil of Kentucky – through his brother-in-law, Frank D. Carley. A widower since 1892, Chess retired as president of Chess & Wymond in 1916.[9] Shortly after, he gave *Winkworth* to his daughter, Grace Mary Chess Robinson.[†] In 1920, Mary Robinson and her husband, Avery, moved to London when Mr. Robinson assumed the position of treasurer of the Royal Philharmonic Society. Chess soon followed, as his other daughter had married an Englishman and also taken up residence in London. In 1923, the Robinsons sold *Winkworth* to stockbroker Henning Chambers and his wife, Mina Breaux Ballard, whose parents, Charles and Mina Ballard, had built *Bushy Park* nearby.[10]

The Chambers owned the estate for over 20 years, during which time they made several notable modifications to the residence. Renaming the property "Boxhill," the Chambers added a second floor to the kitchen wing and a two-story porch on the rear of the house. They also replaced Townsend & Fleming's naturalistic reflecting pool in the rear garden with a swimming pool.[11]

In 1956, *Boxhill* was sold to developer Martin L. Adams & Sons, who proceeded to subdivide the estate into 14 building sites, retaining the mansion and approximately five acres for Joshua Adams and his family.[12] Adams then engaged Louisville architects Stratton and Neal

† In 1932, Mary Chess Robinson founded the Mary Chess Company, maker of perfumes, in New York City.

The library as remodeled by Stratton Hammon, 1978. (© *The Courier-Journal*)

Hammon to modify and update the residence. On the first floor, the kitchen and butlers pantry were remodeled and the study expanded and paneled in cherry. Upstairs, alterations were made to accommodate additional bathrooms and closets. Perhaps the most notable change was the addition of an accessible wrought iron balcony above the front door, which served to join the three-part stair landing window with the door and sidelight assembly below, creating a stronger visual central element between the splayed columns of the portico.[13] Presumably also at this time the current brick, stone and iron gates at the entrance to the mall were constructed. In the early 1990s, the current owners extended and enclosed the east porch as a large solarium.[14]

Winkworth (now *Boxhill*) remains in private hands and in fine condition, although unfortunately without the rooftop balustrade on the main house. The entry gates at River Road exist (widened to accommodate a two-way drive) as does the neoclassical bridge over the Muddy Fork of Beargrass Creek. Townsend & Fleming's terraced gardens at the end of the mall still exist, albeit in a ruined state, and remnants of the formal pond garden are still visible around the swimming pool that replaced it.

Entrance elevation, 2011. (Blackburn)

BUSHY PARK - MELCOMBE

THE ESTATE OF MR. AND MRS. CHARLES T. BALLARD
(LATER OF JUDGE AND MRS. ROBERT WORTH BINGHAM)

John Bacon Hutchings, Architect - Marion Cruger Coffin, Landscape Architect
1909-1911

The story of *Bushy Park* began in 1887 when John E. Green, one of the investor-owners of the famed Glenview Stock Farm, dedicated fifteen acres of the farm's river bluff property to the formation of a summer social and recreation club.[1] Named the Fincastle Club after Fincastle County, Virginia (of which Kentucky was part before achieving statehood), the property featured a large three-story clubhouse wrapped in part by a two-story veranda and surrounded by at least seven individual cottages owned by several of the 60-odd members. Outdoor activities at the Fincastle included trap shooting, croquet, horseback riding and tennis, while the clubhouse served as an inn for gentlemen only, offering its dining room and ballroom for the use of all members.[2]

Among the early members of the club was Charles Thruston Ballard, president and co-founder with his brother, Samuel Thruston Ballard, of the Ballard & Ballard milling company. Born in 1850 and a graduate of Yale's Sheffield Scientific School, C.T. Ballard was married in 1878 to Emilina Modeste (Mina) Breaux, the daughter of a Col. Gustave Breaux, a Confederate commander and prominent New Orleans attorney.[3] Ballard constructed his cottage – "Holiday House" – on a bluff near the clubhouse in 1892-3; S. Thruston, who also had a cottage at Fincastle, would build his own grand residence, *Lansdowne*, on a neighboring bluff seven years later.

The Fincastle Club was disbanded in 1899, and one of its members (and a cousin of Ballard), Judge Alexander Pope Humphrey, purchased the clubhouse and converted it into his private residence. Shortly thereafter, he acquired several of the adjacent cottages, eventually bringing his estate to twelve acres. Simultaneously, Ballard expanded his holdings to an eventual 28 acres and, in 1905, remodeled *Holiday House* with the addition of a fashionable two-story Ionic colonnade.[4]

In 1909, Ballard engaged the prominent Louisville architect, John Bacon Hutchings, to design a substantial and permanent residence, as a replacement for *Holiday House* (which was subsequently torn down), at the edge of the bluff overlooking the Ohio River. The resulting house was a somber modified Georgian, heavily modeled in deep red brick and limestone. The entrance façade was distinguished by an imposing portico of fluted Tuscan Doric limestone columns with a classical architrave of triglyphs, metopes and modillions, surmounted by a comparatively delicate wrought iron railing – a composition that was repeated in the west-facing side porch. To either side, sets of French doors with thick limestone arched lintels framed the main entry, which was unusual in its highly mannered surround of alternating bands of brick and limestone. Centered in the grillwork over the transom was a cartouche bearing a gilded letter "B," a choice that was fortuitous for the subsequent owner

Fincastle clubhouse / Humphrey home, ca. 1910. (Caufield & Shook Collection, University of Louisville Archives and Records Center, Louisville, Ky)

"Holiday House," 1907. (Filson Historical Society)

of the property. The windows of the second floor continued the eclectic nature of the house, being more Federal in design in contrast to the Beaux-Arts nature of the first floor. The slate roof was relatively low in pitch with broad eaves and low, unassuming dormers.

In plan, the house consisted of a large main hall flanked on either side by two identically sized rooms: a music room and billiard room to the west, and a library and dining room to the east. A service ell extended from the rear of the house, while the limestone side porch overlooked an elevated lawn terrace to the west. A pergola was to have graced the east end of the residence, but ultimately was never built. The second floor contained a large living hall surrounded by bedroom suites, as well as servant's quarters and a sleeping porch. An elevator extended from the basement to the second floor.

The focal point of the interiors was the main hall, an Edwardian expanse that suggested the first class salons of the great transatlantic liners of the era. The space, which measured 33 feet by 43 feet, featured richly carved beams, wainscoting and pilasters; great arched doorways with mullioned transoms; a pair of stout Ionic columns; and a grand bifurcated stairway with elaborate iron railings. Opulent torchères and gilt wood chandeliers illuminated the room, which boasted sumptuous furnishings made especially for the Ballards in Italy. The music room, billiard room and library were virtually identical in fenestration and plan, while the dining room was distinguished by a large carved marble fireplace set in the north wall and a triptych of French doors leading to the east terrace. Although each room was distinctive in its architectural finishes, the billiard room deviated from the predominantly Georgian theme of the others, and was fitted in a more Germanic manner with oak paneling and a heavy beamed ceiling.

Requiring two years to build, the house was completed in 1911. Ballard christened the estate "Bushy Park" after the late 17th century Virginia homestead of his great-great grandfather, Armistead Churchill, whose name would later attach to the fabled racetrack of the Kentucky Derby, Churchill Downs.[5] The estate quickly caught the attention of the local press and was featured in an expansive photo essay in *The Courier-Journal* on March 3, 1911, and Hutchings, clearly proud of the project, included the house in the April 1912 exhibit of the Louisville Chapter of the American Institute of Architects.[6]

The general landscaping plan for the site, including the long drive that wound gently uphill from the road to the house, was executed by the English landscape engineer Cecil Fraser, who was responsible for carrying out the Olmsted schemes for Louisville's new parks.[7] Although Ballard initially engaged Olmsted Brothers of Boston to design gardens for the estate, an ensuing disagreement led him to employ New York landscape architect Marian Cruger Coffin for the project. Coffin, who was in Louisville at the time working on the restoration of the gardens at Oxmoor Farms and who would later help design the gardens for Henry DuPont's Delaware estate, *Winterthur*, created at *Bushy Park* a formal Italian garden that featured large "Italien Oil Jars," or urns, and an armillary sun dial, and terminated in a semicircular arbor which afforded views down the knoll toward the creek valley separating *Bushy Park* from *Lansdowne*. The garden, completed in 1912 and named "Broken Flags" after its rustic stone paths, was featured in the October 1917 issue of *House & Garden* magazine.[8] In addition to Broken Flags, Coffin designed a small "giardino segreto," or secret garden (later called the "Green Garden"), at the north side of the main house. Set below the picture window between the twin stairs in the main hall, this intimate parterre of clipped boxwood hedges and octagonal reflecting pool presented an unexpected surprise for the viewer from above.

In 1918, Charles Ballard suffered a heart attack and died at age 68.

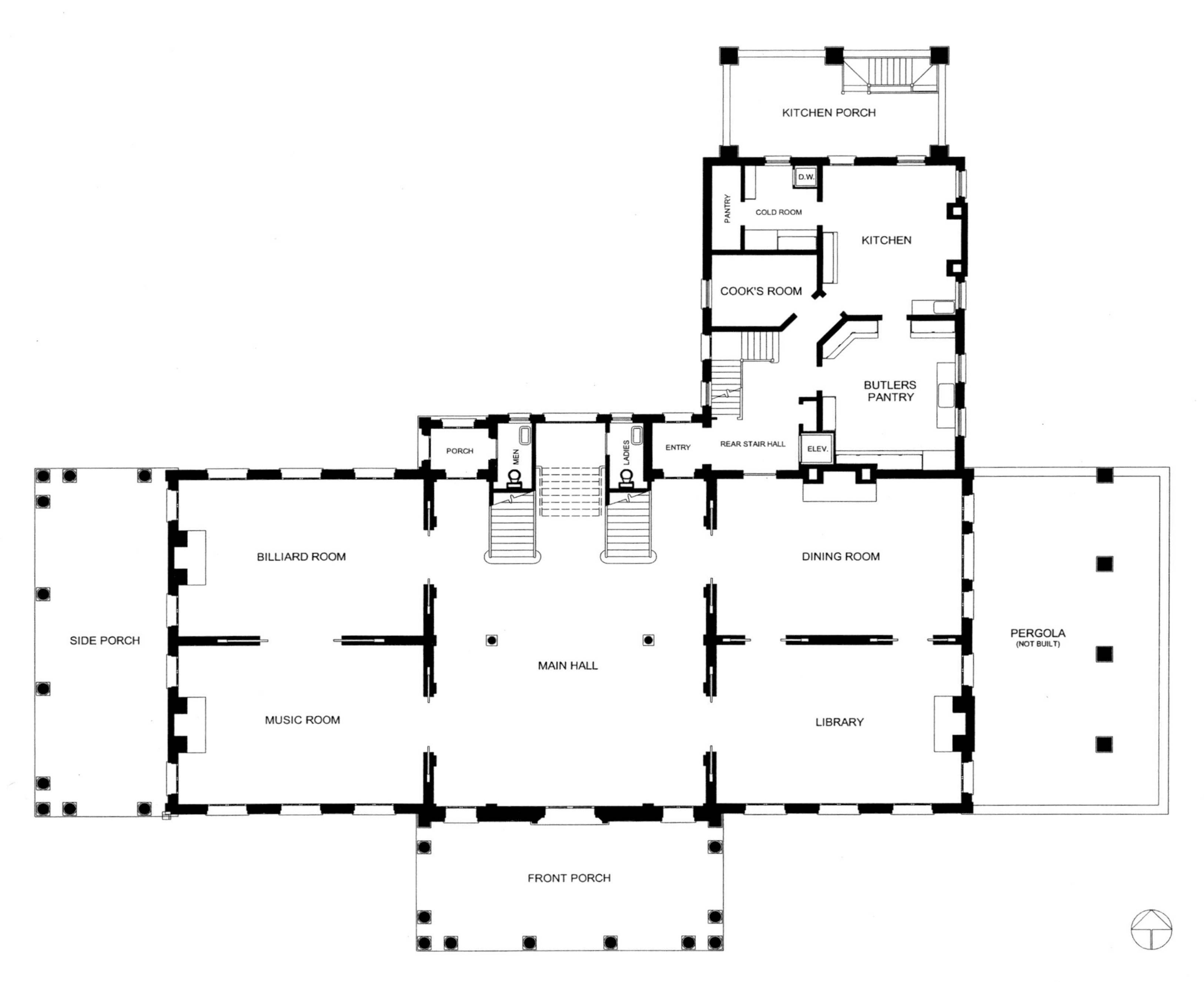

First floor plan

Original music room, ca. 1960. (Private Collection)

Not long after, Mina Breaux Ballard sold *Bushy Park* to Judge Robert Worth Bingham and moved to Cherokee Park where she purchased the Italian villa of Mrs. Ernest Allis, who had also recently passed away. It was Bingham who would proceed to lead the estate into its golden age.

Robert Worth Bingham was born in 1871 in North Carolina and came to Louisville in the mid-1890s. A lawyer by education and practice, he attended the universities of North Carolina, Virginia and Louisville, and was subsequently appointed Mayor of Louisville and later circuit court judge. In 1916, Bingham took as his second wife Mary Lily Flagler, the widow of Standard Oil co-founder and Florida railroad and real estate magnate Henry Flagler. Less than a year later, Mary Lily Bingham died, leaving

Main hall, 1911. (Private Collection)

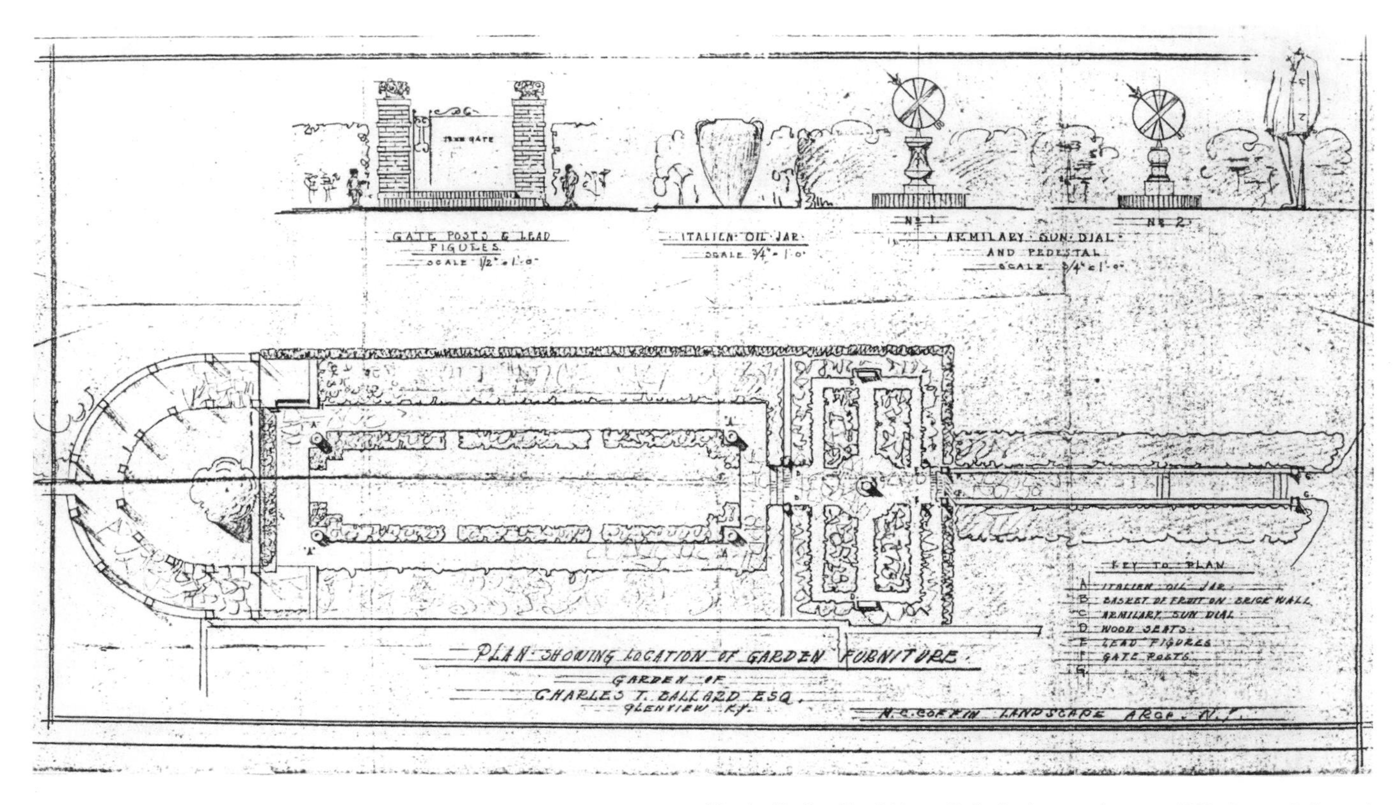

Plan for "Broken Flags," Marian Coffin, landscape architect, ca. 1912. (Private Collection)

a $5 million bequest to her new husband. Bingham went on to acquire Kentucky's two leading newspapers, *The Courier-Journal* and *The Louisville Times,* creating a powerful, highly respected and Pulitzer Prize-winning media empire. In 1924, he was married again, to Aleen Lithgow Hilliard, the widow of Louisville banker and stockbroker John James Byron Hilliard. In 1933, President Franklin Roosevelt appointed Bingham Ambassador to the Court of St. James, a position he held until his death in 1937, when he was succeeded by Joseph Kennedy.[9]

Bingham followed his acquisition of the Ballard estate with a series of improvements that would require over a decade to complete. He began by renaming the property "Melcombe Bingham," or simply "Melcombe," after the family seat in Dorsetshire, England.[10] In 1924, he added a swimming pool, complete with dressing pavilions and arbor, to the designs of Nevin-Wischmeyer & Morgan of Louisville. Within the residence, he made minor alterations to the great hall, but also converted the music room into a glittering salon through the addition of a marble and lapis lazuli fireplace mantel and four slender crystal chandeliers. Shortly after the death of Judge Humphrey in 1928, Bingham acquired the balance of the old Fincastle Club property, including the clubhouse, gardens and nearby cottage Humphrey had built in 1916 for his daughter, Mary Churchill Humphrey.

Bingham demolished the old clubhouse and built in its place a monumental Greek theatre, designed by the celebrated New York firm of Carrère & Hastings. The firm would have been well known to Bingham,

"Broken Flags." The tennis court is at the left. (*House & Garden* Magazine, 1919)

The Secret or Green Garden, ca. 1938. (Private Collection)

having completed Ross Todd's *Rostrevor* near Cherokee Park in 1908 and the Louisville Memorial Auditorium in 1929, as well as Henry and Mary Lily Flagler's palatial Florida palazzo of 1902, *Whitehall*. The theatre proscenium was constructed of limestone as a blend of antique classicism in which academic Greek Doric columns were paired with decidedly Roman arches, set beneath a Greek entablature stylized with a frieze of alternating discs and triglyphs. A shallow pool with twin fountains separated the grass stage from the semicircular seating area, which was constructed, as were the enclosing walls and entry archways, of brick and flagstone. Behind the massive colonnade was a formal boxwood garden, quite possibly a reincorporation of the garden Judge Humphrey planted behind his clubhouse-cum-residence. Hastings died and the firm closed its doors not long before the theatre was completed in early 1930, and Bingham subsequently hired noted landscape architect Arthur W. Cowell of State College, Pennsylvania, to execute the final planting and garden design.[11]

Shortly after building the Greek theatre, Bingham hired English architect S. Tomlin to design a new set of entrance gates for the estate.[12] Humphrey's daughter's cottage, dubbed "Red Flower Cottage" or "Little Melcombe," was converted into an additional residence for family use. A tennis court, greenhouses, working barn, gardeners' cottages and carriage house with chauffeur's quarters completed the estate. In 1933, not long after Judge Bingham was appointed Ambassador to Great Britain, *Country Life* magazine featured the gardens and Greek theatre in an article entitled, "Melcombe Bingham at Glenview, Kentucky."[13]

Today, *Melcombe* consists of approximately 55 acres, not including land acquired later as a nature conservancy from the old *Lansdowne* property. For years a destination of distinguished visitors to Kentucky, the estate has been host to David Lloyd George, Prime Minister of Great Britain; the Duke and Duchess of Windsor; Princess Margaret and Lord Snowden; as well as major figures of the American art, theater, literary and political worlds. Well-maintained, it remains in private hands.

Mary Churchill's "Red Flower Cottage," 2009. (Blackburn)

The Greek theatre, 1930. (Private Collection)

Entrance elevation, 2011. (Blackburn)

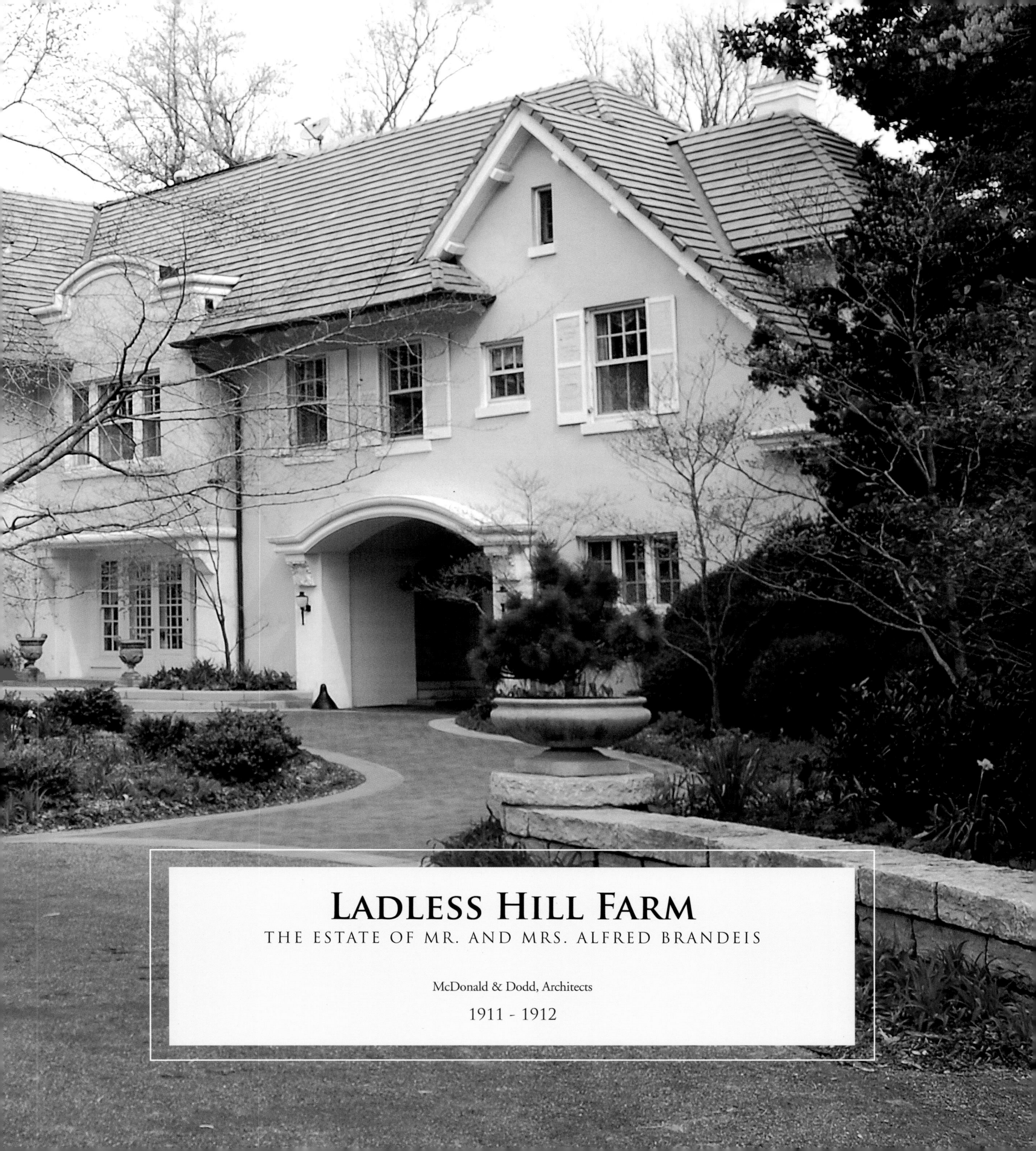

Ladless Hill Farm

The Estate of Mr. and Mrs. Alfred Brandeis

McDonald & Dodd, Architects

1911 - 1912

Alfred Brandeis was born in Louisville in 1854, the son of Adolph and Frederica Dembitz Brandeis, who had immigrated to the United States from Prague five years earlier.[†] In 1852, the senior Brandeis co-founded the grain brokerage firm of Brandeis and Crawford, which was renamed A. Brandeis & Son after young Alfred joined it a number of years later. By the time Alfred took the helm of the business following his father's death in 1906, A. Brandeis & Son had become a very substantial enterprise credited with "contributing largely to the making of Louisville a large grain market." A prominent member of Louisville's business elite, Brandeis was one of the organizers and directors of the Louisville Board of Trade as well as the Lincoln Bank and Trust Company. He took as his wife Jennie Taussig of St. Louis, whose father was the builder of the St. Louis Union Station. The couple had four daughters.[1]

Brandeis enjoyed farming as a hobby and, beginning in 1898, started assembling what would become by 1913 a 67-acre bluff top estate situated between William R. Belknap's *Lincliff* and W.E. Chess' *Winkworth.*[2] A family with no sons, Alfred and Jennie Brandeis named their country house *Ladless Hill Farm.*

As was fairly typical of the era, Brandeis early on had built a relatively modest clapboard home at the edge of the bluff, a broad porch offering sweeping views to the Ohio River beyond. However, this large cottage succumbed to the fate recently suffered by the nearby Caperton and S.T. Ballard houses, burning to the ground in 1909 or 1910.[3] Following the footsteps of his neighbors, Brandeis promptly set out to replace the lost structure with a new, much grander and fireproof mansion. To accomplish this task, the family turned to the Louisville firm of McDonald & Dodd, architects – who, perhaps not coincidentally, had just completed the post-fire houses for both Caperton and Ballard.

The new Brandeis house was designed in an unusual blend of influences drawn from the currently fashionable Arts and Crafts and Mediterranean movements – an approach similar to that the architects had taken at Caperton's *Rio Vista.* Like *Rio Vista, Ladless Hill* was constructed using a concrete frame with hollow tile walls, a stucco exterior and tile roof. The two houses shared a similar fenestration typology (single shuttered sash windows on the second floor above grouped shutterless windows below), broad-eaved roof form and main entrance articulated by a seemingly incongruous mission style pediment above. While the exterior of *Rio Vista* was relatively devoid of ornament, that of *Ladless Hill* was starkly so: only the bracketed lintels and archways above the entry and service doors and porte cochère provided relief from the otherwise taut stucco walls. Interestingly, the shallow arch of the porte cochère formed a design theme throughout the house, reappearing in the screened and service porches, service entrance and river side gable window of the exterior, and stairway arcade, dining room china cabinets and library overmantel in the interior.

Within, the house was finished – as was *Rio Vista* – with primarily Colonial Revival-inspired details, including fluted Tuscan Doric columns at the stairway arcade, rich modillioned crown moldings in the stair hall and dining room and a lavish dining room chimney breast that featured bas reliefs suggestive of the work of the late 17th century English wood

† Brandeis' younger brother was Louis Brandeis, the well-known and distinguished Associate Justice of the United States Supreme Court from 1916 to 1939.

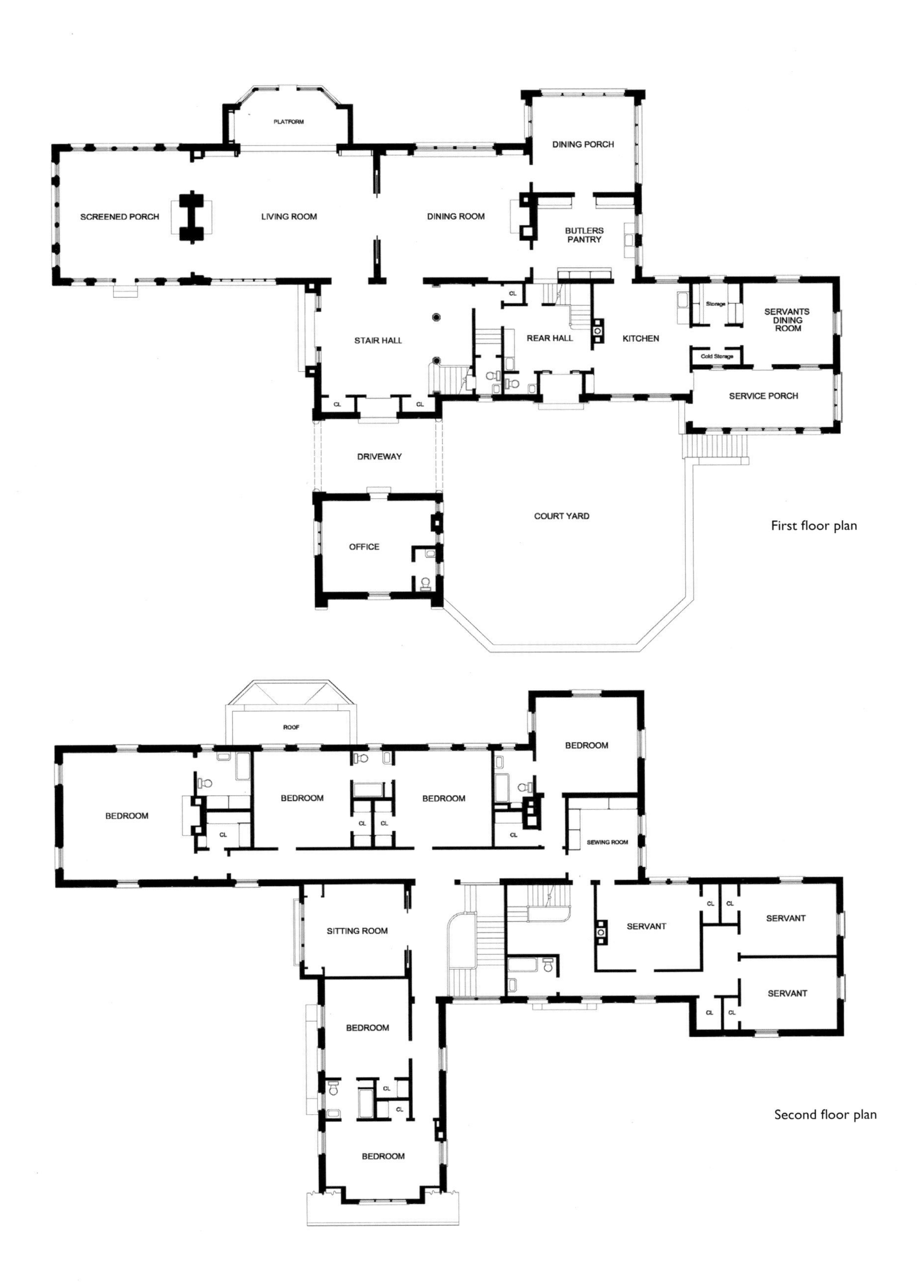

First floor plan

Second floor plan

Stair hall, after removal of arcade, 2010. (Blackburn)

carver, Grinling Gibbons. Stained glass windows, attributed to the Alberts Studio of Louisville, illuminated the stairway.[4] The library was a more Germanic "gentleman's retreat," with dark paneling covering the lower three-quarters of the walls and an equally dark beamed paneled ceiling.

The most distinctive and surprising aspect of *Ladless Hill*, however, was its architectural plan, which seemed to anticipate the rectilinear simplicity of the forthcoming modern movement. Almost pinwheel in shape, the plan consisted of intersecting and adjacent rectangles (the latter which appeared to slide past one another) – an approach that reflected virtually none of the patterns or precepts of the Colonial Revival or Beaux-Arts schools of design then so popular. Perhaps the form was dictated by the nature of the concrete structural frame, or perhaps by the

Original dining room, now used as the living room, 1988. (*Southern Accents* magazine, September/October 1988, Paul Beswick, photographer)

need to fit the house on a narrow ridge along the bluff, but in any event it was a plan fundamentally unlike any other employed in Louisville's country houses of the era.

Alfred Brandeis passed away in 1928, leaving a farm that was "equipped with every modern improvement and farm implement and [was] noted for its fine stock, including blooded Duroc swine."[5] Jennie Brandeis continued to live in the house for several more years – at least long enough to see *Ladless Hill* published in the *Herald-Post* in 1930.[6] Thomas Bullitt, prominent attorney and heir to the fabled Oxmoor Farms in Louisville, subsequently acquired the estate. In about 1959, Bullitt mirrored the efforts of the Collis family at nearby *Malvern House* and engaged the local architectural firm of Louis and Henry to modify and downsize the house. The eastern wing containing the servants' dining room, service porch and servants' bedrooms above was removed, as were the viewing 'platform,' or raised alcove, off the living room and the arcade at the main stairway. The living room was converted to a library and the dining room to a new living room. The dining porch was enlarged into a portion of the butlers pantry and transformed into the formal dining room. In 1983, the current owners engaged Louisville architects Stratton and Neal Hammon to enlarge the dining room by removing the balance of the butlers pantry.[7] A new formal garden and terrace were constructed on the site of the former lawn terrace on the river side of the residence.

Still presiding over much of its original acreage, *Ladless Hill Farm* survives today in excellent condition as a private residence.

Rear service court and servants' wing (since removed), ca. 1912. (Private Collection)

Rear elevation with later landscaping additions, 2011. (Blackburn)

Entrance elevation, 2009. (Blackburn)

Lincliff

THE ESTATE OF MR. AND MRS. WILLIAM R. BELKNAP

McDonald & Dodd, Architects - Olmsted Brothers, Landscape Architects, 1905-1912
Bryant Fleming, Landscape Architect, 1933-1934

1905 - 1934

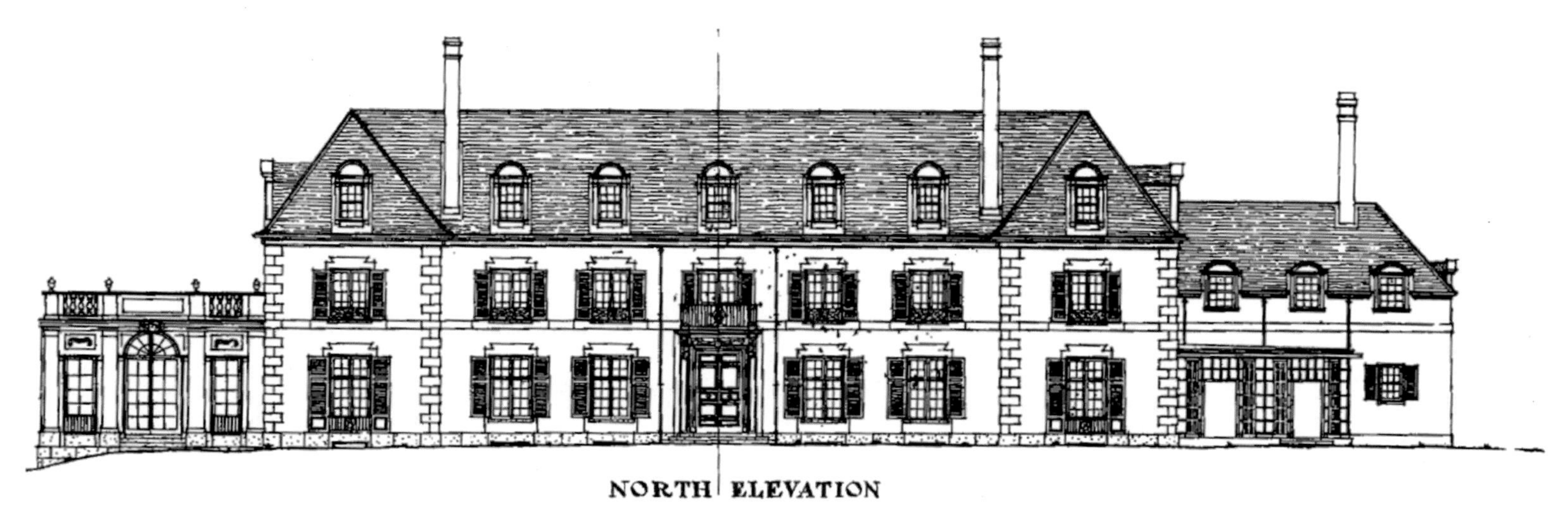

Charles Platt, William Maxwell house, Rockville, CT, 1906-1908. (*The Architecture of Charles Platt*, 1913, republished by Acanthus Press, 1998)

In the early autumn of 1905, John C. Olmsted, principal of the celebrated Boston landscape design firm that bore his name, met with Mrs. William R. Belknap in Louisville to discuss plans for her family's new country estate. Clearly Mrs. Belknap, who was directing the project, had given careful thought to how the estate should take shape – "she has been reading up on preparation for country life," Olmsted noted. At their meeting, Mrs. Belknap provided her landscape architect with a memorandum outlining her scope of work, wishes and questions.

> NAME – LINCLIFF. ROAD. ... SITE FOR HOUSE, BARN, GARDENER'S HOUSE, WOOD-HOUSE, TENNIS COURT, LOOKOUT, CISTERNS, WATERWORKS, LIGHTING; GROUPS OF TREES, PINES, WHITE, RED OR NORWAY. TULIPS; MAPLES, SWEET GUM, OAKS, BEECHES. ORCHARDS, VINEYARDS, FLOWER GARDEN. VEGETABLE GARDEN. EXTENT OF LAWN; WHEN TO SOW. HOW TO PREPARE SOIL. ... FENCES, HOW MANY TO ABOLISH. WHAT KINDS TO SUBSTITUTE. LEAVE PART OF VIRGINIA RAIL FENCE. HOUSE TO BE COLONIAL. BACK AS PRESENTABLE AS FRONT. KITCHEN GARDEN. MUCH PORCH. PORTE COCHÈRE. VENTILATION FIRST CONSIDERATION. PLENTY OF CLOSETS AND STOREROOMS.[1]

Lincliff consisted of 54 acres of former farmland atop the Ohio River bluffs and shared an access road with its neighbor to the north, Alfred Brandeis' *Ladless Hill*. At their 1905 meeting, Olmsted and Belknap were quick to agree on the site of the residence; however, Olmsted's plans to redirect a creek that constituted the boundary between *Lincliff* and *Ladless Hill* in order to provide a scenic approach drive was rejected by Brandeis, leaving Olmsted with no choice but to carve the road discretely into the creek valley hillside. Moving quickly, by year-end the firm was already directing the trimming of trees and installation of new plantings – even though the design of the house existed in concept only.

Gallery hall, 2010. (John Nation)

The site landscape architect and client decided on for the residence was at the peak of the bluff, a generous distance back from its steep edge. In so locating the house, Belknap and Olmsted allowed for both a broad front or approach lawn and a sweeping glade to the rear that terminated in a carefully crafted view of the Ohio River. Olmsted, in the notes from his 1905 visit, suggested placing the house on a north-south axis, and further recommended the form it should take in order to meet his client's wishes:

> I ADVISED THAT THE HOUSE BE LONG AND NARROW SO THE SOUTH EXPOSURE CAN BE TAKEN ADVANTAGE OF BY AS MANY ROOMS AS POSSIBLE AT THE SAME TIME THAT THE NORTH VIEW IS COMMANDED, AND THAT THE LIVING ROOM BE AT WEST END, RUNNING NORTH AND SOUTH, HALL NEXT RUNNING THROUGH, STAIRS AND A STUDY NEXT, DINING ROOM NEXT, RUNNING THROUGH AND SERVANTS DINING ROOM AND VERANDA AT EAST END. ... I ADVISED A GRASS TERRACE ON NORTH FRONT WITH ENOUGH PAVED AREA NEXT [TO] HOUSE FOR SITTING OUT IN SHADE OF HOUSE.[2]

Olmsted worked on *Lincliff* through mid-1906, after which the firm appears to either have completed its responsibilities or been placed on hold by the Belknaps. Although work had ceased, client and landscape architect continued to correspond, but even that came to an end in 1911, the year construction began on the house.[3]

To shape the architecture of *Lincliff*, Mrs. Belknap selected Louisvillian William J. Dodd, who worked hand-in-hand with Olmsted in the early years on the form and placement of the residence.[4] *Lincliff* was the first of Dodd's great country house commissions in Louisville, all of which he would execute during his brief partnership with Kenneth McDonald, an association that lasted from 1906 to about 1913.

The design of the house was completed by mid-1911, after the curious 5-year interregnum that followed the end of Olmsted's documented work. In plan, the residence generally conformed to the layout specified by Olmsted in 1905 and to Mrs. Belknap's dictates that ventilation be the "first consideration" and the "back [be] as presentable as [the] front." Long and narrow, the structure was placed such that the primary axis through the front door was aligned to the north, and the transverse axis traveled east-west. As Olmsted suggested, the living room and open porch were placed at the west end of the house and oriented on a north-south basis, and the dining and breakfast rooms were similarly positioned at the east end. In between, a grand gallery hall, noted for its elegant, shallow vaulted strapwork ceiling, opened at the north to a terrace overlooking the river, and to the south gave access to a paneled study and billiard room, each symmetrically placed on either side of the central entrance vestibule and stairway. To the far west, adjoining the living room, was a glass-enclosed sun porch finished in the fashionable latticework of the day, and to the far east was found the kitchen and service wing. All primary rooms, as stipulated by Olmsted, enjoyed at least partial southern exposure.

The exterior of the house – most notably the front façade – was undoubtedly modeled after the Rockville, Connecticut, mansion of William Maxwell, built between 1906 and 1908 to the designs of New York architect Charles Platt and published in the *Architectural Review* in late 1909.[5] Based on 17th century English and French precedents, the main elevation of the Maxwell house was virtually identical to that of *Lincliff*. In fact, the only significant variations between the two were the thickness and height of the chimneys and the design of the entrance door and surround. Otherwise, both houses were organized around an elongated H-shape plan, shared the same order

Main staircase and entry vestibule, 1920. (Caufield & Shook Collection, University of Louisville Archives and Records Center, Louisville, Ky)

and detail of fenestration, were finished in stucco and surmounted by a tile roof. Even the Palladian sunrooms were indistinguishable from each other. Clearly a copy of the Maxwell design had made its way to either Mrs. Belknap or her architects, and was enthusiastically adopted for *Lincliff.*

The house and outbuildings, which consisted of a central stable and carriage house flanked by identical caretakers' cottages, were organized at opposite ends of a long rectangular lawn that was in turn outlined by the driveway – a composition that resulted in an enormous green forecourt. The house sat upon an expansive, elevated lawn terrace, to the

Living room, 1920. (Caufield & Shook Collection, University of Louisville Archives and Records Center, Louisville, Ky)

Dining room, 2010. (John Nation)

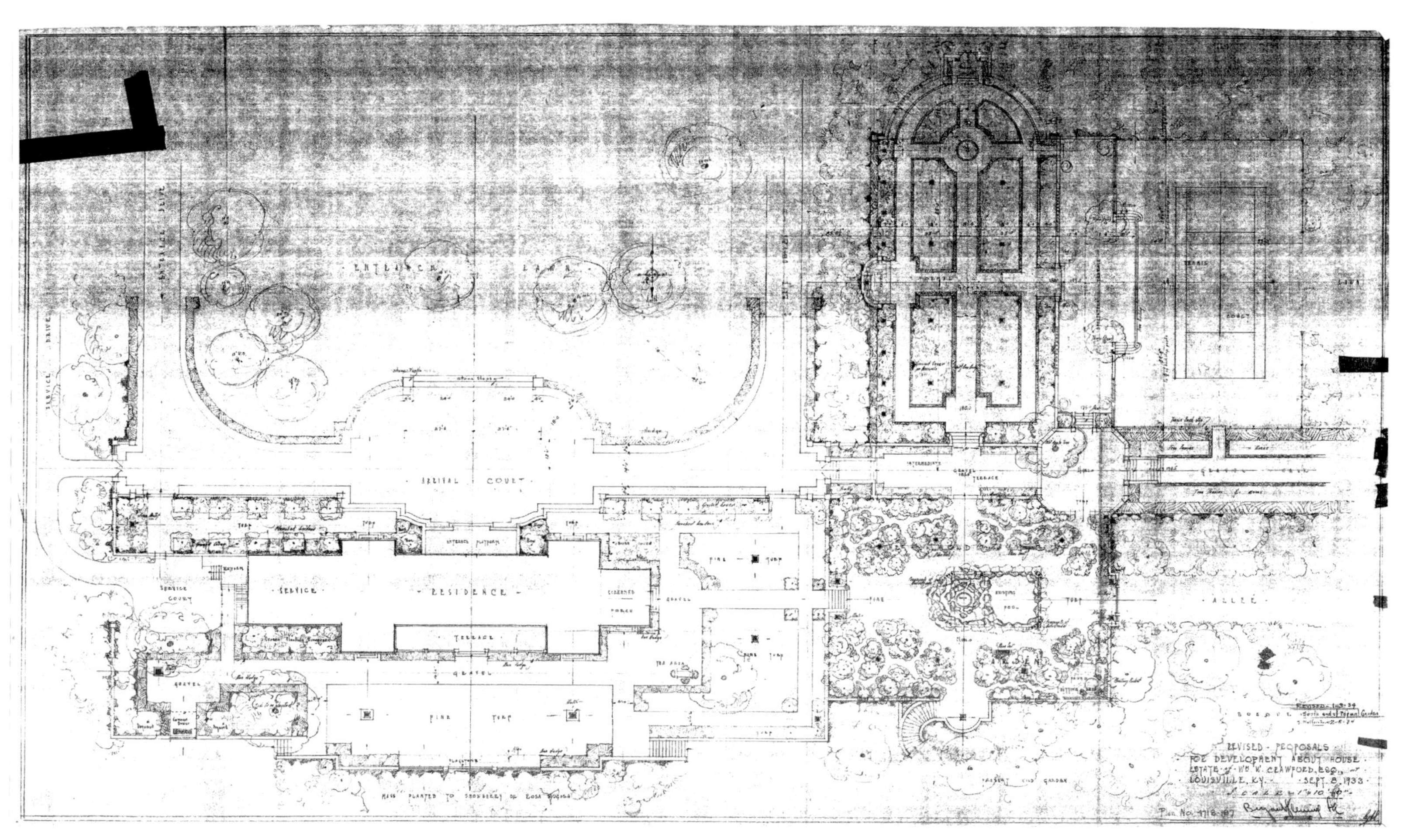

Landscape plan, Bryant Fleming, landscape architect, 1933. (Private Collection)

immediate west of which was a walled sunken garden with rectangular reflecting pool at its center; Mrs. Belknap's tennis court was constructed to the southwest of the residence. Upon completion in 1912, *Lincliff* was unquestionably one of the most impressive of Louisville's rapidly growing collection of country estates.

William Richardson Belknap was the son of William Burke Belknap, the founder of the Belknap Hardware and Manufacturing Company, one of the nation's largest hardware and building material businesses of the time. The younger Belknap graduated from Yale University and later, upon the death of his father in 1889, became president of the family enterprise. He first married Alice Sillman of New Haven, Connecticut, with whom he had five children. Alice passed away in 1890 and four years later, Belknap remarried, this time to Juliet Rathbone Davison.[6] It was Juliet Belknap who directed the planning and construction of Lincliff.

William R. Belknap died in 1914, and Mrs. Belknap left *Lincliff* for a new, smaller residence near Cherokee Park. The executors of the estate transferred about seventeen acres at the western edge of the property to Belknap's daughter, Christine Belknap Robinson, who proceeded to build her own country house, "Blankenbaker Station" (later "Pelham"), on the site. *Lincliff* and its remaining 36 acres were left to Belknap's son, William B. Belknap.[7]

The house initially remained vacant, which provided a timely opportunity for a prominent newlywed couple seeking a temporary place to live. In 1916, Louisville attorney, former mayor and circuit court judge Robert Worth Bingham married Mary Lily Flagler, the widow of Standard Oil co-founder and Florida rail and real estate tycoon Henry Flagler. Considered the wealthiest woman in America, the new Mrs. Bingham was planning to build a mansion in New York City, but in the meantime wanted a suitable house to rent in Louisville. The Binghams leased *Lincliff* and, following a whirlwind of galas opening the Palm Beach social season at Mrs. Bingham's famed *Whitehall*, threw a lavish summer party for 400 at their Louisville estate. The event, according to *The Louisville Herald*, was "one of the most brilliant entertainments ever given" – praise which reputedly led a delighted Mrs. Bingham to give her caterer a platinum and diamond pin as well as a bonus equal to the price of a new car.[8]

Mary Lily Flagler Bingham passed away just over a month after her glittering gala, in July 1917, under circumstances which triggered much local and national speculation. Robert Bingham remained at *Lincliff* until early 1918, following which William B. Belknap and his family moved into the house, staying there until 1922, when he sold the property to Dr. Robert L. Woodard. Woodard owned *Lincliff* for ten years, selling it in 1932 to attorney William W. Crawford and his wife, Mary LaClaire Crawford.[9] It was the Crawfords who would breathe new life into this grand estate through the creation of a magnificent set of gardens by the celebrated landscape architect Bryant Fleming.

Bryant Fleming, of Buffalo, New York, had executed numerous projects in Louisville, starting in 1911 under his partnership, Townsend & Fleming. By 1933, he was operating as a sole practitioner when the Crawford family called on him to work at *Lincliff*. Employing a distinctly more conservative approach than he had used in 1913 at his fantastical gardens for Robert Carrier nearby, Fleming completely reworked and expanded *Lincliff's* formal landscape in a uniquely imaginative way.

Fleming's gardens for *Lincliff*, while based on classical European examples, were designed as an interconnected geometric sequence of outdoor 'rooms' separated by 'hallways.' Each garden, or 'room,' was distinct from the next, just as each 'hallway' or transition space that

Formal garden, 2011. (Blackburn)

separated the gardens had its own character. Fleming's first such room was created from the original sunken garden to the immediate west of the house, which he subsequently dubbed the "old garden." Fleming transformed this predictable garden into an exotic, private Eden by first reconfiguring the rectangular pool into an irregular pond bordered in large rocks, placing at one end of the pond a fountain that bubbled from a pedestal set atop a studied pile of stones. At the east end of the pond he placed two "fragments" of stone balustrades, lending the garden the romantic quality of a ruin or folly. Densely planted for intimacy, Fleming increased the wall height at the west end and inserted within it a tripartite window adorned with molded garlands and fitted with an iron grillage – an architectural element that only heightened the sense of enclosure.

From the old garden one passed across a transverse "intermediate terrace" which functioned as a hallway or vestibule before entering the new, formal garden. Based on the traditional French parterre, the formal garden stretched southward on axis with the fountain at the center of the old garden. Itself a room, the garden of six boxwood-framed beds was enclosed at the east by a tall hedge, to the north and west by a low balustraded wall, and at the south by a similar crescent-shaped wall at the middle of which rose a garlanded gateway that led to the open lawn beyond. Fleming called for statuary in both this and the old garden; in the formal garden, the pedestals were regularly placed with precision, in the old garden, they were randomly sited – their positions reflecting the respective character of the spaces.

Alcove within the formal garden, 2011. (Blackburn)

The last garden space Fleming created was the grass tennis court, reached either from the hallway of the afore-mentioned intermediate terrace or the alternate hallway that was the spectators' platform separating the court from the formal garden. Surrounded by fencing, the tennis court was the third of Fleming's distinct and interconnected rooms at Lincliff.

Apparently at the same time he was creating new gardens, Fleming, in appreciation of Olmsted's original vision, removed a garden the Woodards had added to the north side of the house, thereby restoring the expansive vista across the rear lawn. Additionally, as if completing his mark at *Lincliff*, Fleming designed an imposing set of stone gateposts and iron gates to guard the entrance to the estate.

Sometime between 1941 and 1945, the Crawfords sold *Lincliff* to Mr. and Mrs. C. Edwin Gheens, owners of the Bradas & Gheens Candy Co. and beneficiaries of an oil discovery on their ranch, Golden Ranch Plantation, in Gheens, Louisiana.[10] The Gheens owned the estate for almost forty years, during which time Louisville landscape architect Mary Louise Speed made various modifications and improvements to the gardens. In the late 1960s, Interstate 71 sliced through the south end of the property, fortunately a safe distance away from the house, gardens and outbuildings.

Today, *Lincliff* remains in private hands, the house and gardens impeccably restored and maintained. The mansion itself has, rather surprisingly, undergone very few changes over the years, the only significant modification being the transformation at some point of the living room – likely during either the Crawford or Gheens years – from a brooding library with walls half-paneled in bookcases to a decidedly more English drawing room complete with Adamseque marble mantelpiece. Outside, the current owners continue to expand the gardens in the spirit of Bryant Fleming, adding yet another "room" – a maze – beyond the old garden as well as a new "hall" in the form of an elegant alleé. Continually evolving, *Lincliff* is unquestionably one of the last, intact great country houses of Louisville, if not the country.

South gate to the formal garden, 2009. (Blackburn)

The "old garden" looking toward the Ohio River, 2011. (Blackburn)

Entrance court, ca. 1914. (Brenner Collection, University of Louisville Archives and Records Center, Louisville, KY)

ROCKLEDGE

THE ESTATE OF MR. AND MRS. GEORGE W. BABCOCK

Townsend & Fleming, Architects / Landscape Architects

1911 - 1912

George Wheeler Babcock was born in 1878 in Neenah, Wisconsin, the son of Havilah Babcock, a founder of the Kimberly-Clark Corporation, and his wife, Frances Kimberly. Following his graduation from Yale in 1902, Babcock moved to Louisville where, in 1906, he married Anne Mason Bonnycastle Robinson, more affectionately known as Bonnie.[1] Three years later, he founded the Puritan Cordage Mills, a maker of rope and related products, with partners Avery Robinson and Charles Todd Wolfe. In 1911, the Babcocks acquired 18.5 acres of alluvial plain and bluff top land in Glenview and set out to build their new country estate, *Rockledge*.[2]

The architect selected by the couple was the firm of Townsend & Fleming of Buffalo, New York (Townsend & Fleming in turn hired Meyer & Brenner of Louisville to be their on-site representative). 1911 marked the beginning of the firm's work in Louisville, which – either as a single entity or as Bryant Fleming alone after the partnership's dissolution in 1915 – would ultimately include commissions for at least seven of the city's major country places.[†] How Townsend & Fleming came to Kentucky is a matter of some conjecture. It is possible that Robert Carrier, a former resident of Buffalo, may have introduced Fleming to Louisville at the time Carrier purchased the site for his own estate in 1911. It is also possible that the connection originated from Chicagoan Lydia Avery Coonley Ward – a Louisville native – with whom Fleming had consulted for a retreat in Wyoming, New York, and for whose son, Avery Coonley, he had collaborated with Frank Lloyd Wright on the gardens of Coonley's new house in Riverside, Illinois.[3] Nevertheless, 1911 saw Townsend & Fleming working on two significant projects in Louisville, *Cold Spring* for Samuel Henning near Cherokee Park and *Rockledge* in Glenview for the Babcocks.

Townsend & Fleming, especially in their early years, focused primarily on landscape design; *Rockledge* was one of the few architectural commissions they accepted as a partnership.[4] The particular site the designers chose reflected their interest in topographic opportunity: rather than build the house on flat land, it was instead set atop a narrow ridge between a sinkhole or depression and the stone cliff of the bluff. It was, quite literally, on the rock's ledge.

The sinkhole was central to the architects' design, serving not only as a grand sunken forecourt but also establishing the distinctive entry sequence and consequent internal circulation for the house. One

† These included houses and/or gardens for Babcock, Samuel Henning (*Cold Spring*), Robert Carrier, William Chess (*Winkworth*, attributed), Louis Wymond (*Shore Acres*), Arthur Allen (*Robinswood*, unbuilt pavilion and gardens), H. Boone Porter (*Ridgeley Farm*) and William Crawford (*Lincliff*).

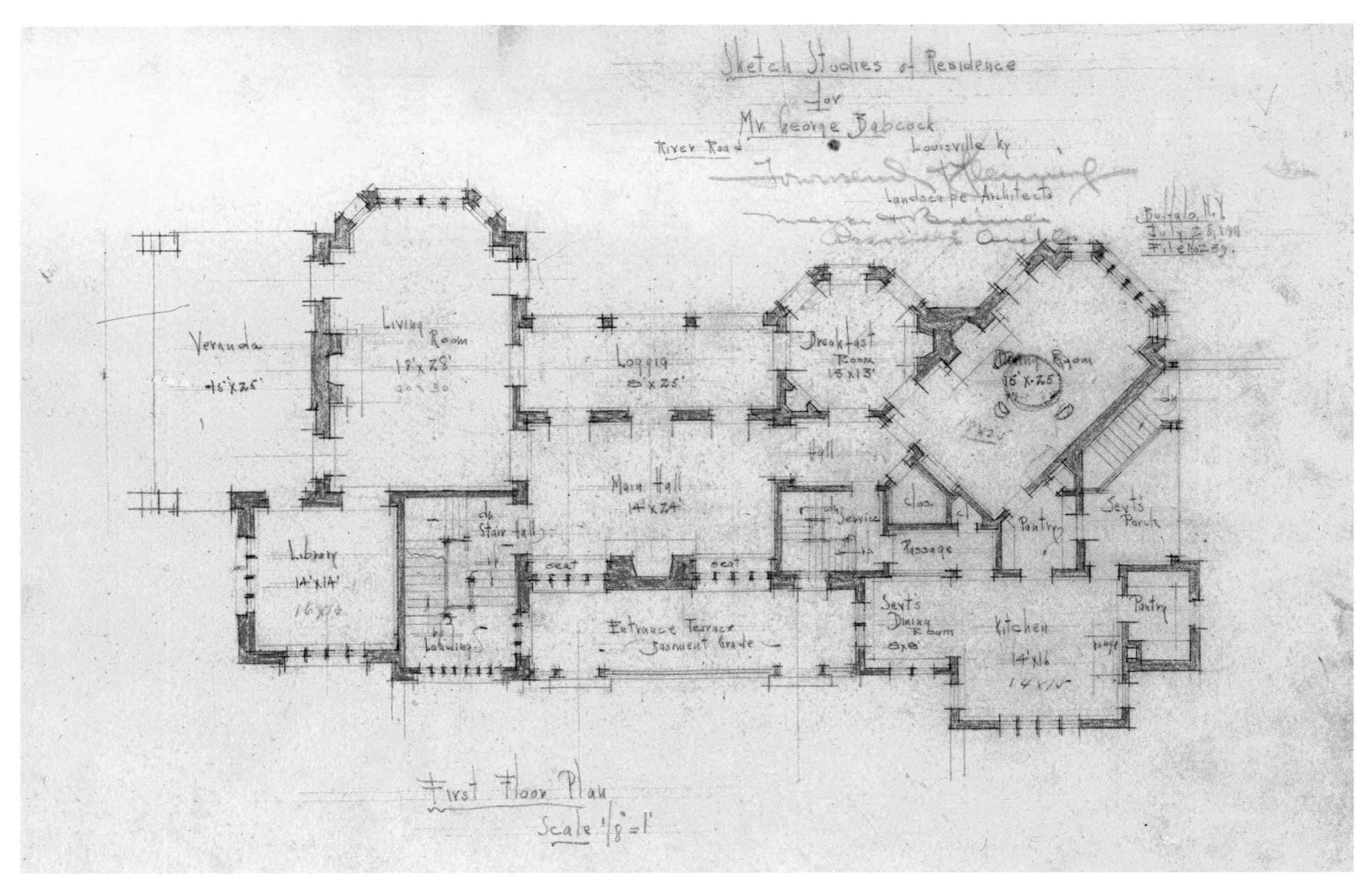

Preliminary floor plan, showing dining and breakfast rooms as originally intended (the breakfast room was ultimately eliminated), Townsend & Fleming, 1911. (Filson Historical Society)

approached the residence up a long, dramatic drive, cut from the stone bluff, that turned in a broad arc before descending into the forecourt through massive stone walls. There the main façade of the house rose three floors, the stone of the lowest level dissipating above the ground floor into a blend of stone, brick and stucco. A tall triple stack chimney firmly anchored this rather stoic wall that, surprisingly, at first glance lacked a visible front door (only a service door was evident upon arrival). In a coy game of hide and seek – not unlike the whimsical approach Townsend & Fleming used later with their gardens for Robert Carrier – the entrance to the house had to be "found," and was tucked discretely into the side of a projecting bay to the left of the central chimney.

Upon entering *Rockledge*, the visitor was confronted with a ponderous oak staircase that wound first to the main floor of the house, and then continued upwards past a grand leaded glass window to the private quarters. The ground level contained service functions; a billiard room was intended though never constructed. One entered the main floor from the grand stair into a large living hall that was dominated by a great stone fireplace with heraldic crest. Heavy, hand-hewn beams distinguished the ceiling and intimate window seats – complete with

Main stair, 2011. (John Nation)

Living hall, 2011. (John Nation)

arm rests – concealed radiators beneath the windows flanking the fireplace. Opposite the fireplace were three sets of French doors that opened to a loggia (since enclosed) overlooking a terrace garden and the Ohio River beyond. The hall gave access at the west to a spacious living room, graced with a late 16th century-style strapwork ceiling and Gothic Revival fireplace mantel. Abutting the living room were a glassed-in sunroom and intimate library. To the east was the elegant dining room, decorated in a decidedly more formal idiom that recalled 18th century English interiors rather than the Elizabethan aesthetic of the other rooms on the floor.

Stylistically, *Rockledge* was a Tudor Revival structure that reflected the nuances of the Arts and Crafts movement that emanated from England at the turn of the century. Most particularly, the design could

LIving room, 2011. (John Nation)

Dining room, 2011. (John Nation)

have been influenced by the work of English architect M.H. Baillie Scott, whose projects and own treatise on architecture, *Houses and Gardens*, had been widely disseminated by 1911. The blend of stone, brick and half-timbering; leaded glass windows; roof of red, green and grey slates; and, of course, the distinctive and surprising entry – not to mention the dramatic siting - rendered *Rockledge* a particularly lyrical work of architecture.

One of the surprises about *Rockledge* – given that it was the work of Bryant Fleming, who excelled at landscapes – was the relative lack of gardens. A flat lawn or flower terrace, bounded by low stone walls, extended from the house to the cliff's edge, and at the motorcourt, opposite the front of the residence, stone steps led to a slope that rose to the carriage house. Perhaps a garden was intended for this space, but if so, it was apparently never built. Whatever the case, the drama of ascending the bluff past the sheer stone of the cliff and entering the remarkable sunken forecourt were alone remarkable gestures indicative of the firm's exceptional creativity and imagination.

Bonnie Babcock passed away at the young age of 37 in 1923, and George remarried a year later, to Blandina Griffiths. In 1928, *Rockledge* was prominently featured in a photo essay in the Louisville *Herald-Post*, which for a number of years gave generous attention to the city's new country estates.[5] The Babcocks continued to live at *Rockledge* until Blandina Babcock died in 1949, followed in 1950 by George. After George's death the Babcock family sold the estate out of the family. In the 1980s, new owners expanded the house to the northeast with the addition of a new kitchen, family room and swimming pool. The front door was shifted at this time to the main floor through the addition of an exterior stone stair.[6] Although the estate was subdivided in the late 1990s into three additional parcels,[7] *Rockledge* and its carriage house remain on substantial acreage in excellent condition.

River-side elevation, 2011. (Blackburn)

Entrance elevation showing the balustrades added by Townsend & Fleming, ca. 1918. (Private Collection)

SHORE ACRES - GREYSTONE

THE ESTATE OF MR. AND MRS. LOUIS H. WYMOND

Lawrence Buck and Edwin B. Clarke, Architects - Townsend & Fleming, Landscape Architects

1911 - 1914

Aerial view, 2002. (Private Collection)

Mr. and Mrs. Louis Wymonds [sic] have a new country house facing Goose Island, on the River road. The building has on the river side battlements and turrets and odd little balconies. In the basement bathhouse facilities and a billiard room form a new departure. The kitchen suggests a clubhouse in its culinary possibilities and, with its big dormitories on the third floor, it seems that the Wymond family expect to uphold their reputation for hospitality. With its boundary wall of brick, tennis courts, and river bank location this charming home in English style might well be on the banks of the Thames.[1]

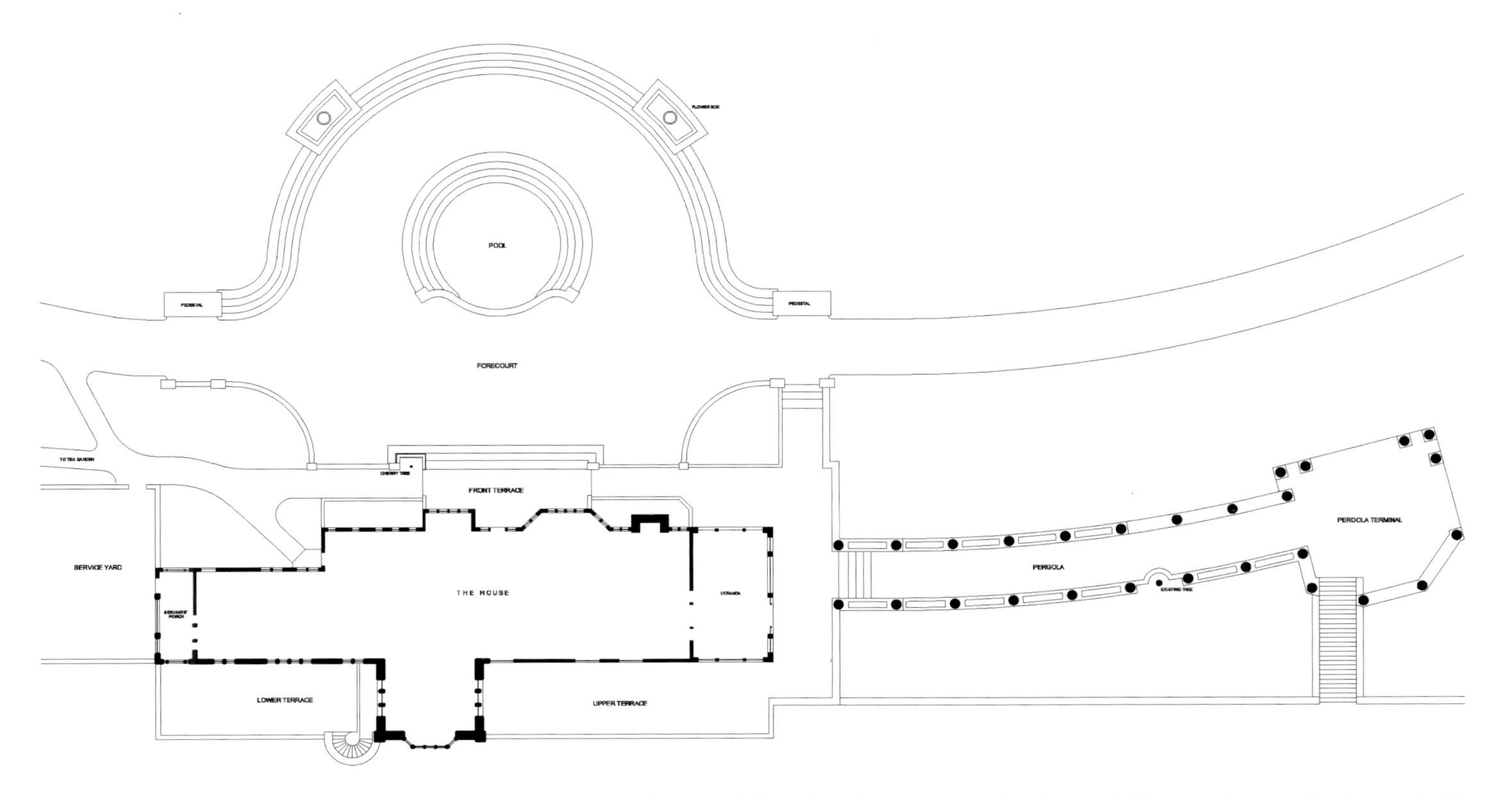

Site plan showing Townsend & Fleming's circular motorcourt and garden pergola. The tea garden was to have been to the left

In 1902, Louis and Margaret Wymond acquired their first parcel of what to the sensible person of the time would seem almost worthless land: a narrow 7.4 acre slice of the ancient Ohio River flood plain, between River Road and the water. Over the next eight years, while their contemporaries were assembling estates safely out of harm's way on the high bluffs, the Wymonds expanded their holdings on both sides of the road and then announced their remarkable intention to build a substantial new country house...right on the embankment of the river.[2]

Louis Wymond was born in Madison, Indiana, the son of W.J. Wymond, co-founder with W.E. Chess of the Chess and Wymond Cooperage Company, one of the nation's largest manufacturers of whiskey barrels. At the time he and his wife, the former Margaret Moore of Memphis, Tennessee, embarked on their construction project, Wymond was Vice President of the cooperage; he would later become president.[3]

Clearly a contrarian, Wymond shunned both the conventional wisdom about building in a flood plain as well as the custom of employing one of a handful of Louisville architects or, if venturing outside of Kentucky, hiring an East Coast design firm. Instead, he engaged Lawrence Buck and Edwin H. Clarke of Chicago, progressive architects whose offices in the Steinway Hall Building introduced them to revolutionaries such as Dwight Perkins and Frank Lloyd Wright. Buck was a master illustrator who excelled in Arts and Crafts as well as Shingle Style residences, and whose work had been included in such well-regarded publications as *House Beautiful* and *Ladies' Home Journal*.[4] He was clearly the leader of the design team, as the Wymond house bore distinct similarities to the architect's previous projects as well as

The house from the river, ca. 1914. (Private Collection)

to the new house he was designing contemporaneously for himself in Highland Park, Illinois. To assist them in Kentucky, Buck and Clarke hired Louisville architect J.J. Gaffney (whose earlier work included the second iteration of *Rio Vista* for J. H. Caperton).

Built on the river embankment atop a massive steel reinforced concrete foundation that was invisible from the front but extended downward a pronounced two full stories at the rear, the Wymond house stretched out along the ridge in a carefully composed blend of the Shingle and Arts and Crafts styles. As with most houses of those two movements that enjoyed ample sites, it was really a large and luxurious cottage – a mix of the English Tudor Revival idiom of the Arts and Crafts and the rambling, classicized Queen Anne of the American Shingle. It was emphatically horizontal, as if to acknowledge the linearity of the river; the consistent height of the stuccoed first floor, parallel shingle coursing, strong roof line that tapered down at either end and low chimney stacks all served to visually elongate the structure. Texturally, in both the literal and more abstract senses, the house was compositionally rich. The coarse grey stucco of the ground level was speckled with pieces of coal, shells and river pebbles, and strong shadows produced by the shingle laps, staggered eaves and projecting bays lent the façade a lively rhythm. Reflecting the underlying romantic nature of both styles, the juxtaposition of roof types – gable, shed and hip – as well as the play of varied casement windows, grouped in pairs, threes and fours and all painted a contrasting white, combined with the irregular and asymmetrical massing of elements to ensure that this was domestic architectural poetry at its best.

On the river side, the same romantic vocabulary was continued – with the addition of the exposed massive concrete foundation walls that held the house firmly in place. Pierced by pairs of arched openings that led to the men's and women's shower rooms, and buttressed by corner piers (and even a central pier that reached up between the billiard room windows to support the dining room bay), the raw structure of the foundation walls – formwork patterns were left exposed – contrasted markedly with the comparatively refined exterior finishes of the residence above. Rather ingeniously, the architects minimized the visual impact of the concrete mass by employing a series of terraces to transition the house from bluff top to waters edge. They began with the broad balcony off the master bedroom above the dining room, then stepped down to the "upper terrace" above the shower rooms and further again to the "lower terrace" below the kitchen windows.[†] Following the lead of the descending roofline, comparatively low retaining walls extended out to the east and west. Finally, a pair of broad, stepped terraces – the upper planted with lawn and the lower left more indigenous to the native shore line – reached outward from the rear of the house to complete the march to the river.

One entered the house into a large hall that extended back to the upper terrace. To the immediate left, or west, was the intimate study, whose bay window overlooked the front lawn. Just past the study was the large living room, which on the water side opened to the upper terrace, and on the River Road side made an ell turn around the study to a cozy paneled inglenook with a broad fireplace. Beyond the living room to the southwest was the glass-enclosed veranda. To the immediate right of the front door was the main stair, whose detailing – including built-in light fixtures atop the railing newel posts – reflected the Prairie or Craftsman influences of the Chicago School. Past the stair, also to the northeast, was the dining room, at one end of which was a fireplace, the other a bay window overlooking the river. On either side of the bay window were French doors, one set leading to the upper terrace, the other leading to a distinctive spiral stair – formed as part of the concrete foundation – that wound down to the lower terrace. To the northeast of the dining room were the kitchen and related service rooms, as well as the rear stair and elevator.

The first floor was finished in a simple manner that revealed the architects' penchant for the Arts and Crafts and even, as mentioned above, Craftsman movements – both in stark contrast to the more conservative European trends predominant at the time. Sturdy wood beams distinguished the ceilings, and rich paneling and bordered wallpaper decorated the walls; the light fixtures throughout were decidedly of Craftsman origin. Colonial details and moldings, so prevalent within Shingle Style interiors, were virtually non-existent in the Wymond residence.

Beneath the living room, in what might be called the first basement, were the billiard room, boilers, servants' sitting room and vegetable cellar. In the lowest level, reached by a stair leading down from the billiard room, were a series of cellars – including a vault guarded by two steel doors – and the afore-mentioned shower rooms.

Upon its completion in 1912, Louis and Margaret Wymond's new country house was published in a lavish photo spread in *The Courier-Journal*.[5] At the same time, it was featured in the First Exhibition of the Louisville Chapter of the American Institute of Architects, which was held downtown in the Starks Building.[6]

In 1913, wishing to put more distance between his new residence and River Road, Wymond petitioned the Jefferson County Court to shift the road to the southeast. He volunteered to pay all costs associated with the relocation and, already owning the land through which the easement would pass, noted there would be no issues related to the taking of anyone's property. Securing the consent of his neighbors, including the

† Interestingly, the "upper terrace," despite being above the shower rooms, was planted with grass rather than paved.

Living room, 2002. (Private Collection)

Allen, Babcock, Brandeis, Carrier and Chess families, the court granted his request and River Road was rerouted into a gentle arc that gave Wymond the yard and privacy he desired.[7]

Once River Road was relocated, the Wymonds in 1914 engaged the services of Townsend & Fleming of Buffalo, New York, to design landscape features appropriate for their new estate. The firm was already well known in Louisville, having recently completed work for Samuel Henning, George Babcock, Robert Carrier and W.E. Chess, and was currently in the process of designing gardens and a library

Dining room, 2002. (Private Collection)

pavilion for Arthur Allen's *Robinswood.*[8]

Townsend & Fleming designed four major landscape elements for the Wymond estate, three of which were completed or partially completed. The first such element consisted of stout stuccoed gateposts at the north and south River Road entrances to the driveway, which swept in a graceful curve past the front of the house. The second element was a highly distinctive circular motorcourt that transformed one's arrival at the residence into an impressive event. Ninety-six feet in diameter and framed within cut stone steps on the far side and a stone balustrade toward the house, the forecourt had at its center a twenty-seven foot wide reflecting pool set within yet another ring of stone steps. Large stone pedestals, presumably intended to support sculptures of some sort, guarded each of the two entries into the court.

The third landscape feature was a pergola extending southward in a gentle arc from the veranda to a pavilion or "pergola terminal" that served as a belvedere overlooking the river. Taking the form of a gravel walkway framed on either side by low walls – or "parapets" – with planters recessed within, the pergola was to be made of slightly tapering concrete columns set atop the parapets and supporting a wood trellis; the pergola terminal was to be similarly constructed. Ultimately, only the parapets were built, without the columns and trellis.[9]

The last garden element designed by Townsend & Fleming was a "tea garden" intended for a curious existing trapezoidal recess in the river

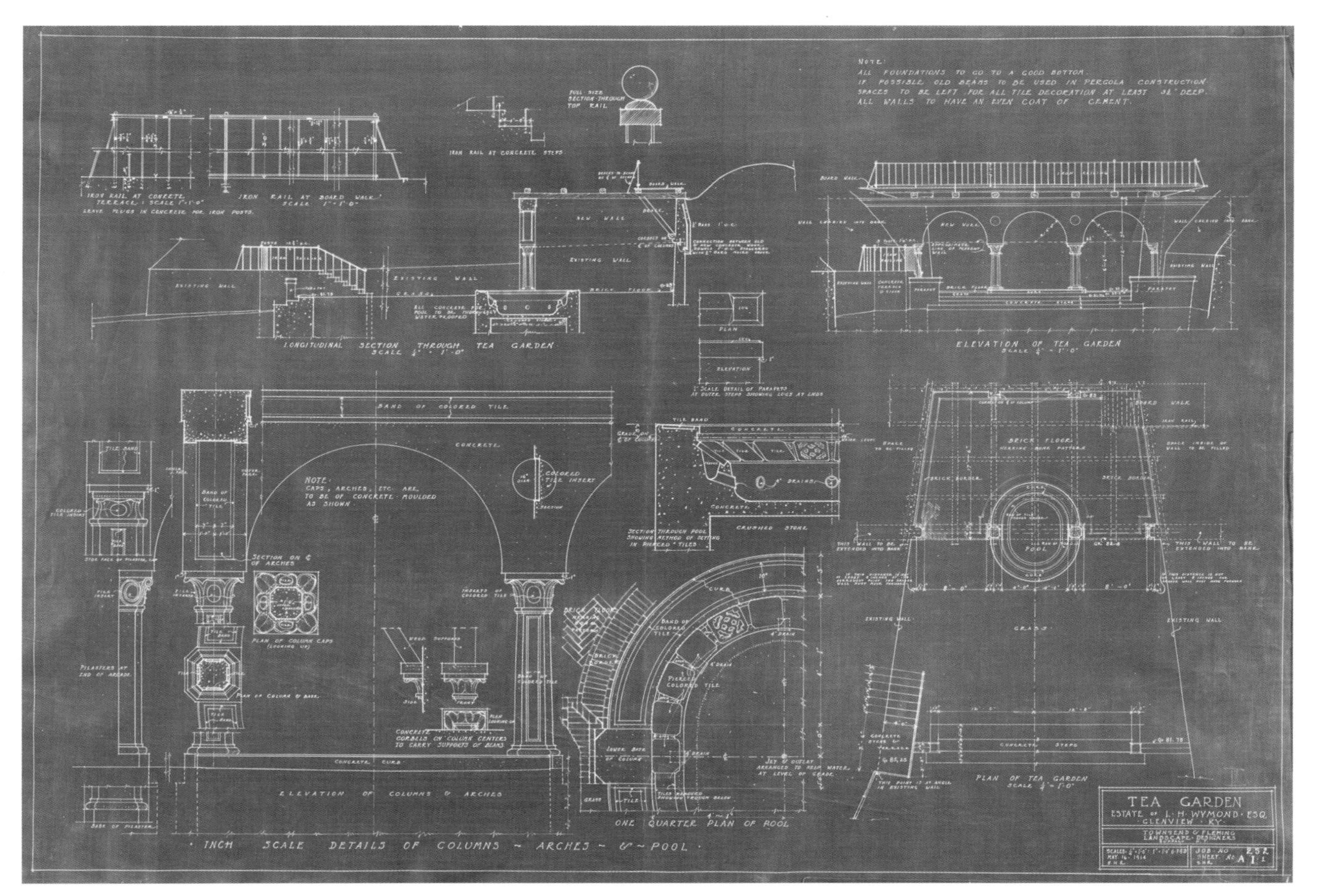

Proposed tea garden (unbuilt), Townsend & Fleming, 1914. (Courtesy of the Division of Rare and Manuscript Collections. Cornell University Libraries)

The western approach to the house, ca. 1918. (Private Collection)

embankment to the east of the house. Whatever the original reason for this "slot" formed by concrete retaining walls, the landscape architects chose build within it an exotic contemplation garden, consisting of a Byzantine arcade – an extrapolation of Richardsonian Romanesque architecture – that traversed a reflecting pool and supported a wood trellis above which a "board walk" balcony passed. Open to only one side – the other three being retaining walls set within the embankment – the garden looked out over a lawn and down broad steps to the river. Unfortunately, the tea garden was never built.

Louis Wymond passed away in 1922, and in 1923 his widow sold the property to Theodore E. Mueller, president of the American Standard Company.[10] Following completion of their new horse breeding farm, *Shady Brook*, not far away off River Road, the Muellers sold the house to Mr. and Mrs. Wright Barr, who may have given it its first name, "Shore Acres."[11] Mr. and Mrs. M.G. Whitley acquired *Shore Acres* from the Barrs, and were the occupants in 1926 when the McAlpine Dam near downtown Louisville opened, causing both Goose Island and the lowest terrace to disappear permanently beneath the water. In 1958, the Whitleys hired Olmsted Brothers to design a reflecting pool and surrounding terrace as the initial phase of an intended larger garden project, none of which was ultimately built.[12]

Today, the house has its seventh owner in its 100-year life, and is now renamed "Greystone." Although the estate was reduced in size somewhat over the years, the house remains in excellent condition on ample land. A swimming pool and garage have been added, the "slot" for the tea garden filled in and the Townsend & Fleming forecourt and pergola meticulously restored – a trellis finally built on top of the low parapet walls. It remains the only of Louisville's great country houses built defiantly on the banks of the Ohio River.

Entrance elevation 2010. (Blackburn)

The Midlands

The Estate of Mrs. Morris Belknap

John Bacon Hutchings, Architect - M. Vernon Cassel, Landscape Architect

1912 - 1914

> POST: RECENT PURCHASES OF REAL ESTATE ALONG THE RIVER ROAD, TOGETHER WITH THE ANNOUNCEMENT OF BUILDING PLANS OF AN UNUSUALLY WIDE EXTENT, SHOW THAT A BUILDING BOOM IS IN PROGRESS IN THAT FASHIONABLE RESIDENCE DISTRICT OF JEFFERSON COUNTY.
>
> THE MOST NOTABLE PURCHASE OF REAL ESTATE WAS BY MRS. MORRIS BELKNAP, WHO HAS SECURED FORTY ACRES OF GROUND UPON THE RIVER ROAD ABOUT A MILE BEYOND THE NEW COUNTRY CLUB. MRS. BELKNAP WILL ERECT A HANDSOME RESIDENCE UPON THE PROPERTY, THE WORK PROBABLY BEGINNING IN THE SPRING.[1]

Marion Stewart Dumont Belknap was the daughter of railroad executive and New York broker John B. Dumont of Plainfield, New Jersey.[2] In 1900 she became the second wife of Col. Morris Burke Belknap, the son of Belknap Hardware & Manufacturing Company founder William Burke Belknap.[3] Morris Belknap passed away in 1910 at the age of 53, and shortly thereafter his youthful widow elected to build a new residence next door to the estate of her brother-in-law, William R. Belknap. To do so, she acquired land not only from W.R. Belknap, but also from the neighboring Waters and Brandeis families. She would name her new estate "The Midlands."[†]

In early 1912, Mrs. Belknap hired Townsend & Fleming of Buffalo, New York, to work on the project. The firm, more customarily recognized for landscape design than residential architecture, had recently completed *Rockledge* for George Babcock a short distance away in Glenview. The architects drafted an elaborate stable/gardeners' cottage for Mrs. Belknap that was never built; whether they designed a house as well is unknown.[4] Ultimately, Mrs. Belknap engaged the distinguished Louisville firm of John B. Hutchings & Sons as her architects for *The Midlands.*[5]

The house Hutchings designed might loosely be described as Georgian in style, and was distinguished by several prominent architectural elements that set it aside from most Colonial Revival residences of the era. From the front, the house was composed as a massive main primary block with a subsidiary side service wing – typical of large colonial residences. Atypical, however, were the two stout chimneys that protruded slightly from the façade and pierced the roof eaves, steadfastly anchoring the building to the ground. Additionally, a muscular, academically detailed Greek Doric front portico served as a pronounced entrance to the house. Seemingly symmetrical, the main block of the mansion was actually subtly off balance: the chimney stacks were slightly different from each other, and the south, or living room side, of the house was a bit longer than the north, or dining room, end. The hip roof, dormers, single story Doric porch and modified Flemish brick bond (two stretchers, rather than one, alternating with each header) all bore a striking resemblance to similar elements Hutchings had employed in his recently completed design for Charles T. Ballard, *Bushy Park*, in Glenview.

† Mrs. Belknap became known as a great civic leader in Louisville, heading the city's branch of Bundles for Britain during World War II as well as serving on the boards of numerous local and regional charitable and arts organizations. ("Mrs. Marion S. Belknap, Civic Leader, Is Dead," *The Courier-Journal*, May 7, 1966.)

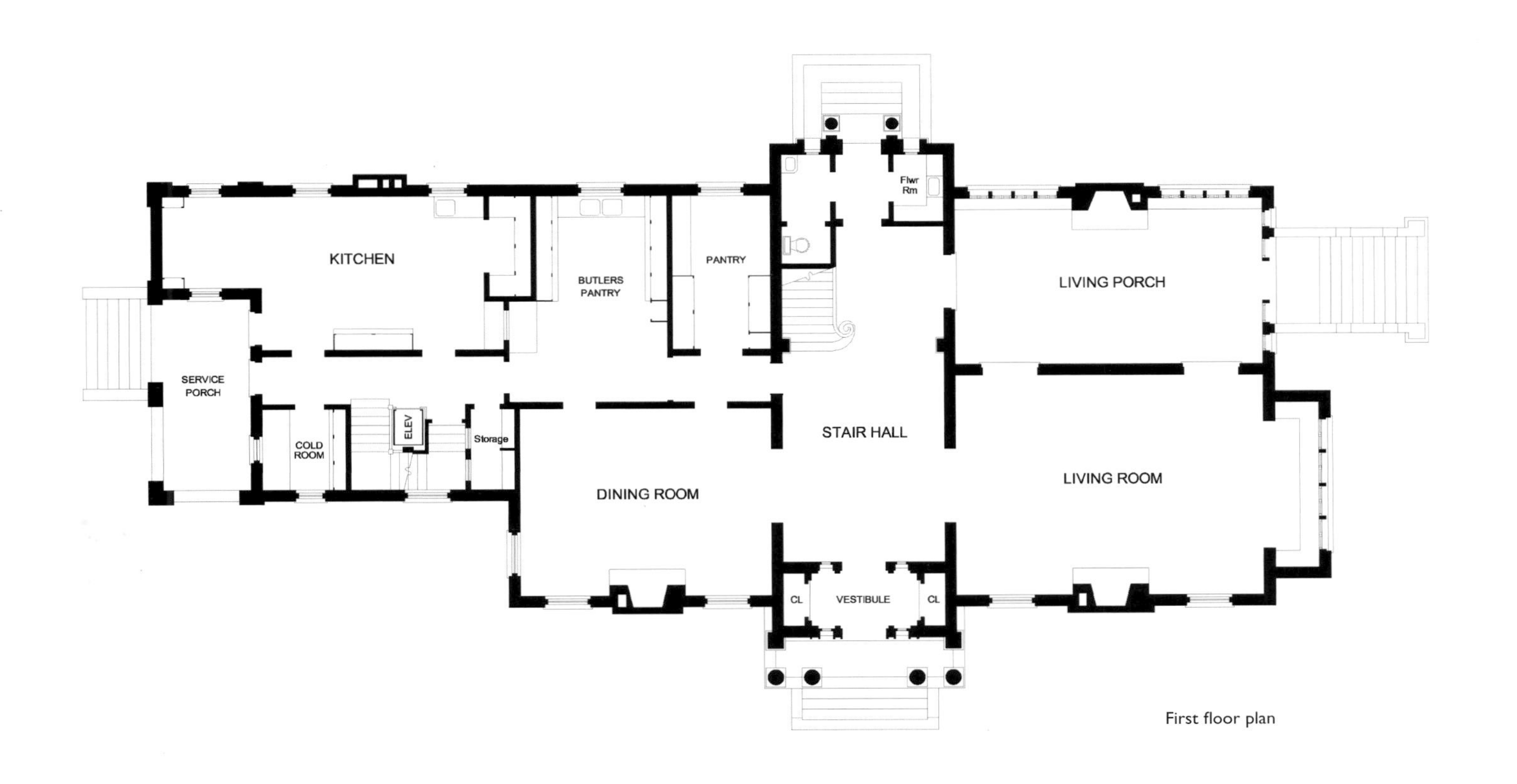

First floor plan

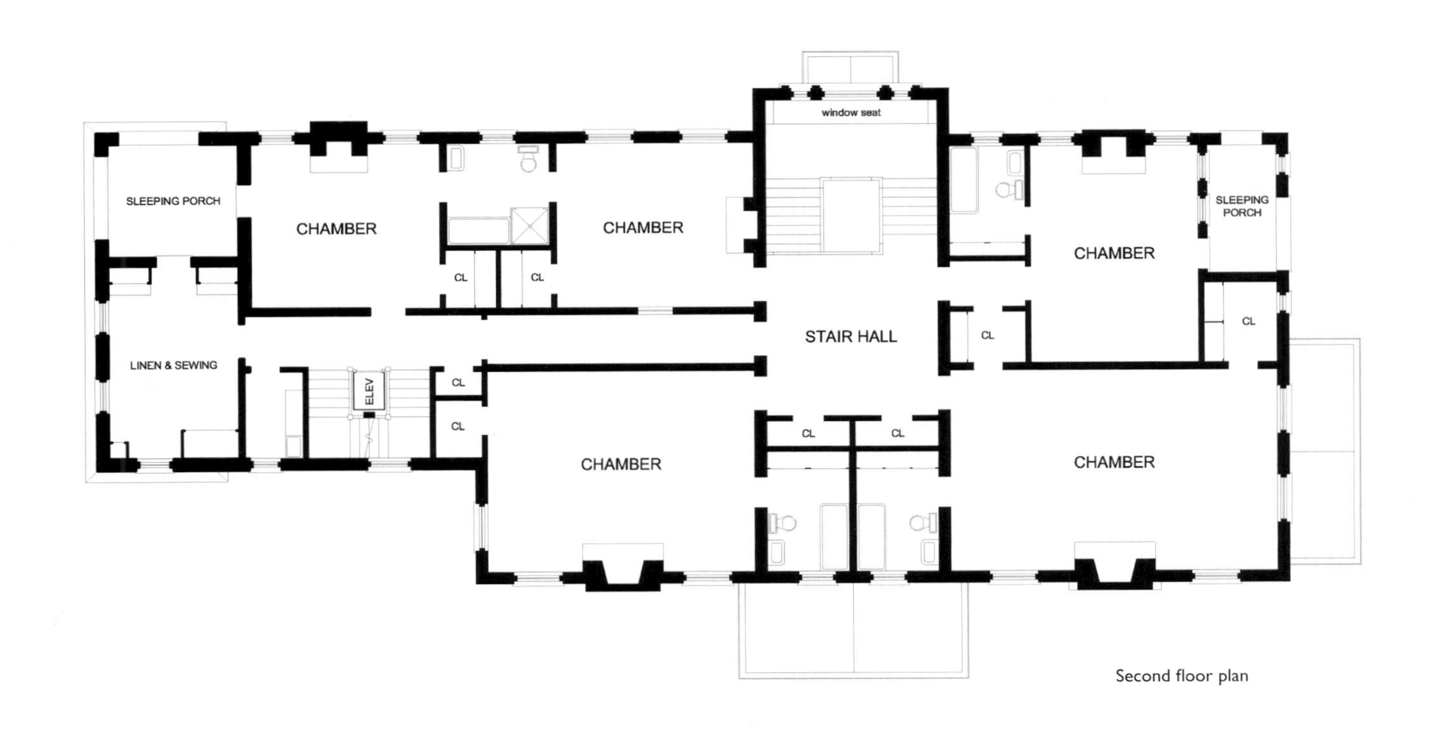

Second floor plan

Dining room, 2010. (Blackburn)

Stair landing, 2010. (Blackburn)

Stair hall, 2010. (Blackburn)

Rear elevation, with swimming pool added later, 2011. (Blackburn)

The rear of the house differed from the front in that the entire structure was treated as one unit, rather than a conjoining of the main block and an attached wing. Further, the center hall and stair within were articulated by a two-story bay containing a Colonial Revival door and Palladian window composition that additionally sported a more modest rendition of the Greek Doric portico seen on the entry façade. The rear fenestration was less tightly organized than that on the front; however, two prominent chimneys, similar to those on the front, provided a needed visual balance that prevented the elevation from appearing arbitrary or monotonous.

Within, the plan of the house was simple and straightforward, the stair hall and north service halls serving as organizing axes for both primary floors. The rooms were relatively few in number but spacious and well ventilated, with large windows; there was an especially sunny living porch on the main floor. Upstairs were five bedrooms – one for Mrs. Belknap and the others for, perhaps, her four stepchildren – as well as the sleeping porches that were requisite in almost every country house of the day.

Perhaps the single most impressive element of the interiors was the grand staircase that rose elegantly above the rear entry vestibule and past an impressive Palladian window to a commodious second floor hall. Framed behind a proscenium created by two fluted Ionic pilasters and a prominent cross beam, the stair, with broad steps, deep treads and a finely detailed railing that terminated in a wide curving flourish, was certainly the focal point of the mansion. High paneled wainscoting decorated the walls of the stair hall and dining room and an elegant composite crown molding finished the ceilings of the primary public areas.

The house and garage were completed by late 1914, but it wasn't until 1930 that Mrs. Belknap constructed the gardens for her estate. In that year, Louisville landscape architect M. Vernon Cassel completed designs for a set of terraced gardens that descended from the south side of the house, terminating in a round pavilion with Tuscan Doric columns and a conical roof. Additionally, Cassel called for a path from these gardens that led southward to a rectangular

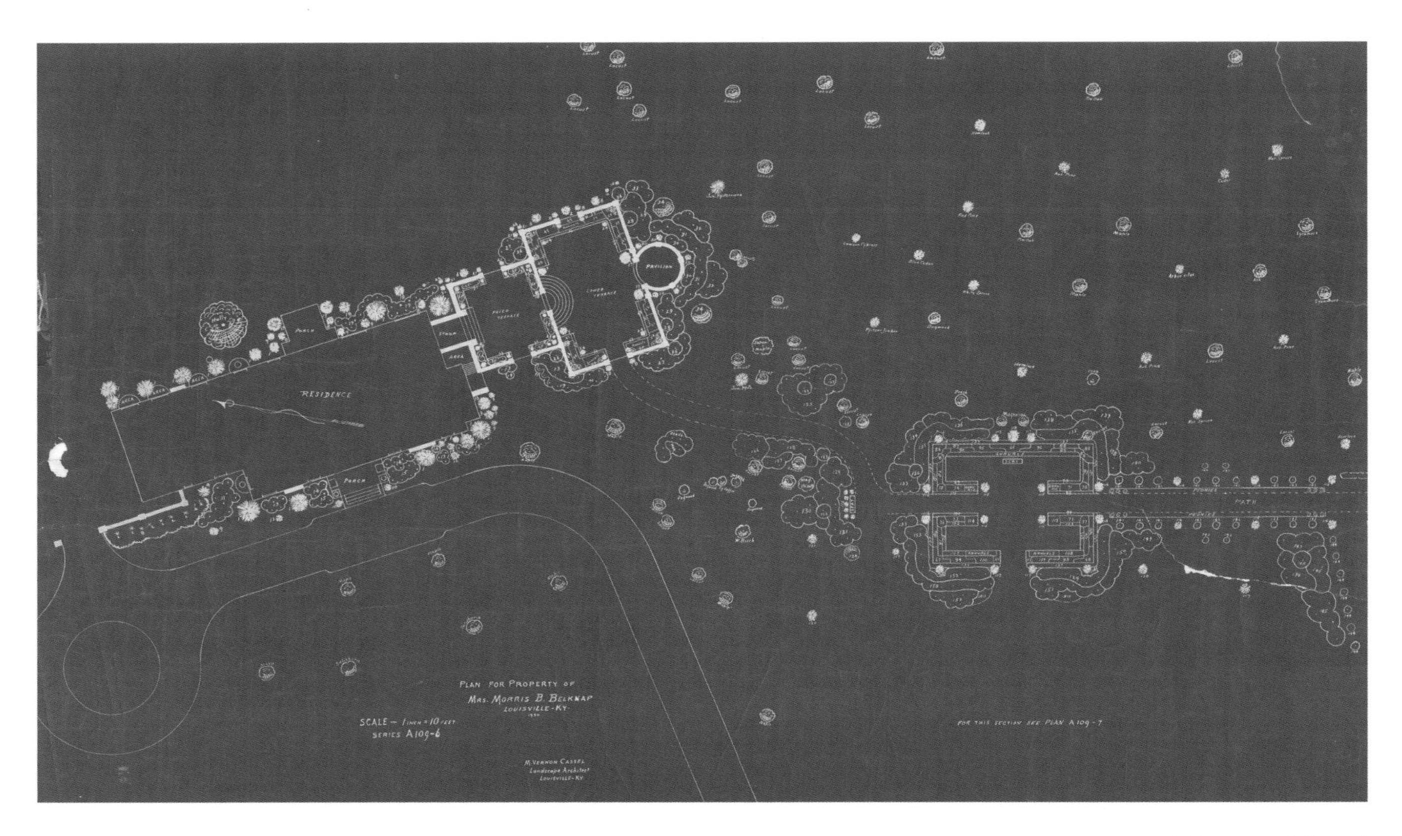

Landscape plan, M.Vernon Cassel, 1930. (Private Collection)

Landscape architect M. Vernon Cassel's lower terrace and pavilion, 2011. (Blackburn)

formal flower garden and then proceeded further to a vegetable garden. The landscape architect also designed a wall and gateposts to screen the view of the service court from the front entrance.[6]

Marion Belknap passed away in 1966, leaving an estate valued at $3 million.[7] Two years later, *The Midlands*, which now consisted of some 58 acres, was sold and subsequently subdivided.[8] The house, garage and terraced gardens remain, with the addition of a swimming pool, in excellent condition on a still-spacious six-acre site.

The tea garden, undated. (Woodside Collection, Filson Historical Society)

THE ESTATE OF MR. AND MRS. ROBERT M. CARRIER

Townsend & Fleming, Landscape Architects

1913

> MR. ROBERT CARRIER HAS PURCHASED FOR $35,000 THE NINETEEN-ACRE TRACT OWNED BY MR. A.R. COOPER, AND IT IS STATED THAT THE COOPER RESIDENCE WILL SOON BE DEMOLISHED AND A HANDSOME RESIDENCE ERECTED THEREON BY MR. CARRIER.
>
> – *The Jeffersonian*, August 31, 1911[1]

So began the story of what was to have been one of Louisville's most splendid country estates, a place created as an integrated whole of landscape, architecture and interiors by one of the country's foremost landscape and architectural designers. Unfortunately, it was an endeavor that was only partially realized.

Robert M. Carrier was a somewhat enigmatic character, beginning his life in Buffalo, New York, and migrating over time to Sardis, Mississippi, where he founded the Robert M. Carrier Lumber & Manufacturing Company. By 1910, the obviously quite successful Carrier was president of the Hardwood Manufacturers' Association and on the Board of Governors of the National Lumber Manufacturers' Association.[2] At some point prior to 1911, he married Alice Bridgeford of Louisville, granddaughter of the founder of the stove and grate foundry, Bridgeford & Co.[3]

The house the Carriers acquired was likely built as a summer home for Albert R. Cooper around the turn of the century. It was a comfortable two-story frame structure with a tall central portico flanked by single-story porches.[4] What made the site attractive to the Carriers, however, was not the house but the exceptional bluff-top knoll that offered magnificent views to the Ohio River; it was a site that, properly developed, would rival the other great country estates that were then rising above the River Road. To achieve their goal, the couple hired the firm of Townsend & Fleming, landscape architects and architects, of Buffalo, New York.

Townsend & Fleming, and more specifically the firm's well-known principal, Bryant Fleming, were already working on several projects in Louisville at the time the Carriers bought the Cooper property. Near Cherokee Park, the firm had executed plans to transform Samuel Henning's late 19th century farmhouse, *Cold Spring*, into a sumptuous Italian villa with gardens, and immediately next door to the new Carrier estate the designers were constructing a large Tudor revival manor, *Rockledge*, for George Babcock. For Fleming in particular, the topography of this particular site offered an ideal palette for his style of design:

the rolling terrain, with its wooded slopes, scenic vistas and crowning summit, meant the gardens could be rendered in three dimensions rather than just planted on flat land.

Bryant Fleming, working with Townsend and then later on his own, became known as the "consummate country place designer," whose facility in landscape design, architecture and interior design enabled him to create a wholly integrated scheme.[5] This was clearly the intent of the Carriers when they engaged Fleming's firm, and the landscape drawings made it quite evident that, although the gardens were to be constructed first, a grand house was to complete the composition at a later date.

Fleming arranged the gardens so as to fan down the hillside to the southwest from the crest of the knoll, the center point of which was a round fountain set within a slightly raised lawn terrace framed within walls and balustrades of dressed limestone. Far from being static, this most formal of the garden group was enlivened at the west end by the addition of a Jacobean wellhead (likely acquired in Europe) and tall, dressed stone gateposts flanking stairs down to the more informal gardens, and, to the southeast, by the insertion of a red brick side wall of the adjacent Georgian greenhouse. Fleming extended the gardens down the sides of the knoll through the use of broad planted terraces supported by sturdy retaining walls of coarse stone intermingled with red brick – an aesthetic he used to great effect at neighboring *Rockledge.* It was in the design of these terrace gardens that Fleming revealed his most distinctive talent as a landscape architect.

In the early twentieth century, virtually all gardens constructed for Louisville's great country houses fell into one or more of three types: the formal garden of clipped, structured parterres; the English cutting flower garden; or the garden as a contrived pastoral vista. Fleming's work for the Carriers, which anticipated his much larger design at *Cheekwood* in Nashville 20 years later, broke with these norms by creating multi-faceted architectonic gardens of surprise, whimsy and unusual delight. Movement through the gardens was both lateral and vertical, direct and meandering, the adventure unfolding further around the next curve. A visitor could stroll from garden space to garden space down gently arced, low steps set between tall stone and brick walls and beneath a vine-covered trellis; he could descend more purposely along axially-placed stair sets, passing through an arched wrought iron arbor to confront an intended vista; or a turn might find him facing carved wood gates beyond which another alluring "room" awaited – a space such as the sunken tea garden with its quiet oval pool at its center. A gazebo emerged from one of the high stone retaining walls just uphill from a fanciful layered stone and brick birdhouse that sprouted from the top of one of the wall's piers. A small grotto was tucked within a terrace wall, waiting to be discovered by the unsuspecting passerby. These unorthodox elements of playfulness, surprise and innocence enlivened the landscape at the Carrier estate in a way no other Louisville country place would enjoy.

Fleming took extra care to integrate the estate's service structures into his plan. The carriage house and motor court were aligned with one of the gated garden entrances, and the potting shed was built into a perimeter wall in the manner of an old English hamlet. A freestanding gardener's cottage contributed to the sense of a small village clustered near the courtyard wellhead. Surprising was the greenhouse, set deliberately within the gardens and whose stiff Georgian facades marked the building as a type of folly that stood out in distinct contrast to the otherwise rustic architecture of the gardens.

Perched on the edge of the bluff overlooking the river, at some distance from the gardens and house site, and on axis with the fountain in the Jacobean lawn terrace, was an arcaded belvedere, from which narrow paths descended the cliff to the roadway below as well as to the drive of neighboring *Rockledge.*

Stairs descending from the gazebo to the lower lawn terrace, undated. (Woodside Collection, Filson Historical Society)

Gazebo with bird house barely visible to the left, undated. (Woodside Collection, Filson Historical Society)

The belvedere overlooking the Ohio River, undated. (Private Collection)

Bird house, 2009. (Blackburn)\

On this axis, between this belvedere and the lawn terrace, was to have been the Carriers' new house. One can only imagine its intended appearance, given a biographer's observation that Fleming "intermarried architecture with landscape through the use of a common stylistic design language; [he] balanced house and garden by blending the two to make a single, unified design statement."[6] Perhaps it would have been a Tudor Revival structure like *Rockledge*, incorporating a similar stone and brick architectural vocabulary. Perhaps, too, it may have been a Jacobethan manor, relating more to the formal terrace garden and anticipating the English mansion Fleming built for Robert Carrier 10 years later in Memphis. Whatever it was to be, construction of the final element of Fleming's grand plan was cut short by Robert and Alice Carrier's divorce in 1916.[7]

Four years after the end of her marriage, Alice Carrier sold the unfinished estate, including an additional 8-acre parcel the couple had acquired from Louis Wymond in 1913[8], to William A. McLean, co-founder of the Wood-Mosaic Corporation, for the sum of $65,000.[9] The MacLean family owned the property until selling it in 1986 to a developer, who razed the house and subdivided the estate in a remarkably sensitive manner, leaving virtually all Fleming's work intact. The garden walls and follies, cottages and belvedere are privately maintained and remain today in surprisingly good condition.

Gate to gardens opposite carriage house, 2009. (Blackburn)

Door leading to the tea garden, undated. (Woodside Collection, Filson Historical Society)

The lawn terrace. Georgian greenhouse is on the left, Jacobean wellhead on the right, undated. (Woodside Collection, Filson Historical Society)

Wall carving, 2011. (Blackburn)

Malvern House as rebuilt during the renovation of 2009-2010. (stephenphotography.com, 2010)

Malvern House

THE ESTATE OF MR. AND MRS. ATTILLA COX, JR.

Ogden Codman, Jr. and E.T. Hutchings, Architects - Olmsted Brothers, Landscape Architects

1914 - 1924

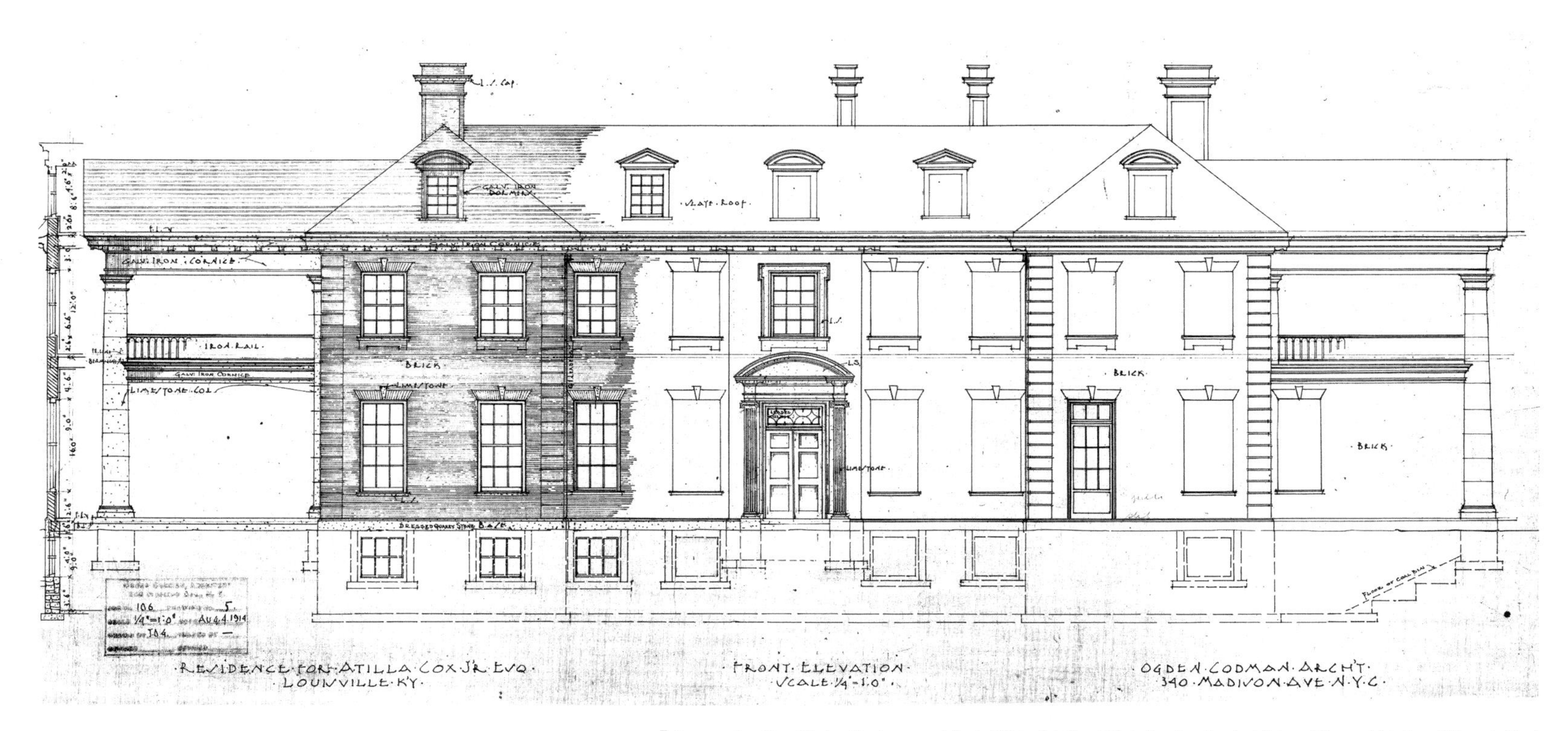

Entrance elevation, Ogden Codman, architect, 1914. (National Park Service, Frederick Law Olmsted National Historic Site)

Entrance elevation, 1959. (Family Archives)

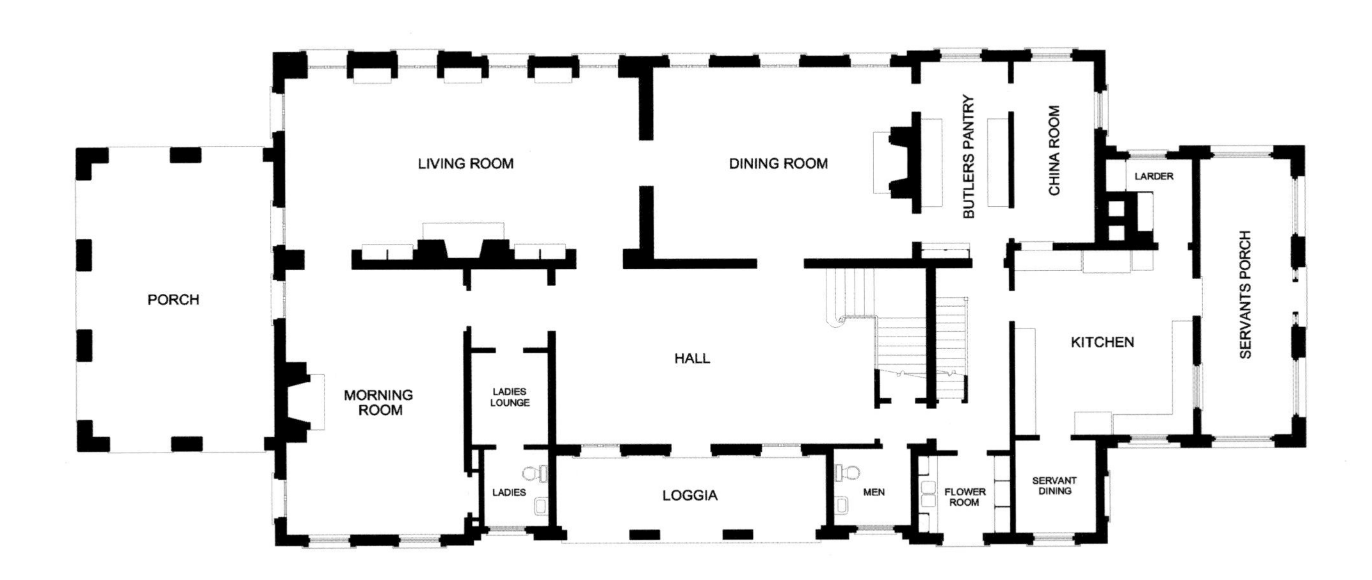

First floor plan

Malvern House, the supremely imposing Georgian manor built in 1922 by Attilla Cox, Jr. and his wife, Carrie Gaulbert Cox, was one of the grandest houses built on the bluffs overlooking the Ohio River. Its story is one of the most unusual, a narrative that continues to add chapters even to this day.

In 1898, twenty-three-year-old Attilla Cox, Jr. married Carrie Rogers Gaulbert, the only child of George and Harriet Rogers Gaulbert. Described as "one of the wealthiest men in Louisville," George Gaulbert was co-founder of the Peaslee-Gaulbert Company, one of the nation's largest paint products manufacturers.† Cox was the son of Attilla Cox, Sr., a savvy entrepreneur who had parlayed an early success with his brother in the dry goods business into significant investment positions in the country's burgeoning railways – including partnerships with August Belmont of New York – as well as in a multitude of Louisville's preeminent financial institutions, including the Columbia Finance and Trust Company, of which he was president.[1] *Malvern House* was the fortuitous result of the eventual confluence of these two great fortunes.

The young newlyweds initially lived with Carrie's parents in their downtown Louisville mansion. In 1905, they engaged the architectural firm of Clarke and Loomis to design a summer house east of the city near the recently-built Louisville Country Club. Now named "Ledgelawn," the new summer place was completed in 1906.[2]

George Gaulbert died in 1908 and Attilla Cox, Sr., passed away one

† In 1928, the paint and varnish business of the Peaslee-Gaulbert Company was sold to the Devoe & Reynolds paint company, which ten years later also acquired Louisville's Jones-Dabney paint company; in time, Devoe was acquired by Celanese Corporation.

year later. Shortly afterwards, Attilla and Carrie Gaulbert Cox embarked on their plans to build a new house near *Ledgelawn* on land inherited from George Gaulbert. The site was a 17.6-acre parcel that stretched along the north ridge of the bluff that rose above the alluvial plain of the Ohio River, a location that afforded expansive and unobstructed views up, across and down the river.

The Coxes hired Ogden Codman, Jr., of New York as their architect, a selection undoubtedly influenced by the family's business association with Belmont and personal friendships within Manhattan society. Codman was perhaps best known as the co-author with Edith Wharton of *The Decoration of Houses*, a treatise first published in 1897 that outlined specific rules for the proper planning and finishing of interior residential spaces. Codman had enjoyed considerable success in his field, designing various townhouses and country estates in the northeast, and most notably interiors for Cornelius Vanderbilt II at *The Breakers* in Newport and John D. Rockefeller, Jr., at *Kykuit* in New York. His work for the Cox family would be his only project in Kentucky.

Hall, 2010. (John Nation)

Dining room, 2010. (Nation)

Detail of the antique Adam mantelpiece in the dining room, 2010. (Nation)

Living room, 2010. Note the bay window on the right, added during the 1959 renovation. (stephenphotography.com)

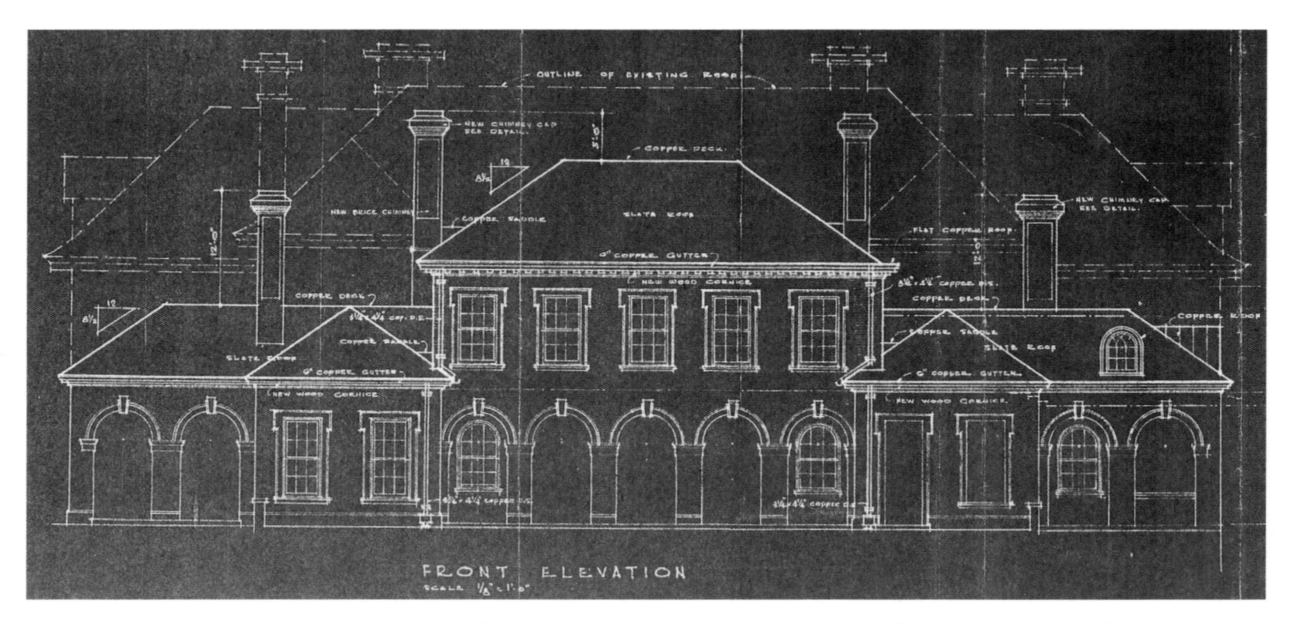

Detail from renovation plans showing outline of original house, Nevin & Morgan, 1959. (Family Archives)

Codman completed his initial design for *Malvern House* in late 1914.[3] A combination of a Georgian country house and a Palladian villa, the residence invoked many of the themes from *The Decoration of Houses.* The authors' assertions that "according to the best authorities, the height of a well-proportioned doorway should be twice its width" and that said doorway should preferably be of the French type were clearly applied to the terrace and certain interior doors, and the dictate that the classical architecture of the ancients was tested, proven, and therefore appropriate was evident in the monumental Doric columns that framed the side porches.[4]

In plan, Codman's scheme called for a large rectangular front hall, finished with black and white marble floors and plastered walls, presumably molded or incised to resemble paneling or dressed stone. The hall was enclosed on three sides by a library to the west, living and dining rooms to the north, and breakfast room and service functions to the east. Again obeying his treatise, Codman employed paired doors throughout his interior (recalling that, "between two rooms destined for entertaining, a double door (à deux battants) is always preferable to a single one"), carefully locating each opening so as to facilitate movement and the convenient placement of furniture. An exception to his axiom that "there is no good reason for uniting [the stair and hall]" was the magnificent sweeping curved staircase that dominated the east end of the front hall.

In 1916, Cox hired the Olmsted Brothers to determine the final location of Codman's planned residence and carriage house, as well as to plat the drives and gardens. The firm's initial study sited the house near the ridge of the bluff, and called for an oblique driveway approach that expanded into a broad oval roadway in front of the mansion. The plan also included a second drive that climbed up the face of the bluff, from east to west, and turned back on itself once on top to join the oval forecourt road. The carriage house was to be placed away from the house

Morning room, 2010. (stephenphotography.com)

itself, to the southwest. Olmsted's last work on the Codman plan was the design of a flower garden in 1917.[5]

Attilla Cox enlisted in the War effort in the fall of 1917. During his two years overseas, virtually all work on the design of *Malvern House* and its gardens came to a halt. Following the end of the War, Ogden Codman closed his business and, in 1920, moved permanently to France, where he lived until his death in 1951. Shortly after returning to Louisville in mid-1919, Cox resumed his building project, but quickly learned he would have to find a new architect, which he did in the accomplished Louisvillian, E.T. Hutchings.

It is evident that Hutchings was instructed to work with the drawings left behind by Codman, for in massing and in plan, the house as built under Hutchings was virtually identical to that designed by Codman. In plan, the arrangement of rooms closely mirrored that of the preceding

The former west porch, enclosed in 2009 as the music room, 2010. (John Nation)

scheme, with the one notable exception that the grand curving staircase was deleted in favor of a simpler, yet still elegant, rectilinear rendition. It was with the exterior that Hutchings took liberties to assert his own design ideas.[6]

The changes were many. Hutchings replaced the monumental Doric porches with wings that extended the brick walls of the house, but still accommodated the functions of open porch with sleeping porch above to the west and service rooms below on the east. In lieu of the imposing classically framed front door proposed by Codman, Hutchings substituted an arcade, the three central openings of which led to a recessed front porch. Hutchings eliminated Codman's proposed brick jack arches above the windows in favor of heavily molded limestone frames (the design for which was borrowed from Codman's north elevation); similarly, Codman's brick quoins were replaced by variants in alternating stone. At the roof level, Hutchings constructed three rather clumsy dormers with unusually simplistic 45-degree pediments in place of Codman's five decidedly more graceful versions. On the north, terrace elevation, Hutchings essentially repeated the design of the south façade, but incorporated Codman's cherished French doors in place of the arcade while also inserting a pediment above the center door to break the potential monotony of the bands of windows and doors. Massive chimneys with unusually broad caps punctuated the roof.

Within, *Malvern House* was finished with a distinct bow to *The Decoration of Houses*, which would lead one to believe Codman's drawings were complete enough to allow the implementation of his ideas. The front hall was outfitted with a black and white marble floor, plaster walls incised to resemble stone and a marble stairway with an iron railing of a stylized harp design – all in accordance with the rules articulated in the book. The antique pine paneling for the morning room was purchased in England and customized as necessary to fit the room, and the living room was completed with oak walls and bookcases, as well as Codman's favored drapery pockets at the French doors. A pair of doors joined the living room with the dining room, the walls of the latter being executed with box moldings and painted a neutral color, wallpaper being considered "objectionable" and "inferior" by Mr. Codman and Ms. Wharton. A carved marble fireplace mantle by the

Third floor Canadian cabin room, 1959. (Family Archives)

18th century Scottish architect Robert Adam, acquired by the Cox family in England, and elegant Georgian overmantle served as the focal point of the room. Beyond the dining room, at the northeast corner of the house, was a breakfast room, the exact size and finishes of which were lost in a renovation. Hutchings was understandably quite proud of this project, for he included it in a 1931 exhibition of his work at the J.B. Speed Memorial Museum in Louisville.[7]

Olmsted Brothers resumed work on *Malvern House* in 1922, designing the entry gateposts and grand axial drive that terminated in a low-walled square forecourt, as well as the ballustraded lawn terrace overlooking the River. In a departure from the firm's earlier plans, the drive up the bluff was eliminated and the garage moved to the east side of the property. In 1924, Olmsted created a formal garden – the "green rarden" – enclosed by high, clipped hedges and centered on a rectilinear reflection pool. An octagonal gazebo stood at the east end. Together with a large vegetable garden, the formal garden occupied a space at the front of the property near the roadway, to the west of the gates.

Attilla and Carrie Gaulbert Cox's great construction project was essentially complete by 1922, the year they sold nearby *Ledgelawn.* The gardens continued to attract their attention, however, and in 1930 they engaged landscape architect and Pennsylvania State University professor Arthur W. Cowell to explore alterations to the landscape. Nothing seems to have come of this effort, however, for from 1932 to 1939, noted Louisville landscape architect Anne Bruce Haldeman revised Olmsted's gardens and designed several new additions. Her work included a 'wildflower bowl' in a depression at the west of

The wildflower bowl, Anne Bruce Haldeman, landscape architect, undated. (Private Collection)

Olmsted's vegetable garden, a reshaped pool garden on the site of Olmsted's original formal green garden and a panel cutting garden that replaced a portion of the vegetable garden.[8]

Attilla Cox, a "prominent attorney, realtor, capitalist and humanitarian," lived at *Malvern House* until his death in 1938.[9] Carrie Gaulbert Cox continued to reside at the estate until she passed away eleven years later in 1949, at which point the house passed to the Cox's only child, Harriet Cox (Mrs. John V.) Collis, who had been living next door with her family in a Tudor Revival house designed in 1936 by Nevin-Morgan & Kolbrook of Louisville.[10] In what amounted to a remarkable effort at downsizing, the Collises in 1959 hired architects Nevin & Morgan to substantially reduce the size of the house. The entire third floor was removed, taking with it the distinctive rustic Canadian cabin room tucked behind the dormers, and the second floor was torn off the east and west wings, leaving only the five-bay central portion of the house intact. The roof was then lowered, and rectangular bay windows added to the living room and, symmetrically, to the pantry/china room off the dining room. In this greatly altered state the house remained for another fifty years.

In 2009, the current owners – she the great granddaughter of Attilla and Carrie Gaulbert Cox – rebuilt the second floor so that the entire nine-bay main block is now restored. The garage, long ago sold off as a private residence, remains today in excellent condition. Work at *Malvern House* continues on the restoration of the gardens, drives and terraces as the family continues to honor the distinguished legacy left by Mr. Codman, Mr. Hutchings, the Olmsteds and Ms. Haldeman.

The green garden as originally designed by Olmsted Brothers, undated. (Private Collection)

Entrance elevation, 2011. (Blackburn)

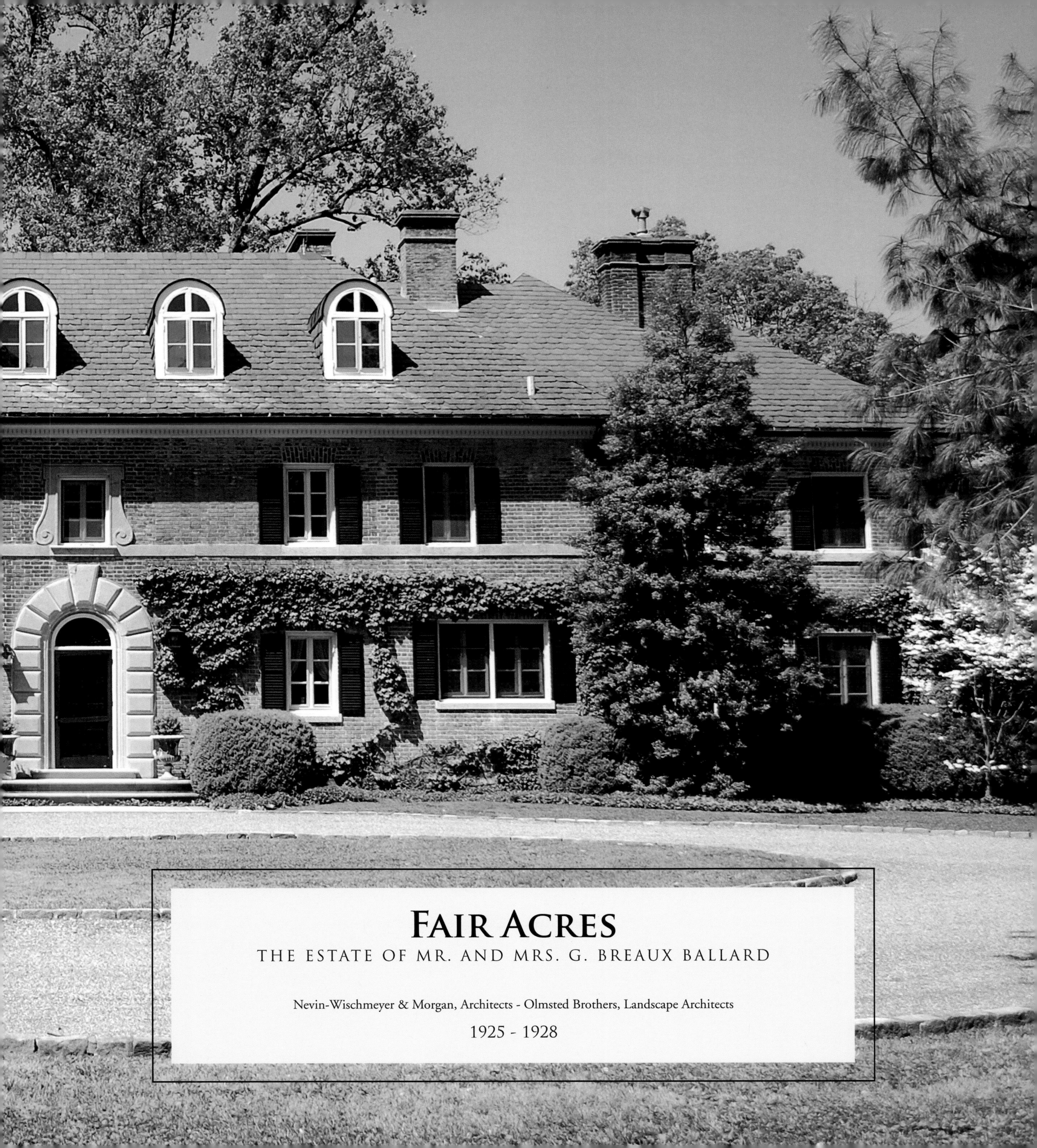

Fair Acres

THE ESTATE OF MR. AND MRS. G. BREAUX BALLARD

Nevin-Wischmeyer & Morgan, Architects - Olmsted Brothers, Landscape Architects

1925 - 1928

Proposed approach landscaping and motorcourt entry scheme (unbuilt), Olmsted Brothers, 1927. (National Park Service, Frederick Law Olmsted National Historic Site)

On September 27, 1913, in a lavish ceremony in South Bend, Indiana said to include 1,000 guests, Gustave Breaux Ballard married Mary Jane Fish. Ballard was the son of Charles Thruston Ballard, co-founder of the Ballard & Ballard Company of Louisville, and Emilina Modeste Breaux, the daughter of prominent New Orleans attorney Gustave Breaux. Ms. Fish was the daughter of Frederick Samuel Fish, chairman of the Studebaker Corporation, and Grace Anna Studebaker, whose father was John Mohler Studebaker, one of the five brothers who together established the famous eponymous automobile manufacturer. The newlyweds were introduced through Ballard's sister, Mina, who had attended New York's Farmington School with Mary Jane.[1]

Ballard was born in Louisville in 1888. Following graduation from Yale's Sheffield Scientific School, he worked for his father and uncle at the flour mills before departing for military service as a captain in France. At the end of World War I, he returned to America and moved with Mary

Jane to Pennsylvania, assuming the position of president of the Studebaker Sales Co. of Philadelphia. In the early 1920s, the Ballards came back to Louisville, where Breaux founded the Studebaker Sales Co. of Kentucky.[2] Not long after their return, the couple set out to build a new country home befitting their prominent position within the city's elite.

The site the Ballards acquired consisted of approximately 20 acres in Glenview, a short distance south of the former estate of Breaux's father, *Bushy Park*. Apparently, the parcel included a large 19th century brick residence, which the family chose to retain and use as the starting point for a much-expanded mansion.[††] Completed in 1925 to the designs of Louisville's prestigious Nevin-Wischmeyer & Morgan architects, *Fair Acres*, as the new house was called, conveyed a gracious aura of relaxed gentility through an unusual and idiosyncratic eclecticism.

Nevin-Wischmeyer & Morgan typically worked within the boundaries of stylistically pure precedents.[3] *Fair Acres* stood out in contrast to the architects' customary approach, as it was a blend of Italian, Georgian and even French influences; in short, it had no established architectural model. An Italian Renaissance front door surround was placed beneath a scroll-framed second floor window (which could have been either English or Italian in origin); tall French doors denoted the living room; and three rounded dormers stood in a neat, if asymmetrical, row atop the east portion of the house, recalling those of 18th century pavilions outside of Paris (and also, incidentally, standing in interesting counterpoint to the three segmental half-dormers of the living room wing). The tall chimneystacks were assuredly Georgian as was the brickwork, carefully executed in Flemish bond.

The architectural arrangement was uncharacteristically romantic for these most academic of architects. Varying wall and roof planes, a shifting eave line, a subtle melding of the symmetrical living room wing (likely an addition to the original house) with the asymmetrical remainder of the house, and a scattered forest of chimneys lent this elongated mansion an air of studied informality, as well as a sense that this house could very well have evolved and grown over the years. Tying the entire composition together was a broad limestone stringcourse, which helped assure the viewer that this was indeed a unified design concept.

Entrance hall, 2009. (Blackburn)

Within, one entered a rectangular hallway, at the east end of which was a dramatic curving stairway rendered in stone with a heavy wrought iron railing. In a continuation of the stylistic eclecticism of the exterior, the stairway reflected the fashionable Mediterranean architecture that was then so popular in the well-known resort communities of Florida and Southern California. The hall opened, at the west end, to the grandest room in the residence, a 25-foot by 45-foot living room. Set several steps lower than the hall, the room featured a heavy coffered ceiling of rich butternut and had as its focal point a massive stone chimneypiece, likely of English origin from the Jacobean or Jacobean revival period. Also radiating from the entrance hall were a small library and the dining room, the latter finished in a modified Colonial Revival style with fluted pilasters at the walls and a carved antique English mantel.

† See, for instance, *Breeze Hill*, built for Mr. and Mrs. Bruce Haldeman immediately following *Fair Acres*.

Living room, 2002. (stephenphotography.com)

Library, 2002. (stephenphotography.com)

In 1927, the Ballards again engaged Nevin-Wischmeyer & Morgan, this time to enhance and expand the recently completed residence. On the interior, the architects outfitted the library with elegant raised paneling and matching bookcases executed in their preferred Georgian idiom. Outside, at the east end of the mansion, they crafted a new service courtyard and garage structure, complete with guest apartment and chauffeur's quarters above, to replace a frame structure that stood to the west of the house. The architecture of the garage reflected that of the living room wing of the house, and served to balance the entire composition of residence, service court and garage outbuilding. Simultaneously, the architects engaged Olmsted Brothers to assist with the design of a new entry forecourt and gardens.[4] The paneling and garage projects were finished by 1929, and the house was presented to an ever-curious public in an expansive photo essay in the Louisville *Herald-Post.*[5] Olmsted's plans never came to fruition, however, and were likely a casualty of the stock market crash and Depression that followed.

The Ballards continued to live at *Fair Acres* until some time in the 1950s, when they built a new, smaller home at the south end of the estate. Both Breaux and Mary Jane passed away within months of each other in 1961, and by the end of the decade the property had been sold to a developer and subdivided.[6] Today, the house and garage remain in excellent condition on approximately four acres, along with the addition of a swimming pool and formal boxwood garden by Louisville landscape designer Mary Webb.

Garage, 2009. (Blackburn)

House from the west, 2011. Mary Webb's garden is in the foreground and a recently added solarium is to the left. Note the unusual positioning of the massive chimney directly above the living room window. (Blackburn)

Entrance elevation, 2011. (Blackburn)

Breeze Hill

THE ESTATE OF MR. AND MRS. BRUCE HALDEMAN

Nevin-Wischmeyer & Morgan, Architects - Anne Bruce Haldeman, Landscape Architect

1927 - 1928

The great country houses of early 20th century Louisville tended to follow European or East Coast American design precedents; it was less likely for the architecture to reflect Kentucky or Southern regionalism. An example of one such exception was *Breeze Hill*, the imposing 'Southern Colonial' mansion built for newspaperman Bruce Haldeman and his wife, the former Annie Ford Milton, in 1928. Designed by the distinguished Louisville architecture firm Nevin-Wischmeyer & Morgan, the estate consisted of over 20 acres of rolling hillside in the exclusive enclave of Glenview, on a site just north of G. Breaux Ballard's *Fair Acres*.

Bruce Haldeman was the son of Walter Haldeman who, with Henry Watterson,† merged their respective newspapers in 1868 to form *The Courier-Journal*, Louisville's major daily broadsheet. Born in 1862 in Knoxville, Tennessee, where his family had moved during the Civil War due to their "Southern sympathies," Bruce Haldeman graduated from the University of Virginia and promptly entered his father's business.[1] In 1902, he became president of *The Courier-Journal* and Louisville Times Company, a position he held until 1918 when Robert Worth Bingham (see "Bushy Park / Melcombe") acquired the enterprise. Haldeman lived until 1948, passing away after a brief illness at his Glenview home.

The design of *Breeze Hill* had its roots in the English Palladian style of the mid-Georgian era that would ultimately become so identified with the American South. Domestically, its immediate precedents lay in the American Classical Revival of the early 19th century, which provided rich material for the subsequent Colonial Revival that, by the 1920s, was taking hold as the country's preferred architectural sourcebook. Houses and commercial buildings designed by Nevin-Wischmeyer & Morgan tended to be rigidly academic; that is, the firm followed historical models rather precisely. *Breeze Hill* was no exception, and could very well have been influenced by the remarkably similar *Sabine Hall* in Virginia.[2]

The house was approached by a long sweeping drive that rose gently southeast along the contour of the hill and then turned to the north, ending in a broad circle in front of the portico. Dignified and impressive, the residence was composed as a large central block with a smaller, recessed wing extending from each side, resulting in a virtually symmetrical composition. The exterior walls were solid brick painted white; a slightly protruding stringcourse extended around the entire house, denoting the location of the second floor. Careful attention was paid to proportions and the impact the house would make on the viewer. For example, all second floor windows were slightly narrower than their first floor counterparts to prevent a top-heavy appearance. Atop the house was a high-pitched slate roof bracketed by stone-capped paired chimneys, which in turn enclosed two attic windows. Copper downspouts featured special conductor heads designed with a sunflower motif that was popular in the Colonial Revival pattern books of the time.

The front elevation of the house was notable for its two-story Tuscan Doric tetrastyle (4-columned) portico, which sheltered a relatively modest paneled front door with delicate leaded fanlight above. With the rear elevation, however, the architects indulged in more stylistic freedom, creating a two-story recessed loggia flanked by decidedly more

† Henry Watterson (1840 – 1921) was born in Washington, D.C., fought for the Confederacy in the Civil War and edited a pro-Confederate newspaper, the *Chattanooga Rebel*. Following the war, Watterson edited newspapers in several states before moving to Louisville in 1867 to purchase – and edit – the *Louisville Journal*. In 1868 he merged the *Journal* with Walter Haldeman's *Daily Courier* to form the Louisville *Courier-Journal*. In 1918 Watterson won the Pulitzer Prize for his editorials supporting American involvement in World War I. In 1919, following a dispute with Robert Worth Bingham (who had recently acquired the daily) over Watterson's opposition to the League of Nations, he resigned from the paper and retired.

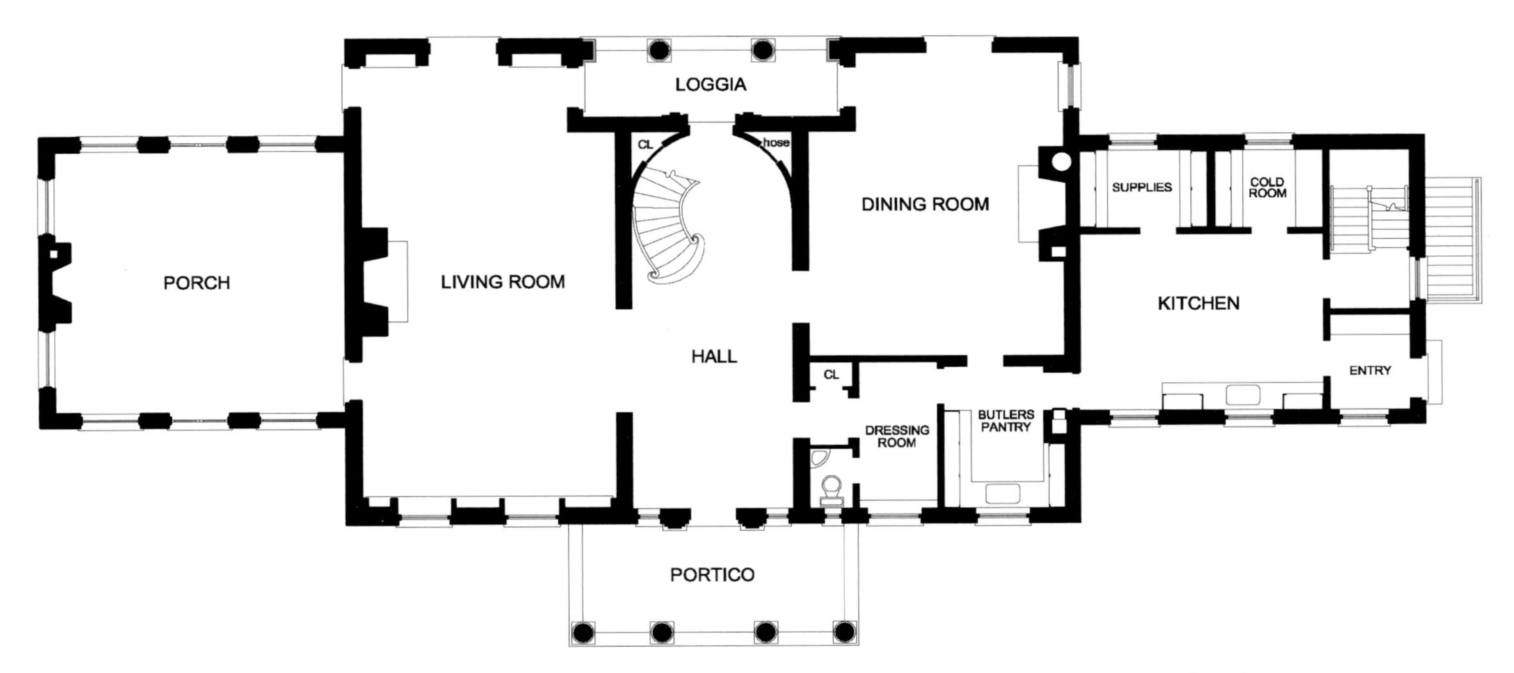

First floor plan

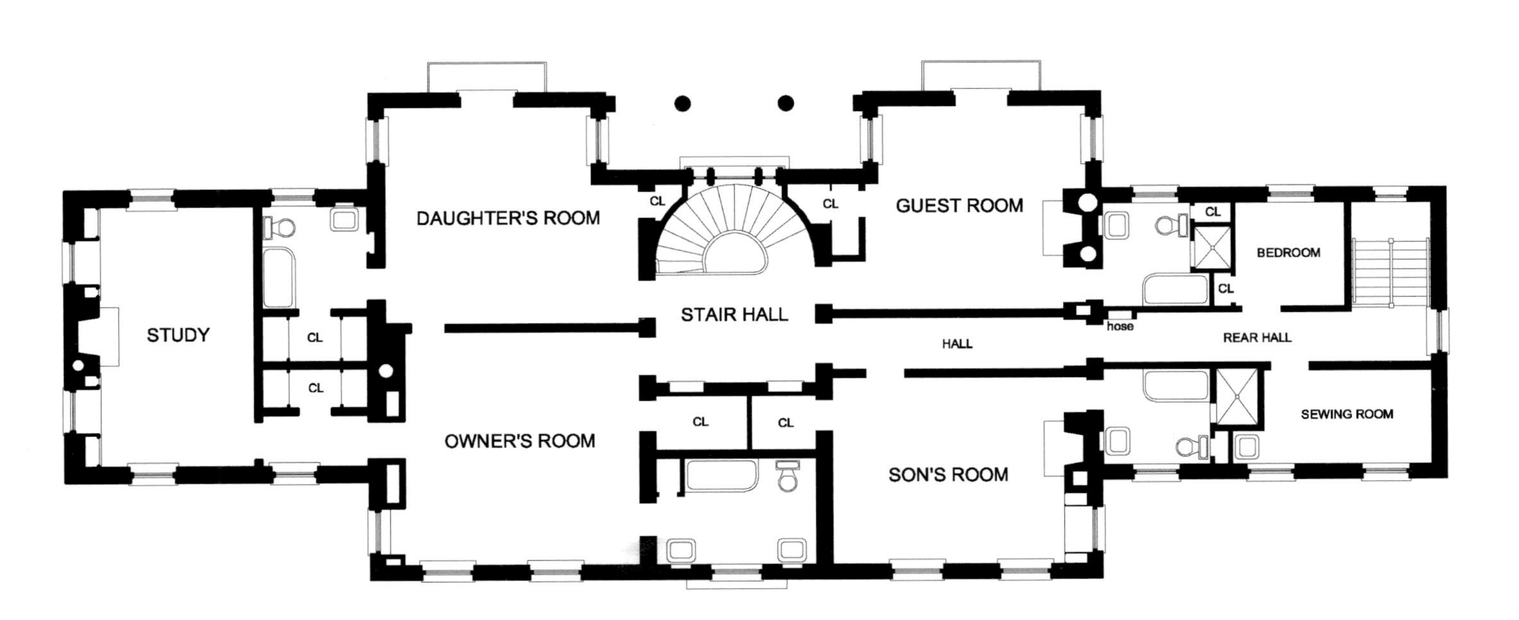

Second floor plan

Hall, 2009. (Blackburn)

contemporary broad-paned French doors and wrought iron balconies. The lintels above the ground floor doors, unlike their brick counterparts in the rest of the house, were of stone with exaggerated key and end stones, not unlike those at the Nathaniel Russell house in Charleston, South Carolina.[3]

The plan of *Breeze Hill* was simple and straightforward, and while the rooms were relatively few in number, their scale was notably impressive. One entered into a wide center hall, at the rear of which a graceful curving stair wound upward past a large Palladian window. To the west of the hall was the living room, which in turn opened to a screened porch

Living room, 1930s. (Filson Historical Society)

with fireplace. To the east of the hall were the dining room and kitchen. It is interesting that each opening leading to a room off the hall was articulated differently: the entry to the living room was through a broad paneled elliptical archway flanked by fluted Doric pilasters, the door to the dining room was surmounted by a richly detailed classical pediment atop a pulvinated (pillow-shaped) frieze and the passage to the dressing room and kitchen was defined by a simple cased arched opening. An elegant dentil crown molding was used throughout the first floor.

The second floor rooms were oriented off the central stair hall, which featured two recessed book niches in the south wall. There were four primary bedrooms, each with its own bathroom – the master additionally enjoying a private study – and a service wing with a bedroom and sewing room.

The grounds of the estate consisted of the house and a large garage outbuilding with quarters above. Additionally, at the rear of the house to the northeast was a sunken garden centered on a stone-bordered reflecting pool designed by Haldeman's daughter, acclaimed landscape architect Anne Bruce Haldeman.

Breeze Hill remains essentially as it was originally designed and constructed. A swimming pool was added at the rear of the house in the 1960s and a substantial pool house was constructed after 2000. Although there have been several renovations of the interior, the disposition of rooms and the building envelope are unchanged. And while the property has been subdivided into several parcels, the house, garage, gardens and swimming pool are still together as one, albeit slightly smaller, country estate.

Sunken garden, Anne Bruce Haldeman, landscape architect, undated. (Private Collection)

Rear elevation, 1930s. (Filson Historical Society)

Entrance elevation, 2010. (Blackburn)

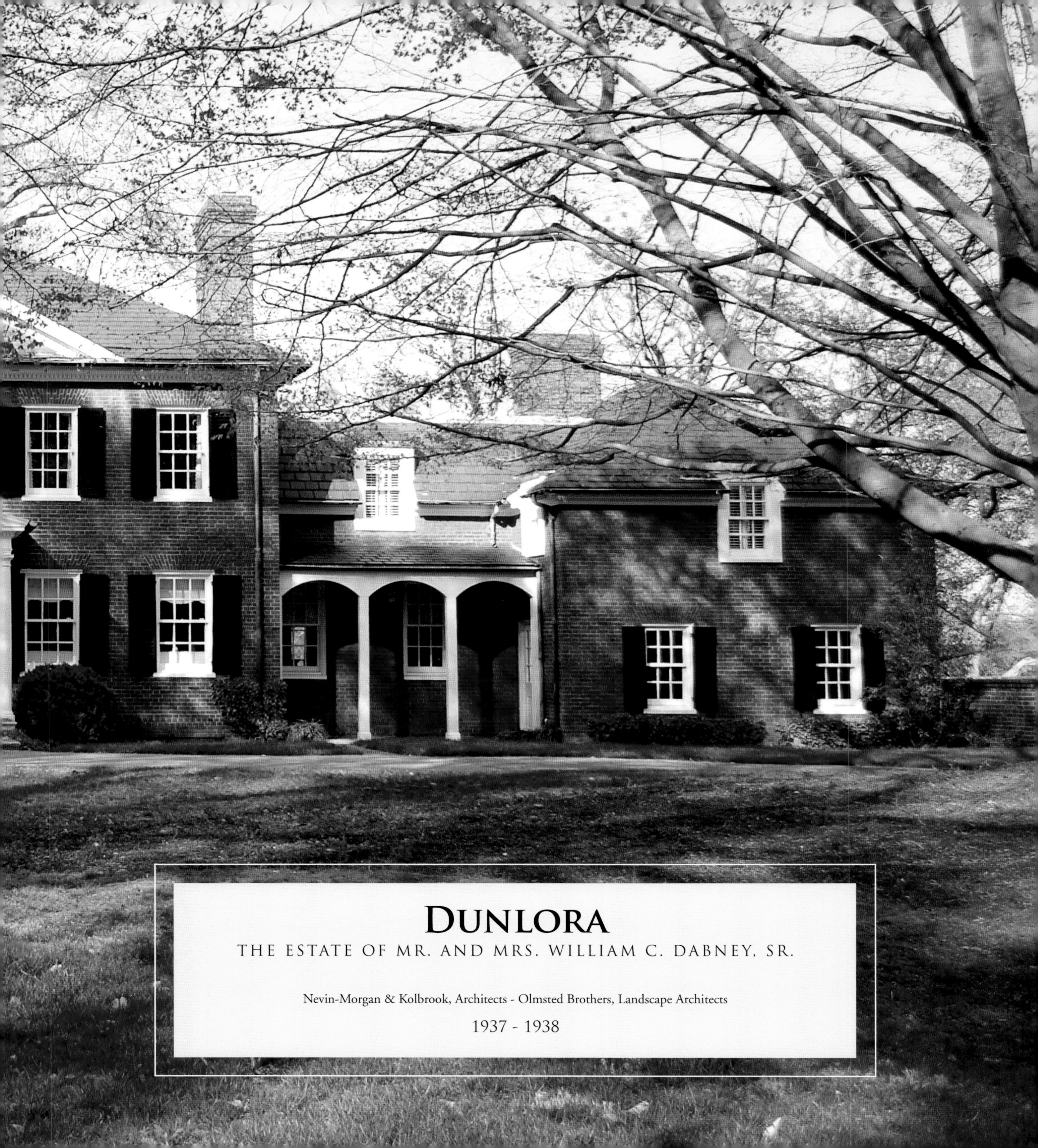

DUNLORA

THE ESTATE OF MR. AND MRS. WILLIAM C. DABNEY, SR.

Nevin-Morgan & Kolbrook, Architects - Olmsted Brothers, Landscape Architects

1937 - 1938

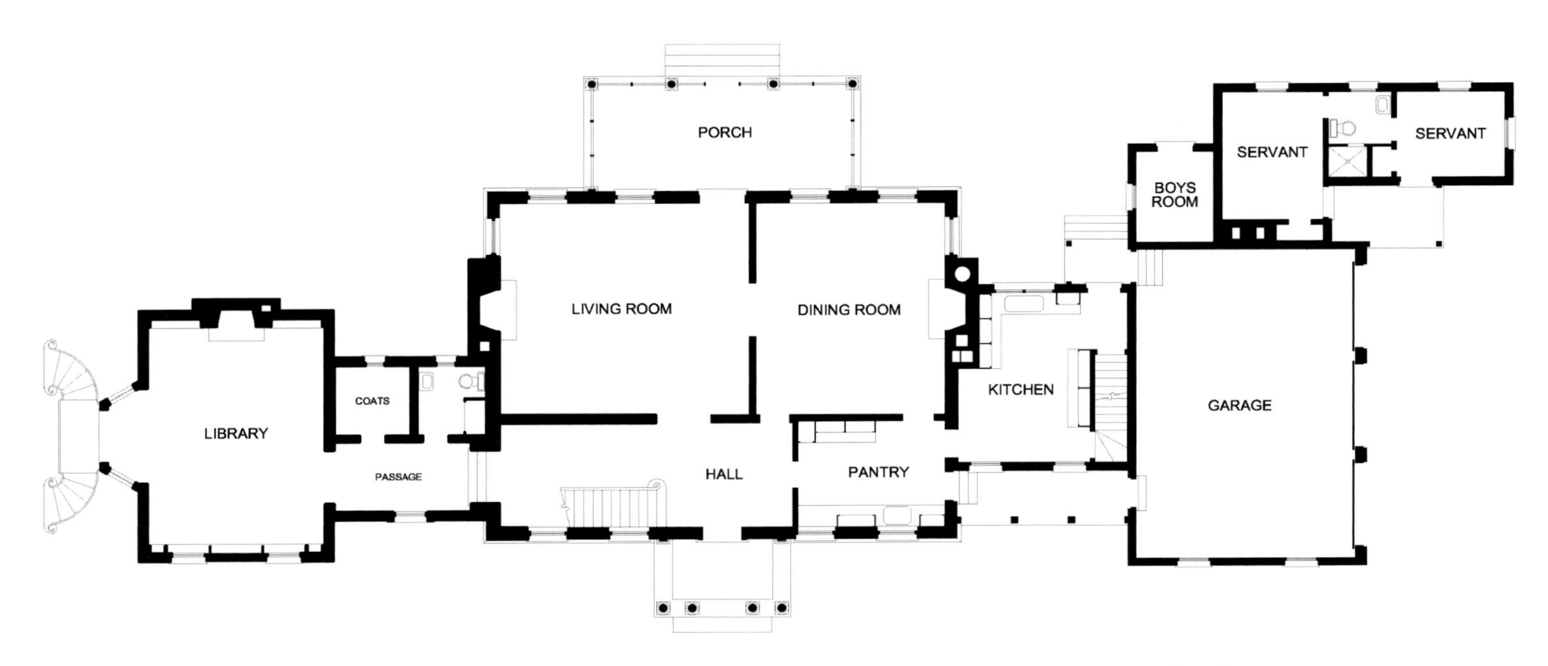

First floor plan

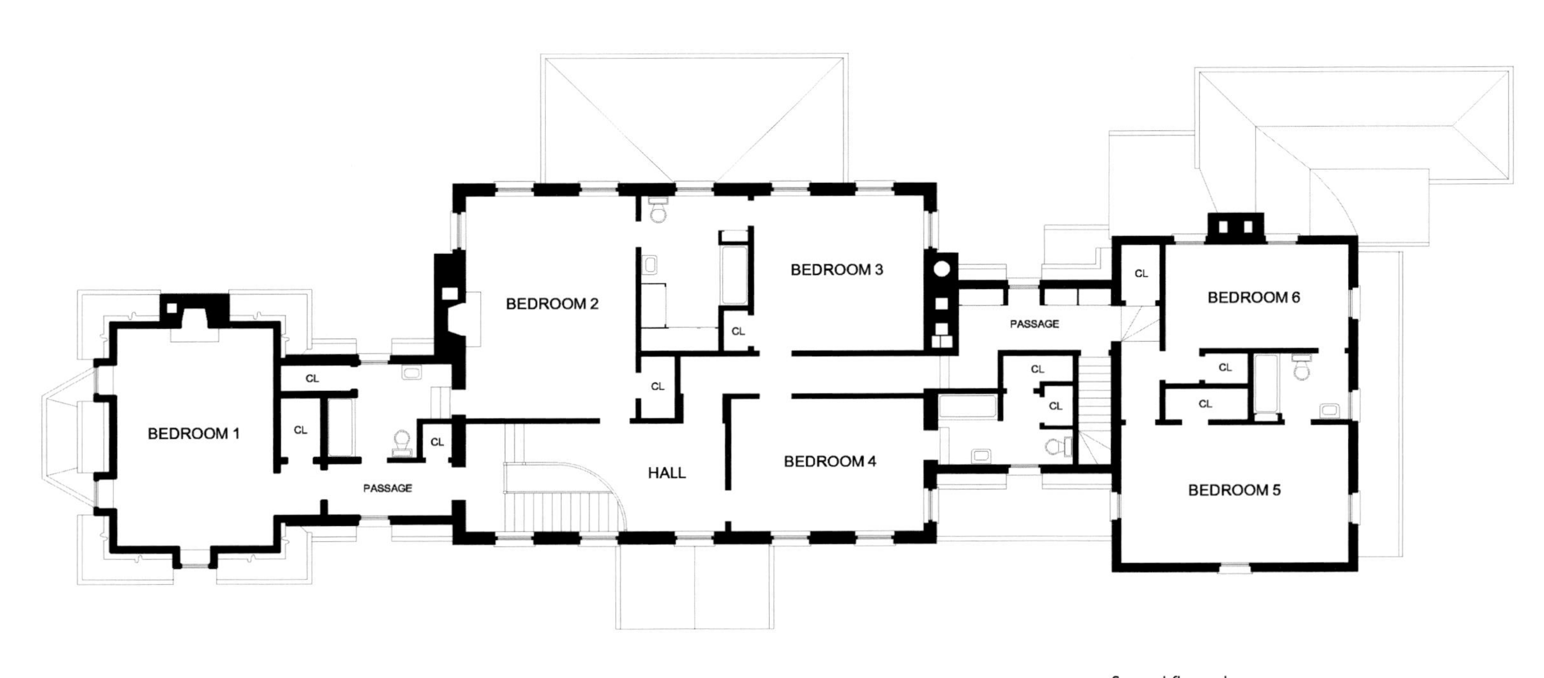

Second floor plan

Much of the bluff overlooking the Ohio River between Mockingbird Valley Road and what would become Indian Hills Trail had long been the property of the Gaulbert family, whose fortune stemmed from the Peasley-Gaulbert paint and varnish company. Louisville businessmen of a certain set enjoyed a gentlemanly camaraderie as competitors, and therefore it should come as little surprise that William C. Dabney, the co-founder of the Jones-Dabney paint company, would in 1937 purchase a portion of the Gaulbert land as the site for his new homestead, *Dunlora*. It is also quite possible that Dabney was then in the throes of negotiating the sale of his business to the Devoe-Reynolds paint company of New York, which had acquired Peasley-Gaulbert in 1928. The upcoming merger would directly link the ongoing financial interests of the Gaulbert and Dabney families.

Whatever the reason, Dabney and his wife, the former Florence Joyes, purchased almost seven acres from the Gaulbert heirs and hired Louisville's most prominent architecture firm, Nevin-Morgan & Kolbrook, to design a fashionable house that was grand in presence but relatively modest in size, reflecting the economic sensibilities of the Depression era.

Dunlora was fashioned as a Palladian five-part villa consisting of a central block bookended by two flankers and their respective connecting hyphens, a pattern typical in Kentucky, Virginia and Maryland in the late 18th and early 19th centuries. The architects tended to take an academic approach to their work, using historical models as the basis for their designs; in this case, the inspiration may very well have come from *Tulip Hill*, the well-known Federal estate near Galesville, Maryland.[1]

In plan, the house was cleverly conceived as a subtle study in pragmatic asymmetry that belied a seemingly balanced exterior. The hyphen and flanker to the west (the library side) were each narrower than their counterparts to the east, and a breezeway connecting the garage with the main house stood in opposition to the simple arched Georgian window to the west and further had the effect of pushing the corresponding hyphen back to the north. In a nod to the new compactness of contemporary living, the east flanker concealed a detached three-car garage and servants quarters.

In many ways, *Dunlora* owed much of its organization and appearance to the architects' 1930 country estate for another Louisville paint industrialist, Boone Porter.[2] As in this much larger five-part predecessor, the living and dining rooms in the Dabney residence stretched across the rear of the house, connected by a pair of French doors surmounted by a mullioned elliptical transom; opposing fireplaces stood at either end of the rooms' east-west axis. Similarly, a paneled library occupied the first floor of one flanker and a broad columned porch extended across the rear center three bays of the main house. Tall, stout chimneys anchored each primary block of the exterior, lending the house an aura of dignified formality. Although not employed at the Porter house, of note was the use at *Dunlora* of semi-recessed dormers which served to break the cornice line of the hyphens and flankers and visually lower them, resulting in a pronounced emphasis on the main or center block of the house.

The Olmsted firm's work at *Dunlora* was limited to elemental

Hall, 2011. (Blackburn)

site work (grading, drives, etc.), the details of the wall surrounding the garage courtyard and the design of a low-walled terrace garden abutting the library flanker.[3]

William and Florence Dabney lived at *Dunlora* with their daughter and three sons. In 1955, Dabney retired from his position as president of Devoe-Reynolds, having commuted regularly to New York rather than leaving his native Louisville. At the time of his death in 1963, the family had sold and moved from their splendid Federal mansion.[4] With the addition of an expanded kitchen and a family room in place of the rear porch, *Dunlora* stands today in excellent condition.

Library wing, 2011. (Blackburn)

CODA

The Gentleman's Farm and the Ex-Urban Exception: A Glimpse through *Fincastle*

The families behind Louisville's great country houses overwhelmingly chose to build in close proximity to one another in either of the two locations discussed in this book. There were, as always, notable exceptions, and in Louisville these took the form of working estates constructed at a fair distance from the city center. More closely resembling the English model of an income-producing farm, these country places – or gentlemen's farms – nevertheless retained much of the leisure-oriented intent and architectural indulgence of their River Road and Cherokee Park siblings. Paint magnate H. Boone Porter's *Ridgeley Farm* (Nevin-Morgan & Kolbrook, 1930, with gardens by Bryant Fleming) and creosote manufacturing heiress Mrs. Alvin T. Hert's *Hurstbourne Farm* (E.T. Hutchings, expansion architect, 1928) are but two notable examples. Perhaps the most distinctive of these estates was *Fincastle*, designed by an urbane Chicago society architect for an equally urbane scion of a distinguished Louisville family. A laudable representative of its genre, *Fincastle* was completed in 1937, and as such helped close the chapter on Louisville's incredibly rich era of the country house.

Rear elevation, ca. 1940. (Private Collection)

Entrance elevation, ca. 1940. (Private Collection)

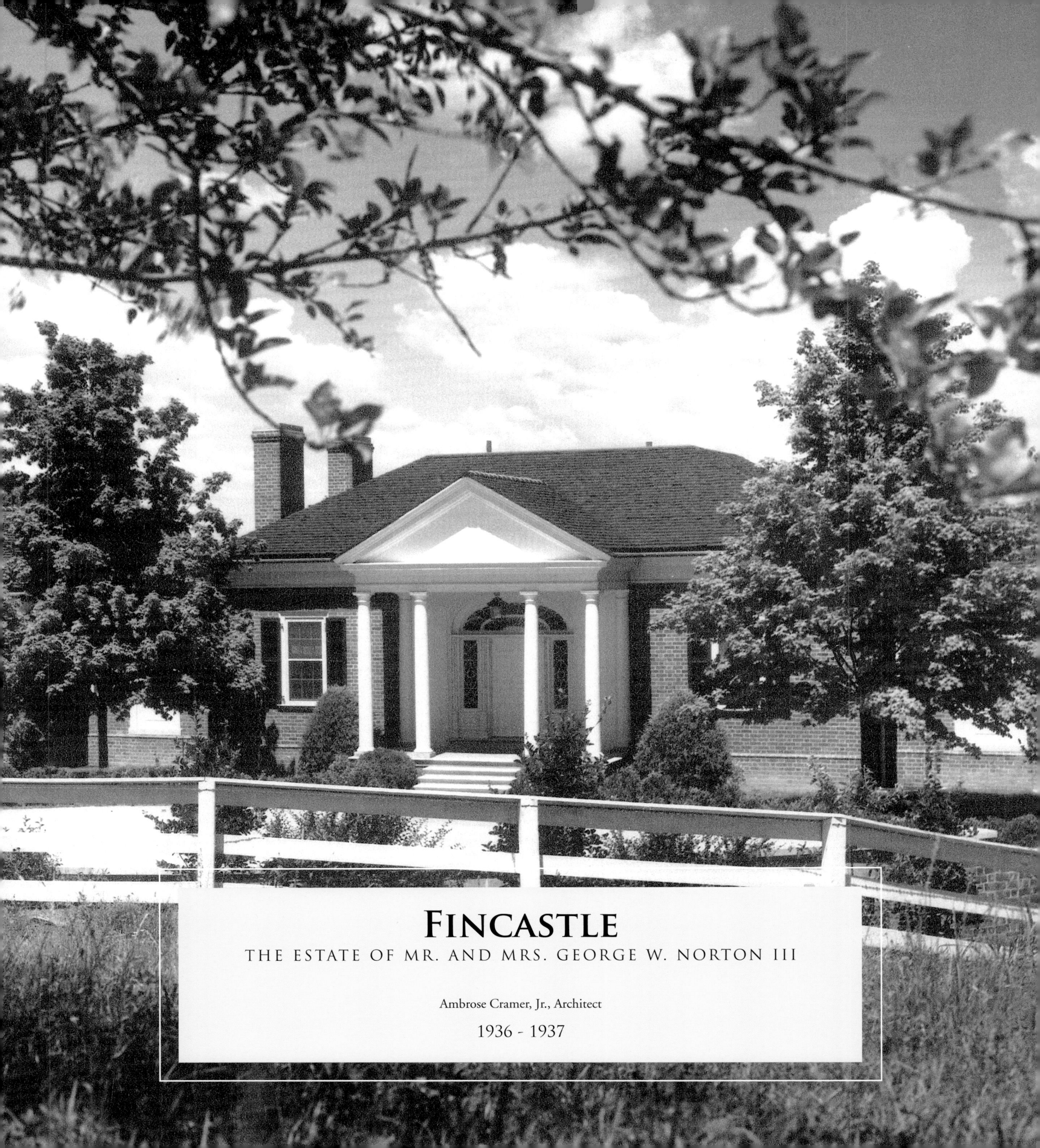

FINCASTLE

THE ESTATE OF MR. AND MRS. GEORGE W. NORTON III

Ambrose Cramer, Jr., Architect

1936 - 1937

The era of Louisville's great country houses that began in 1899 with George W. Norton, Jr.'s, Norton Hall at Cherokee Park and S. Thruston Ballard's Lansdowne in Glenview was reaching its conclusion by the end of the 1930s. World War I, changes in taxation, altering immigration patterns and, of course, the Great Depression had all wreaked their own special havoc on that brief moment in time in which unbridled new wealth, European craftsmen and a structured social order – including a dedicated servant class – allowed the country's elite to indulge in the creation of estates that connoted membership in that European legend of the landed gentry. At Cherokee Park, the era came to an end with the sumptuous renovation and expansion of *Daneshall* for the A. Gilmore Ouerbackers in 1939. Along the bluffs of the Ohio River, it was brought to a close a year earlier with William Dabney's *Dunlora.*

The penultimate great house constructed from the ground up before the advent of World War II was *Fincastle*, the quietly elegant gentleman's farm of George W. Norton, III, and his wife, Jane Morton Norton. Perhaps in deference to the sensitivities of the struggling economy, *Fincastle* was built discretely away from the more visible Cherokee Park and River Road estate areas, and took the appearance (at least on first blush) of a comparatively modest residence. The result of the confluence of two great fortunes, however, the house was – notwithstanding its unassuming façade – a marvelously intriguing work of architecture on which, ultimately, no expense was spared.

The site the Nortons selected for *Fincastle* consisted of over 200 acres abutting a large bend in Harrods Creek, about three miles east of the Ohio River. To design their new house, they selected Chicago society architect, Ambrose Cramer. Cramer perfected his skills under the tutelage of David Adler, one of Chicago's most prominent architects of country estates and city mansions in the first half of the twentieth century. A first cousin to Adler's original business partner, Henry Dangler, Cramer served as Adler's junior partner until branching out on his own some time prior to 1931. He was the son of an affluent Lake Forest family, and took as his wife the daughter of Arthur Meeker, vice president and director of Armour & Company, the enormous meatpacking concern. Financially and socially established, and well-connected through both his family and Adler, it should come as little surprise that he and the Nortons would inevitably meet.

Cramer positioned the new house toward the back of the property, on a gentle slope that fell down toward Harrods Creek, a long drive that meandered through horse pastures leading the visitor in from the road. This particular site afforded the architect with an opportunity to create a truly distinctive residence. Due to the fall of the land, the house upon arrival was a single story structure, yet at the rear was a full two stories, an arrangement not all that unusual in Louisville at the time. What was unusual, however, was that Cramer's design presented, in essence, two different houses to the viewer: the front, single story façade was clearly based on *Ridgeway*, the circa 1818 Federal house not far away in St. Matthews, while the rear was, by contrast, a stylized version of a classic Georgian plantation from 18th century Virginia. The only local precedent for this type of approach was Louis Seelbach's *Barnard Hall*, near Cherokee Park, where McDonald & Dodd similarly designed two façades, one Georgian (at the entrance) and the other Greek Revival (overlooking the park).

The front of *Fincastle* was historically more pure than the rear and was based on two great Kentucky models. The five-part massing, general fenestration, hyphen details and delicate Tuscan Doric portico were unmistakably drawn from *Ridgeway*, and the design of the front door grouping – including sidelights and fanlight – were virtually duplicated from Lexington's *Rose Hill* of circa 1818.[1] On the creek side, Cramer took more artistic license: what now became a grand

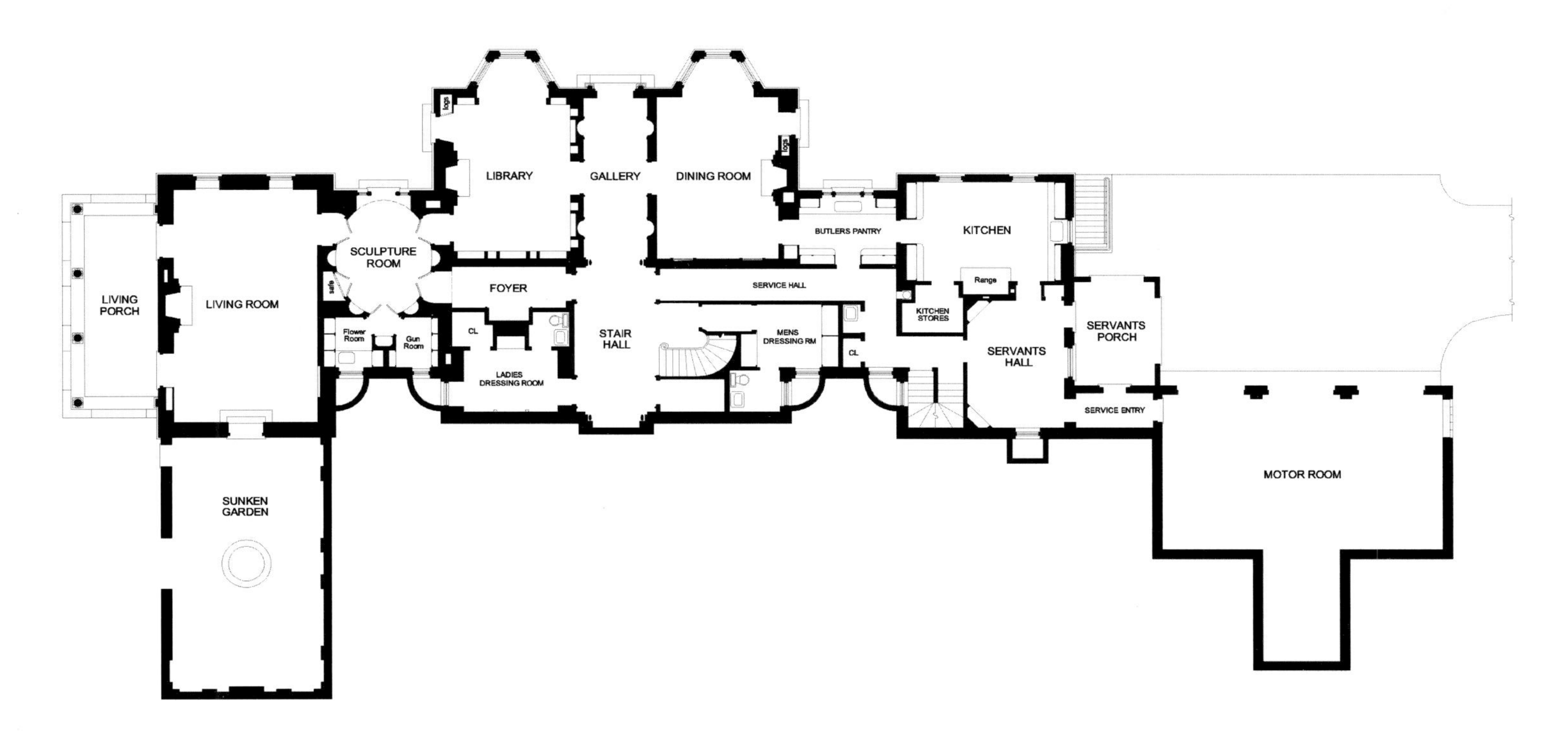

First floor plan

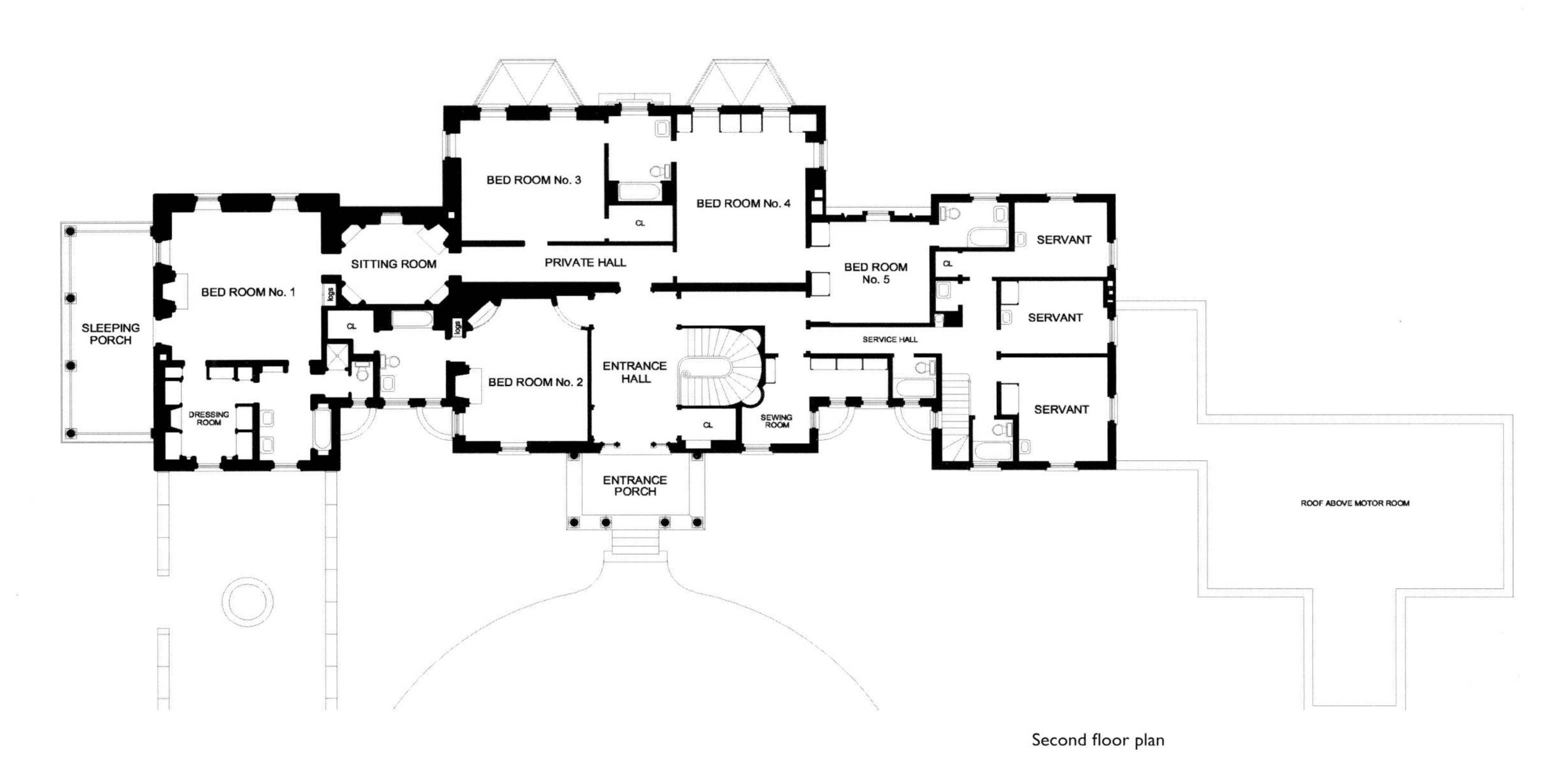

Second floor plan

five-part Georgian plantation house reflected the downsized scale and streamlining typical of the late 1930s. As was to be expected in Cramer's work, the details he did include were executed with a robust plasticity. The brick walls boasted not one but two string courses, creating in essence a wide band and double shadow line across the three mains blocks of the house. The bay windows of the library and dining room, presumably patterned after a nearly identical window at David Adler's own house in Libertyville, Illinois, were rich in their deep, modeled quality, as was the very sculptural pedimented center door and stylized window surround above. Cramer carried this attention to form in the hyphens, where the amply modeled doors, surmounted by projecting lunette hoods, stood below distinctively bracketed dormers likely drawn from Adler's Mrs. Kersey Coates Reed house of 1931-2 in Lake Forest.[2] A heavily textured flat tile roof completed the composition.

Within, the house was organized around an inverted plan; that is, one entered on the bedroom level and descended to the public floor. The millwork details of the entrance hall, and stair hall below, were executed in a rather moderne style reflecting the prevailing fashion of the era. Thin, delicately reeded columns and pilasters supported blind elliptical archways set within the walls as well as

Entrance portico, 2011. (Blackburn)

Detail, rear elevation, 2011. (Blackburn)

Main stair, ca. 1940. (Private Collection)

an arch that bifurcated the lower stair hall and gallery. An artificial skylight illuminated the graceful curving stairway, which was subtly tucked within a large side alcove off the hallways. The design of the main, public floor evidenced Cramer's training under Adler. The plans of the dining room and library were reminiscent of the senior architect's work on plumbing magnate Richard T. Crane, Jr.'s, *Castle Hill* in Ipswich, Massachusetts of 1924-8, and the 1934 Lake Forest estate of Mrs. J. Ogden Armour.[3] Similarly, Cramer's extraordinary millwork detailing – virtually all rendered in a stylistically correct Georgian manner (with the exception of his nod to the moderne in the hallways) – demonstrated the exceptional architectural finesse that emanated from Adler's atelier.

Living room with view to sunken garden, undated. (Private Collection)

As with the exterior, the interior enjoyed a marvelous sculptural quality. Varying wall thicknesses; crescent-shaped niches; unconventional room shapes, such as the oval sculpture room, octagonal master sitting room and chamfered bedroom; archways; columns; pilasters; modillioned moldings and the curving stairway all combined to lend a distinctive three-dimensional character that was quite unusual – and costly – for a structure of this era.

The landscaping at *Fincastle* was relatively simple, apparently designed by Cramer in concert with the house. The roadway to the house terminated in a circular drive, partially cut into the slope of the hill. Extending from the west of the house, on axis with the living porch,

Dining room, ca. 1940. (Private Collection)

Library, 2011. (Blackburn)

View from lower level gallery to stair hall, 2011. (Blackburn)

Sculpture room, ca. 1940. (Private Collection)

Mrs. Norton's studio, ca. 1940. (Private Collection)

was a long, rectangular formal garden at the end of which was an artist's studio for Mrs. Norton. Projecting to the south from the end of the living room, and connected to the formal garden though a raised lawn terrace, was an enclosed sunken garden centered, as was its counterpart off the living porch, on a round reflecting pool. Concealed from view at the front of the house, this set of gardens contributed to the unfolding sense of surprise and unorthodoxy that prevailed in this most distinctive of residences.

George W. Norton, III, the son of George W. Norton, Jr., grew up at *Norton Hall.* Jane Morton Norton, the daughter of Dr. David Cummings and Mary Harris Ballard Morton, often visited her grandparents at *Lansdowne.* Born in 1902, the younger George Norton graduated from Yale University in 1923 and the Harvard School of Law three years later. In 1928, he and Jane Morton were married. In about 1932, he entered the nascent radio business, acquiring the WAVE studios, yet continued to practice law until volunteering for the war effort in 1941. Upon his return from overseas duty in 1944, having achieved the rank of major, Norton devoted his attention full-time to WAVE. Under Norton's stewardship, WAVE expanded to become the first television station in Kentucky, with the largest broadcast area in the state. At the time of his death in 1964, Norton owned not only WAVE but also stations in Evansville, Indiana, and Green Bay, Wisconsin.[4]

Jane Morton Norton was active in WAVE, serving as its vice president during World War II and president following the death of her son, George W. Norton, IV. A trained artist, she was also known as a great philanthropist, founding with her husband the Norton Foundation and with her brother, Senator Thruston Morton, the Morton Center for chemical dependency.

Mrs. Norton sold *Fincastle* to W. L. Lyons Brown, Jr., head of the Brown-Forman Corporation and former American Ambassador to Austria, who lived on the estate until selling it to the current owners. Still on a considerable 80 acres of land, *Fincastle* remains in superb condition with the addition of a family room off the original kitchen and butlers pantry, as well as a swimming pool and pool house. Jane Norton's studio has been converted to a guest cottage, still separated from the living porch by Cramer's elegant formal garden and terrace.[5]

Door panel within the sculpture room, 2011. (Blackburn)

View into the Greek theatre at *Melcombe*, 1933. (Caufield & Shook Collection, University of Louisville Archives and Records Center, Louisville, KY)

Architects' Biographies

LEWIS COLT ALBRO

Lewis Colt Albro (1876-1924) was born in Paris, France to American parents and raised in the family's hometown of Pittsfield, Massachusetts. In 1893, the young Albro moved to New York City where he worked for McKim, Mead & White while pursuing his studies at the Metropolitan Art School. During his thirteen-year tenure at the McKim firm, Albro was involved in the design of several Carnegie libraries, the Columbia University Library and the Manhattan residence of Gibson Girl creator Charles Dana Gibson. In 1906, Albro and fellow architect Harrie T. Lindeberg left McKim, Mead & White to form their own partnership, which lasted until about 1914. From that point until his death in New York, Albro practiced on his own. "His work," observed a writer in the April 1924 issue of *Pencil Points*, "was marked by a versatility and keen appreciation of color, mass and design that won him the distinction of being placed among the most notable architects who have made domestic architecture their specialty."

WILLIAM STRUDWICK ARRASMITH

William Strudwick Arrasmith (1898-1965) was a native of North Carolina who became nationally known for his art deco-inspired Greyhound bus stations, of which he designed over 100. Arrasmith began his education at the University of North Carolina, Chapel Hill, in 1916 but after one year transferred to the University of Illinois, graduating with a degree in architecture in 1921. Shortly after finishing school, Arrasmith traveled to New York City to work with McKim, Mead & White, staying with the firm a brief six months before moving to Louisville where he accepted a position with architect E.T. Hutchings. Following six months with Hutchings, the young architect joined Brinton Beauregard Davis in Louisville as a draftsman. Over the next few years, Arrasmith worked again for Hutchings as well as architect Clarence Stinson before settling into a partnership in 1928 with Herman Wischmeyer, who had just ended his association with the Louisville firm of Nevin, Wischmeyer & Morgan, to form Wischmeyer & Arrasmith. The partnership, which designed Louisville's moderne Bowman Field terminal building in 1935, was eventually known as Wischmeyer, Arrasmith & Elswick upon the 1937 addition of Fred Elswick and, in time, Arrasmith, Judd & Rapp, the name it holds to this day.

LAWRENCE BUCK

Lawrence Buck (1865-1929) was born in New Orleans, Louisiana, the son of Norwegian landscape painter William H. Buck. Little is known about his education or apprenticeship, other than he was listed as a draftsman in New Orleans in the mid-1880s. By 1894, Buck had moved to Chicago, where the *Lakeside Directory* classified him on various occasions as either an architect or an artist. In 1902, Buck became a member of "The Crafters," a loosely organized group of artists located in Chicago's Steinway Hall, the heart of the city's progressive architecture movement where such well-known architects as Dwight Perkins, Robert Spencer and Frank Lloyd Wright also had their offices. In 1908, Buck enjoyed a surge in his architectural career following the publication of his Arts & Crafts Charles Reeves house (Oak Park, Illinois) in the October issue of *House Beautiful* magazine. Additional inclusions in that periodical as well as in *Ladies Home Journal* brought him commissions in Louisville, Pittsburgh, the Dakotas and California. From 1909 until at least 1912, Buck worked in partnership with Edwin Clarke, although for the majority of his career he apparently preferred working alone, occasionally producing architectural delineations for other firms. He passed away in 1929 at his home in Highland Park, just north of Chicago.

CARRÈRE & HASTINGS

John Merven Carrère (1858-1911) was born in Rio de Janeiro, the son of a Baltimore coffee merchant and a descendant of early French emigrants to the United States. He began his formal education in Switzerland at the age of 14, often vacationing in France at the home of his paternal grandmother. In 1882, Carrère received his diploma from the École des Beaux-Arts and joined New York's McKim, Mead & White as a draftsman.

Thomas Hastings (1860-1929) was born in New York City, the son of a distinguished Presbyterian minister and a descendant of the founders of the Massachusetts Bay Colony. Hastings started his training in the architectural design department of Herter Brothers, one of New York's most prestigious decorating and furnishings firms, and then studied architecture at Columbia University for two years prior to enrolling at the École des Beaux-Arts in 1880. Upon his graduation four years later, he too returned to New York to work with McKim, Mead & White.

Carrère and Hastings left McKim, Mead & White to establish their eponymous firm in 1885. Carrère was the business and professional head of the partnership, while Hastings handled most of the design work. Shortly after embarking on their new venture, Hastings' father introduced the young partners to one of his congregants, Henry M. Flagler, who hired the firm to design a lavish new hotel in St. Augustine, Florida. Completed in 1887, the Ponce de Leon Hotel was an artistic triumph that propelled Carrère & Hastings to prominence. Over the next quarter century the firm produced a steady stream of notable hotels, churches, private and public buildings, city mansions and country houses, including the New York Public Library and Manhattan's Henry Clay Frick mansion (now the Frick Collection museum).

Carrère's untimely death in an automobile accident at age 53 brought an end to the firm's rapid growth; nevertheless, Hastings continued to operate the business under the original name, securing numerous prestigious commissions until his own passing in 1929. From beginning to end, Carrère & Hastings enjoyed one of the most distinguished client rosters of their time, counting among their patrons not only Flagler and Frick, but also Alfred I. du Pont, Murray Guggenheim, Frank Goodyear, William Rockefeller, E. H. Harriman and William K. Vanderbilt. Two of the firm's last projects were in Louisville, the War Memorial Auditorium of 1929 and Greek Theatre for Robert Bingham, completed after Hastings' death in 1930.

JOSEPH EVERETT CHANDLER

Joseph Everett Chandler (1864-1945) was born in Plymouth, Massachusetts, to Mayflower descendants. He graduated in architecture from the Massachusetts Institute of Technology in 1889, and immediately embarked on a documentation tour of the American South. His resulting book of large-format photographs, *The Colonial Architecture of Maryland, Pennsylvania, and Virginia*, was published in 1892 and was so popular it was reprinted in 1900. Sixteen years later, Chandler published *The Colonial House*, an architectural history and pattern book that coincided with, as he wrote, the "fortunately widespread and increasingly intelligent interest" in the Colonial Revival.

Chandler was one of the best known and most influential of the first generation of preservation architects who discovered, popularized and restored early American houses. His notable projects included the restoration of the Old State House, Old Corner Book Store and the Paul Revere House in Boston; the House of the Seven Gables in Salem; and the Mayflower House in Plymouth. When designing anew, Chandler generally worked in the Colonial Revival style. His guiding premise was a belief that architectural forms embodied the values of their builders, and that a culture could not survive without preserving reminders of its origins and character.

OGDEN CODMAN, JR.

Ogden Codman, Jr. (1863-1951) was born in Boston to a prominent New England family. From 1872 to 1882, he lived in France, where (along with time in Germany) he received much of his early education before returning to the United States to study architecture at MIT in 1882. His formal training in the field was rather minimal, as he spent but one year at MIT followed by several years with local architecture firms, including that of his uncle, John Hubbard Sturgis. In 1891, Codman opened his own office in Boston, then a branch in Newport, Rhode Island, moving ultimately to a permanent location in New York City in 1893 – the year Cornelius Vanderbilt II chose him to decorate the upper floors of his palatial villa in Newport, *The Breakers*.

Codman's position as a prominent society architect, decorator and tastemaker was solidified with the publication in 1887 of *The Decoration of Houses*, a widely-read treatise on high-end interior design he co-authored with Edith Wharton. In addition to designing numerous elegant interiors and townhouses in Boston's Back Bay and New York's Upper East Side, Codman was responsible for a number of notable country houses, including *Bryce House* (later *Clayton*), the English Georgian mansion of Lloyd Bryce, and *Haut Bois*, the Louis XVI-style petit chateau for Walter Maynard – both on Long Island – as well as the interiors of John D. Rockefeller, Jr.'s *Kyhuit* in Pocantico Hills, New York.

Codman closed his office for the duration of World War I and in 1920 moved to France where he resided, first at his restored *Château de Grégy*, and then at a villa of his own design, *La Léopolda*, until his death in 1951. Looking back, Ogden Codman was a major influence on the transformation of taste from the dark, often cluttered Victorian interiors of the late 19th century to the classical forms and lighter palette of the early 20th. His own designs were drawn from actual examples of high-style 18th century French, English and American houses, and reflected an understanding of classical architectural vocabulary that, despite his limited formal education, often exceeded that of his more extensively trained contemporaries.

MARIAN CRUGER COFFIN

Marian Cruger Coffin (1876-1957) was born in Scarborough, New York, to well-to-do parents. She received her early education at home with private tutors and, in 1901, enrolled in the landscape architecture program at MIT. Coffin graduated in 1904 – one of only four women in a class of 500 students – and moved to New York City, opening her own office after finding that architecture firms were reluctant to hire a female designer. Coffin's career received an important boost from her childhood friend, Henry Francis du Pont, who not only recommended her to well-connected friends, but also ultimately hired her for her largest commission, assisting him with the gardens for his expansive estate near Wilmington, Delaware, *Winterthur*. In addition to being one of the first American women formally educated in landscape architecture, Coffin was part of a movement away from the late 19th century Olmsted-inspired notion of naturalistic picturesque design toward a formal vision inspired by the gardens of France and Italy. She articulated her approach in her 1940 book, *Trees and Shrubs for Landscape Effects*: "In any landscape scheme the designer should think as the architect does, not only of his plan but also of the elevation which expresses this plan and the interrelation between the two." Her numerous notable projects included gardens for *Hillwood*, the Long Island estate of Edward F. Hutton and Marjorie Meriwether Post, and *Oxmoor*, the William M. Bullitt estate near Louisville.

ARTHUR W. COWELL

Arthur Westcott Cowell (1878-1958) graduated from Cornell University in 1903, and worked as a landscape architect in Pittsburgh and Philadelphia before moving to State College, Pennsylvania in 1913 to organize the department of landscape architecture at Penn State. He retired from the university in 1925 to pursue his own professional practice. While most noted for his planting plans for the Pennsylvania highways, Cowell designed numerous public parks as well as gardens of many private estates, including the plan of *Glenhill Farm* for paper manufacturer Ernst Behrend in Erie, Pennsylvania and the formal garden at *Drumanard* for Major and Mrs. Alexander MacKenzie Watson outside of Louisville.

KNIGHT CHENEY COWLES / COWLES & COLEAN

Knight Cheney Cowles (1892-1970) was born in Chicago, the grandson of Alfred Cowles, Sr., an early owner of the *Chicago Tribune* newspaper. He graduated from Yale University in 1916, received his masters degree in architecture from Harvard in 1922 and an Architecte Diplômès par le Gouvernement from the École des Beaux-Arts in 1925. Following his return from Paris, Cowles worked at the noted Chicago architecture firm of Holabird & Roche – which had designed several automobile showrooms for his father, Alfred Cowles, Jr., in downtown Chicago – before establishing his own partnership, Cowles & Colean, in 1929. Cowles worked with Colean (about whom very little has been documented) until 1943, after which time he pursued a private practice. Cowles & Colean's work included several residences in Lake Forest, Illinois as well as commercial projects in Ohio and Chicago. In addition to their work for Arthur Allen in Glenview, the firm designed a small house in Louisville for Morris Belknap, Jr.

AMBROSE CRAMER, JR.

Ambrose Coghill Cramer, Jr. (1891-1970) was born in Chicago, the son of a prominent Lake Forest family and great-great-grandson of Irish immigrants who came to America in 1798. He received his preparatory education at The Hill School in Pottstown, Pennsylvania and the Lake Placid School in New York, and graduated from Yale University in 1913. From 1915 until the outbreak of World War I, he worked as a draftsman in the office of his first cousin, Henry Dangler, and Dangler's better-known partner, society architect David Adler. At the conclusion of the War, Cramer traveled to Paris where he studied architecture for two years prior to enrolling at the École des Beaux-Arts, completing his studies in 1926. Upon his return to Chicago, Cramer again joined David Adler first as a draftsman, then rising to head designer. He remained with Adler until 1929 when, following his marriage to Mary Meeker, socialite daughter of Arthur Meeker, vice president and director of meat packing giant Armour & Company, he left to form his own architectural firm, Ambrose C. Cramer, Inc.

During his peak design years preceding World War II, Cramer designed several notable projects, including *Constantia*, an elaborate Cape Dutch-style country estate for his in-laws in Montecito, California; the John Colman residence in Lake Forest, Illinois; *Brushwood* for steel magnate Edward L. Ryerson, Jr., in Deerfield, Illinois; and a residence for Mrs. D. M. Ryerson in Middleburg, Virginia.

Cramer served in the War effort from 1942 until 1946 as director for the Lend-Lease Administration in Washington, D.C. At the conclusion of the War, he returned to Chicago, closed his architecture business and moved his family to Rockport, Maine, where he became active in historic preservation. Cramer died in Rockport in 1970.

FREDERICK HOYT ELSWICK

Frederick Hoyt Elswick (ca. 1896-1958) was born in Williamson, West Virginia. He studied at Manassas College in Virginia for a year before the outbreak of World War I, following the conclusion of which he worked as a draftsman in Huntington, West Virginia, before moving to Ashland, Kentucky. In 1926, he relocated to Louisville to work with architects W. Earl Otis and Helm Bruce, Jr. and, in 1931, joined Herman Wischmeyer and William Arrasmith to form Wischmeyer, Arrasmith and Elswick, an association that continued until 1945. At the end of World War II, Elswick pursued his own practice under the name of Fred Elswick & Associates. Among his higher profile projects were work on the Henrietta Bingham estate (now Harmony Landing Country Club) in Goshen, Kentucky, and the Kentucky State Fair and Exposition Center in Louisville.

WILSON EYRE

Wilson Eyre (1858-1944) was born in Florence, Italy to American parents. The son of a foreign service officer, he received his early education in Europe; Newport, Rhode Island; and Lenoxville, Canada before studying architecture at MIT for one year in 1877. In 1878, he moved to his family's hometown of Philadelphia where he worked as a draftsman in the office of architect James Peacock Sims. Upon Sims' death in 1882, Eyre continued the firm under his own name, working independently until 1911, when he took as a partner J. Gilbert McIlvaine, an association that lasted until McIlvaine's death in 1939.

Eyre was widely admired for his distinct and novel residential designs, a hybrid of English Arts and Crafts, American Colonial Revival and other architectural styles. He "used ornament – often related to the Arts and Crafts and Art Nouveau movements – sparingly, highlighting relatively plain surfaces and shapes and emphasizing the natural beauty of carefully selected and crafted materials." Eyre was most productive during the 20 years preceding World War I, and found the greatest number of his clients along Philadelphia's Main Line and in the suburbs of New York (where he operated a second office from 1903 to 1918). In addition to his practice, Eyre taught at the University of Pennsylvania from 1890 to 1894 and was a regular contributor to *House & Garden Magazine*, which he co-founded in 1901.

BRYANT FLEMING / TOWNSEND & FLEMING

Bryant Fleming (1877-1946) was born in Buffalo, New York and, following the early death of his mother, spent much of his childhood at his grandparents' farm in northern Niagara County. He showed a precocious interest in nature, studying at the Buffalo Botanic Gardens following graduation from high school and then, at the advice of Frederick Law Olmsted (to whom he had written for guidance) enrolling at Cornell University to study under the widely respected horticulturist, naturalist and author, Liberty Hyde Bailey. Fleming graduated from Cornell in 1901 and promptly joined the Boston office of landscape architect Warren Manning, where he remained for three years. In 1904, Fleming and Bailey established a new Department of Landscape Art as part of Cornell's College of Agriculture, with Fleming appointed the school's first lecturer and instructor in landscape art (he would serve as the head of the department from 1906 to 1915).

At the same time he was working with Bailey at Cornell, Fleming opened his own practice as a landscape architect in Buffalo with Medford, Massachusetts native Frederic de Peyster Townsend (ca. 1872-1951), an architect and planner for Buffalo's 1901 Pan-American Exhibition. The partnership's work included site planning, subdivision platting and landscape and architectural design for numerous private residences and estates – including the landscape design for Frank Lloyd Wright's Avery Coonley house in Riverside, Illinois. In 1915, Fleming and Townsend dissolved their firm, and Fleming moved to the small village of Wyoming, New York, to open his independent practice.

Together with Townsend and then on his own, Fleming and his employees often served as architects, interior designers and landscape architects for a single commission. Fleming's knowledge of art, architectural history and antiques rivaled his command of horticulture and the technical aspects of landscape design, and consequently facilitated a cross-discipline artistic integration that came to define his style. By the mid-1920s, he had projects underway in Chicago, Detroit, Cleveland, Kansas City and Louisville, as well as in small towns in New York, Pennsylvania, Ohio, Michigan, Mississippi, Florida and southern Canada. In 1925, Fleming moved to Ithaca, New York, to be closer to Cornell.

The peak – as well as the conclusion – of Fleming's long design career was undoubtedly his 1929 commission to design the residence, interiors and gardens of *Cheekwood*, the 100-acre estate of Maxwell House Coffee entrepreneur Leslie Cheek in Belle Meade, outside of Nashville, Tennessee. The project, completed in 1932 after the Great Depression brought an effective end to Fleming's business, embodied the retrospective observation that "Fleming's work was extremely individual and unorthodox, at times challenging all rationality, often guilty of the most whimsical exaggeration, yet somehow invariably delightful."

J. J. GAFFNEY

James J. Gaffney (1863-1946) was a Louisville native who received his early architectural training at the offices of Clarke and Loomis in Louisville, followed by a period working with architect Cornelius Curtin. He served as a foreman for McDonald Brothers prior to establishing his own firm in 1898. Gaffney's projects spanned a broad spectrum of types, and included – in addition to houses – the Belvoir and Besten apartment buildings on Cherokee Parkway in Louisville, as well as numerous churches, including St. James Catholic Church in Louisville's Highlands neighborhood.

GEORGE HERBERT GRAY

George Herbert Gray (1874-1945) was born in California, the son of the Rev. Edward P. and Mary Louise Gray. He graduated from Johns Hopkins University in 1895, and attended the École des Beaux-Arts from 1901 to 1906. In 1909, Gray married Mary Belknap, the daughter of Louisville industrialist William R. Belknap and his first wife, Alice Belknap. Three years later, he partnered with Herman Wischmeyer to form Gray and Wischmeyer, an association that lasted until Gray enlisted in the War effort in 1917. After the War, Gray returned to live in Columbia, Connecticut, where he served as head of the department of city planning from 1920 until 1923. His book, *Housing and Citizenship…A Study of Low-Cost Housing*, was published posthumously in 1946.

ANNE BRUCE HALDEMAN

Anne Bruce Haldeman (1903-1999) was born in Louisville, the granddaughter of Walter N. Haldeman, co-founder of the Louisville *Courier-Journal* newspaper. She attended Bennett College in Millbrook, New York, and after graduation studied at the Cambridge School of Architecture and Landscape Architecture, later a part of Harvard University. Following graduation from the Cambridge School, Haldeman worked with Fletcher Steele, a prominent Boston landscape architect, and then with Ellen Biddle Shipman in New York City – the latter an association and friendship that endured until Shipman's death.

In about 1934, Haldeman returned to Louisville to begin her long career in Kentucky, where her first commission was for the redesign of gardens at Mrs. Attilla Cox's *Malvern House*. Her work ultimately included gardens for the J. K. Lilly, III estate, *Newfields*, near Indianapolis; the Chicago Botanical Garden; and private residences in Lake Forest, Illinois, Cincinnati and North Carolina. She was instrumental in the acquisition, preservation and restoration of *Farmington* – the historic Speed family homestead outside of Louisville – where she created a new garden in an 18th century manner. The first woman member in Kentucky of the American Society of Landscape Architects, Haldeman in 1973 was awarded the Mrs. Oakleigh Thorne Medal from the Garden Club of America for outstanding achievement in garden design.

JOHN BACON HUTCHINGS / E. T. HUTCHINGS

John Bacon Hutchings (1859-1916) was born in Louisville, the son of Eusebius Hutchings, a prominent financier, and the former Elizabeth Bacon. The details of his education and architectural training are unknown; however, in 1890 he partnered with Louisville architect Cornelius Curtin to create the firm of Curtin and Hutchings. He remained in that partnership until about 1897 or 1898 when he associated briefly with architect Henry Hawes, and then practiced mostly on his own until 1911. In that year, his two sons, Eusebius Theodore and John B., Jr., joined their father in what would ultimately be called J. B. Hutchings & Sons. John Bacon, Sr. was noted for his residential work, and was an accomplished designer in a variety of styles, ranging from the Tudor and Georgian Revivals to the Shingle Style and the Arts and Crafts. He was quite evidently one of two local architects preferred by Louisville society, the other being McDonald & Dodd. Upon his death in 1916, Hutchings' sons closed the firm; after the end of World War I, John Bacon, Jr. moved to Asheville, North Carolina, and E. T. embarked on his own, independent practice.

Eusebius Theodore ("E. T.") Hutchings (1886-1958) like his father was born in Louisville. He attended the University of Kentucky for two years, and then enrolled at Cornell University, departing in 1909 to continue his studies in Hanover and other European cities. Following his work with his father and brother and service in World War I, Hutchings returned to Louisville in 1919 and opened his namesake firm. His roster of notable commissions included the vast horse farm, *Spindletop Hall*, in Lexington, Kentucky; the restoration of *Federal Hill* (also known as "My Old Kentucky Home") in Bardstown, Kentucky; and the remodeling and expansion of the Alvin T. Hert estate, *Lyndon Hall*, outside of Louisville (now the Hursbourne Country Club). He additionally served as associate architect to Carrère & Hastings for the design and construction of the Louisville War Memorial Auditorium.

MCDONALD & DODD

The Louisville architectural firm of McDonald & Dodd was among the city's most distinguished during its brief existence between 1906 and 1913. It was the culmination of various partnerships – Maury & Dodd, McDonald Brothers, McDonald & Sheblessy and Dodd & Cobb – that had come and gone since about 1886. McDonald & Dodd's client list included many of Louisville's social and business elite, and their residential commissions included a number of the city's costliest town and country houses. The dominant design partner was evidently Dodd, and McDonald apparently oversaw the technical and business sides of the partnership.

William J. Dodd (ca. 1862-1930) was born in Quebec City, Canada, the son of Irish and English immigrants. In 1869, the family came to the United States, settling in Chicago – which Dodd would claim as his birthplace in later years. While little is known about his education, it is certain that Dodd trained under famed architect William Le Baron Jenney, a founder of the Chicago School of architecture, and later under Spencer Beman, another major figure of the Chicago School, with whom he worked on the model corporate town of Pullman, Illinois.

Dodd appears to have arrived in Louisville in 1886. He was initially associated with architect Oscar C. Wehle from 1887 until 1889, and then with Mason R. Maury, with whom Dodd designed the Richardson Romanesque-style Louisville Trust Building in 1891 – said to be the first steel-framed fireproof building in Kentucky – as well as the Colonial Revival Kentucky Pavilion at the 1893 World's Columbian Exposition in Chicago. His partnership with Maury lasted until about 1896, at which time he teamed with Arthur Cobb, an engineer who had come to Louisville from Cleveland in 1889, to form Dodd & Cobb, architects of the lavish Edwin Hite Ferguson mansion in downtown Louisville (now the Filson Historical Society). In 1904, the partnership dissolved and Dodd joined with Kenneth McDonald to form McDonald & Dodd.

Kenneth McDonald (1852-1940) was born in Romney, Virginia and came in Louisville in 1873 shortly after graduating with a degree in civil engineering from the Virginia Military Institute. He initially taught mathematics at the Rugby School and worked with his brother, Harry Peake McDonald, in a firm that ultimately became McDonald Brothers when Kenneth's other siblings, Donald and Roy, entered the business in the 1880s. In 1895, Kenneth left the firm and practiced alone until forming a partnership with John Francis Sheblessy in 1901. This association lasted until 1906, when he joined William J. Dodd in McDonald & Dodd.

Together, McDonald & Dodd designed many notable projects, among them the Weissinger-Gaulbert apartments, Stewart's Dry Goods department store, Atherton Building and Presbyterian Theological Seminary, all in downtown Louisville; the Louisville Country Club;

and the Memphis, Tennessee mansion of banker C. Hunter Raine.

In 1913, McDonald and Dodd dissolved their partnership. McDonald moved to San Francisco, and Dodd relocated to Los Angeles where he worked with Julia Morgan on the design of William Randolph Hearst's Los Angeles Herald-Examiner Building of 1915.

D. X. MURPHY & BROTHER

Dennis Xavier Murphy (1853-1933) was born in Louisville to Irish immigrant parents. Little is known about his childhood and early education other than he began his architectural training at age 16 under noted Louisville architect Henry Whitestone. Following Whitestone's retirement in 1880, Murphy assumed control of the practice, and a year later hired his younger brother, James Cornelius Murphy (1864-1935), as an apprentice. In 1890, the two brothers formed a partnership under the name of D. X. Murphy & Brother, which changed to D. X. Murphy & Brothers when a second sibling, Peter Murphy (1868-1955), joined the firm. In 1962, new owners Jean D. Farley and T. D. Luckett, II renamed the practice Luckett & Farley, the name it carries to this day.

D. X. Murphy & Brother was perhaps best known for designing the grandstand and twin towers for the Jockey Club at Churchill Downs in 1894, as well as the L&N Railroad office building in downtown Louisville.

NEVIN - WISCHMEYER & MORGAN / NEVIN - MORGAN & KOLBROOK / NEVIN & MORGAN

The firm that became known as Nevin & Morgan (and ultimately, after 1967, Nevin, Morgan & Weber) had its beginnings in the nineteen-teens as a partnership named Henry & Nevin, Hugh Lloyd Nevin being one of the principals. In 1920, following J. Earle Henry's death, the firm was reorganized to include Herman Wischmeyer and Frederic Morgan and renamed Nevin-Wischmeyer & Morgan. Approximately eight years later, Herman Wischmeyer left the practice and was replaced by Joseph Kolbrook, and the business was retitled Nevin-Morgan & Kolbrook. At some point prior to 1952 – likely shortly after the end of World War II – Kolbrook also left to establish his own practice, and Hugh Nevin and Frederic Morgan continued on under the name of Nevin & Morgan.

Throughout its various iterations and long existence, the firm was particularly celebrated for its residential architecture, the best examples of which were often attributed to Frederic Morgan as designer. However, the practice also produced a number of notable commercial and institutional buildings, including Louisville's Pendennis Club, Collegiate School, Second Presbyterian Church, Church of St. Francis-in-the-Fields and Broadway Baptist Church – and, perhaps surprisingly, the moderne Lee Terminal Building at the city's Standiford Field Airport.

Hugh Lloyd Nevin (1876-1969) began his working career in Louisville as a plumbing and heating contractor with Henry J. Scheirich in 1898. A decade later, he received his law degree from the University of Louisville, and was admitted to the Kentucky bar. Instead of practicing law, however, he chose to become an architect, designing and marketing house plans and his architectural services in the newspaper. His advertisements and brochures for "Nevin Homes" identified him as a skilled promoter, a talent that enhanced his role as business manager of the firms that were to bear his name. He retired in 1965.

Herman Wischmeyer (1875-1945). Please see separate biography.

Frederic Lindley Morgan (1889-1970) was born in Loda, Illinois, the son of a well-to-do druggist. In 1912, he graduated from the College of Engineering at the University of Illinois, following which he spent a year and a half in Europe, touring in England, France and Italy. Morgan returned to the United States in 1914 and moved to Louisville to work as an assistant to J. Earle Henry, architect and engineer for the Board of Education. Following two years under Henry, Morgan moved to Michigan, where he filled a similar position with the Detroit Board of Education before leaving to serve in World War I. At the conclusion of the War, Morgan returned to Louisville, joining his former employer at Henry & Nevin.

Morgan's design work earned the praise of clients and fellow architects alike. Louisville architect Stratton Hammon described him as one of Louisville's architectural geniuses, and the American Institute of Architects, when elevating him to the status of Fellow, observed that he was an "Able delineator, [and] he has jealously fostered and ably developed the traditional residential design of his native state [sic], animating and vitalizing it with his own peculiar fine discrimination." Morgan bequeathed his estate to the University of Louisville, creating the Frederic Lindley Morgan Chair of Architectural Design.

Joseph Hyde Kolbrook (1891-1976) was born in Louisville as Joseph Hyde Kaltenbach. He was educated in Louisville and Los Angeles, and retired from independent practice in 1968.

OLMSTED BROTHERS

Perhaps no other names are as closely associated with the birth and development of American landscape design as are those of Frederick Law Olmsted and his two sons, John Charles Olmsted and Frederick Law Olmsted, Jr. Vaulted to fame by the 1857 commission to design New York's Central Park, for almost 100 years the senior Olmsted and later his sons helped shape the nation's parks, university campuses and private grounds into carefully conceived and picturesque landscapes.

Olmsted Brothers, created in 1898 by brothers John C. and Frederick Law, Jr. following their father's retirement a year earlier, was responsible for literally thousands of commissions across the country, including some of the nation's most significant residential enclaves and country estates. While the brothers continued to work in their father's preferred naturalistic idiom, they also bowed to the fashion of the era, and created formal gardens that reflected their clients' desires to emulate European models. The mingling of the two design approaches, and a concern for balancing aesthetics and practicality, enabled the firm to be extremely versatile and thus in great demand. By 1920 alone, when John C. passed away, the practice had already secured over 3,500 commissions, which made it the world's largest landscape architecture firm. Olmsted Brothers endured until 1961.

John Charles Olmsted (1852-1920) was born in Vandeuvre, near Geneva, Switzerland, the son of Dr. John Hull Olmsted and Mary Cleveland Perkins Olmsted. By 1859, he had lost his father to tuberculosis, gained a stepfather – his uncle, Frederick Law Olmsted – and moved into a house in New York's Central Park, which was then under construction. In 1862, the family moved to Washington, D.C., and then to California's Sierra Nevada. He spent the summers of 1869 and 1871 in Nevada and Utah as a member of Clarence King's survey party along the 40th Parallel, where he developed his remarkable ability to note and remember the topography as well as geological and botanical features of the land.

Olmsted graduated from Yale's Sheffield Scientific School in 1875 and entered his stepfather's business in New York as an apprentice. From 1877 and 1878, he traveled through Europe, focusing on the study of architecture in London. By 1884, when the Olmsted firm moved to Brookline, Massachusetts, the younger Olmsted had become a full partner with his stepfather. When he formed Olmsted Brothers with his half-brother, Frederick Law, Jr., in 1898, John C. assumed the position of senior partner, a role he held until his death.

John C. Olmsted was a "man of few words, fond of detail, ... [with] a broad grasp of large scale landscape planning" who "carried to completion a vast amount of work quietly and with remarkable efficiency" and who, in addition to his extensive design and planning work, was responsible for developing and advancing the business side of the firm. He was deeply involved in carrying on the partnership's already extensive work with park planning, which led to commissions for residential subdivisions and private homes and estates. His interest in architecture was reflected in his residential work, where he took particular care to fit the residence to the site and available vistas, often making preliminary house designs and collaborating closely with the building architect. Upon his untimely death at age 68, management control of the firm passed to his brother, Frederick, Jr.

Frederick Law Omsted, Jr. (1870-1957) was born Henry Perkins Olmsted on Staten Island, New York, the son Frederick Law Olmsted and Mary Cleveland Perkins Olmsted, his brother's widow. Not long after his birth, his father renamed his only biological son Frederick Law Olmsted, Jr.

Young Olmsted graduated from Harvard University in 1894 after having spent a summer working in the office of Chicago architect Daniel Burham as the "White City" for the 1893 World's Columbian Exhibition was being built. Following graduation, he traveled to Asheville, North Carolina, where he spent thirteen months on the construction site of George Vanderbilt's *Biltmore House*. In late 1895, he formally entered his father's firm in Brookline, and joined his half-sibling, John C., in the partnership of Olmsted Brothers three years later.

Frederick Jr. rose to prominence in 1901 with his appointment to Washington, D.C.'s McMillian Commission, which was charged with interpreting, expanding and implementing the original L'Enfant plan for the capital city. Olmsted levered this project into additional urban planning commissions throughout the country, including work for Detroit; Pittsburgh; Palos Verdes, California; and Lake Wales, Florida. Later in his career, he devoted much of his time to public service, focusing on the conservation of the country's state and national parks and remaining wilderness areas, including Maine's Acadia National Park, the Florida Everglades and Yosemite in California. He was instrumental in the creation of the National Park Service, and contributed key language to the 1916 bill that established the Service. Olmsted retired in 1949.

CHARLES ADAMS PLATT

Charles Adams Platt (1861-1933) was born in Manhattan, the son of a successful corporate lawyer, John Platt, and Mary Cheney Platt, heiress to a Connecticut silk mill. He showed little interest in his general education, instead choosing in his late teens to become an artist. In 1878, Platt enrolled in drawing classes at New York's National Academy of Design and in painting classes at the Art Students League, supplementing his studies with summer sketching trips in the New England countryside. He soon acquired an interest in etching, joining the New York Etching Club at age nineteen and earning a reputation as a skilled etching artist within the year. However, his preference was to develop his talents as a painter, and in 1882 he sailed for Europe, where he studied in Paris for the next five years.

Platt's transition from etching and painting to landscape design and architecture began in 1892, when he and his younger brother spent several months sketching, measuring and photographing the Renaissance and Baroque gardens of Italy. Their images were first published in two articles for *Harper's Magazine* in 1893, and then reissued as a book, *Italian Gardens*, in 1894. The book, a first of its kind, was immensely popular and resulted in several major commissions for American gardens. Platt then moved into architecture as he designed cottages and gardens for friends, initially in the artists' summer colony of Cornish, New Hampshire, where he maintained a house.

Platt was never formally trained in architecture – his application to the École des Beaux-Arts was rejected – but his artist's skill and acute eye for detail and proportion clearly enabled him to absorb the art and translate it with unusual talent to paper. As he gained more and more experience in architecture and landscape design, he was encouraged and supported by two influential friends, Royal Cortissoz, art critic for the New York *Sun*, and Herbert Croly, an editor of *Architectural Record*. In very little time, Platt became one of the preferred architects of country houses and estates and counted among his clients members of the Pratt, McCormick, Rockefeller, Roosevelt and Pulitzer families. He additionally designed numerous townhouses and office buildings, as well as such institutional projects as the Freer Gallery in Washington, D.C., and the campus plan and buildings for the University of Illinois at Urbana. The 1913 monograph of his residential work, *The Architecture of Charles Platt*, became an instant pattern book for architects, and served to extend his influence across the country.

Platt passed away in 1933, and his sons, William and Geoffrey, continued the firm into the 1980s.

SHEPLEY, RUTAN & COOLIDGE

George Foster Shepley, Charles Hercules Rutan and Charles Atherton Coolidge were architects in the office of Henry Hobson Richardson when the great master died in 1886. In an informal, unsigned will, he directed these three trusted assistants to carry out his unfinished work. Together, they formed the partnership of Shepley, Rutan & Coolidge, which survives to this day in Boston as Shepley Bulfinch Richardson and Abbott – the oldest continually operating architectural firm in the country.

George F. Shepley (1860-1903) came from St. Louis, where he attended Washington University. Upon his graduation in 1880, he moved to Boston to study architecture at MIT and was hired into Richardson's office. Shortly after her father's death, Shepley married Richardson's daughter, Julia. **Charles H. Rutan** (1851-1914) was an engineer who received his architectural training in Richardson's office, where he started at 18 as an office boy and rose to become one of Richardson's chief designers. **Charles A. Coolidge** (1858-1936) was a Bostonian and a member of the Harvard class of 1881. He pursued additional studies at MIT before beginning his career in Richardson's office in the early 1880s. In 1889, Coolidge took as his wife George Shepley's sister.

In time, the partnership migrated away from Richardson's signature heavy Romanesque idiom toward a preference for eclecticism. From about 1894 to 1934, the firm typically chose to design in any of three general styles: Italian High Renaissance, Late English Gothic or Tudor and English Post-Renaissance or Georgian, the latter of which the architects tended to prefer for their residential commissions.

Shepley, Rutan & Coolidge produced a significant volume of work across all building types, including the original campus for Stanford University and buildings for the University of Chicago as well as for Harvard and Vanderbilt Universities; the Chicago Public Library (now Chicago Cultural Center) and Art Institute; and country houses for banker N. W. Harris in Lake Geneva, Wisconsin, and plumbing magnate Richard T. Crane, Jr. in Ipswich, Massachusetts.

ELLEN BIDDLE SHIPMAN

Ellen Biddle Shipman (1869-1950) was born into a prominent Philadelphia family, the daughter of Ellen Fish McGowan Biddle and Col. James Biddle. She spent her early years on frontier outposts in Nevada and Arizona, in time returning to New Jersey to live on her grandparents' farm. In 1893, she left Radcliffe College after one year to marry playwright Louis Shipman, and the following year moved to the artists' colony of Cornish, New Hampshire. There she met architect Charles Platt, with whom she would have a long and serendipitous professional relationship.

In 1910, Louis Shipman left Ellen and moved to London. Now alone, she began to pursue her career in earnest. Working frequently with Platt, she became a sought-after designer of country house landscapes. In 1920, Shipman moved to New York City and opened her office. During the close to 40 years she practiced landscape architecture, she developed a dedicated following that resulted in over 650 garden commissions. Her notable projects included *The Manor House* for Standard Oil industrialist John T. Pratt in Glen Cove, New York (with Charles Platt); *Longue Vue Gardens* near New Orleans for cotton merchant Edgar B. Stern; Lake Shore Boulevard in Grosse Point, Michigan; and master plans for the Bronx Botanical Gardens and Duke University.

Shipman maintained a fierce independence and feminist profile throughout her long career, teaching at and only hiring graduates from the Lowthrope School of Landscape Architecture in Groton and the Cambridge School of Architecture and Landscape Architecture – both institutions restricted to women. She asserted that without women, the golden age of American landscape design would not have occurred, and that "until women took up landscaping, gardening in this country was at its lowest ebb. The renaissance of the art was due largely to the fact that women, instead of working over their boards, used plants as if they were painting pictures, and as an artist would."

Ellen Biddle Shipman closed her office in 1946 and passed away four years later at her home in Warwick West, Bermuda.

WALKER & GILLETTE

Walker & Gillette was one of the more prominent East Coast architectural firms of its time. Based in New York City, and in operation from 1906 to 1945, its commissions encompassed all building types and especially included great estates and town houses for prominent members of high society. The firm, which frequently partnered with landscape architects (especially Olmsted Brothers), received numerous awards, including the AIA medal for apartment house design in 1910, the gold medal of the Architectural League of New York in 1922 and the gold medal of the AIA in 1925. Its extensive list of commissions ranged from Manhattan's Art Deco Fuller Building to the lavish Regency-style William Goadby Loew house on East 93rd Street (also in New York) to a grand Mediterranean villa designed for Harry Payne Bingham in Cleveland, Ohio.

Alexander Steward Walker (1876-1952) was born in Jersey City, New Jersey. He received his early education at St. Paul's School in Concord, New Hampshire, and then graduated from Harvard University in 1898. Three years later, he joined Warren & Wetmore as a draftsman, where he met Leon Narcisse Gillette; the two formed their independent practice in 1906. Walker, whose position in New York society and membership in many of the city's prestigious clubs provided him with an enviable contact list, was the salesman for the partnership who was largely responsible for securing commissions.

Leon Narcisse Gillette (1878-1945) was born in Malden, Massachusetts. After studying at the University of Minnesota, he worked at the Minneapolis architectural firm of Bertrand & Keith. In 1899 he received his certificate of architecture from the University of Pennsylvania and then relocated to New York City, where he worked in the offices of Howell & Stokes, then Schickel & Ditmars and ultimately Babb, Cook & Willard. In 1901, he enrolled at the École des Beaux-Arts and, after receiving his diploma in 1903, returned to New York where he joined the prestigious architectural firm of Warren & Wetmore. Gillette contributed a rigorous design talent, enhanced by his Beaux-Arts training, as well as a strong administrative capability to his partnership with Walker

HERMAN WISCHMEYER

Herman Wischmeyer (1875-1945) was born in Baltimore, Maryland, to German immigrant parents. In 1876, his family moved to Louisville where his father was engaged in the wholesale grain trade. Following graduation from high school in 1893, Wischmeyer traveled to Germany where he studied architecture at the polytechnic institutes of Hanover and Munich from 1894 to 1897. Upon his return to Louisville, he became a draftsman and superintendent in the office of D. X. Murphy & Brother, where he remained until leaving in 1905 to study at the polytechnic institute in Dresden. After completing this additional schooling, he traveled briefly in Italy, returning to Louisville in 1906 to open his own office.

Wischmeyer continued as an independent practitioner until 1912, when he formed a partnership, Gray & Wischmeyer, with George Gray. The firm dissolved in 1917 when Gray entered the military, and Wischmeyer remained independent until 1920, when he became a partner with Hugh Nevin and Frederic Morgan in Nevin-Wischmeyer & Morgan. About eight years later, he left to form a new partnership with William Arrasmith in the firm of Wischmeyer & Arrasmith, which became Wischmeyer, Arrasmith & Elswick when Fred Elswick joined the firm in 1937.

The stairway at *Daneshall*, 1968. (©*The Courier-Journal*)

End Notes

INTRODUCTION

1 Kathleen Jennings, "Luxurious Country Houses at the City's Skirts," *The Courier-Journal*, May 26, 1912.
2 Mark Alan Hewitt, The Architect and The American Country House (New Haven: Yale University Press, 1990) page 18.
3 *Art Work of Louisville, Kentucky*, Part 1 (Chicago: Gravure Illustration Co., 1903.
4 George R. Leighton, "Louisville, Kentucky – An American Museum Piece," *Harper's Monthly Magazine*, 1937, page 402.
5 *Art Work of Louisville, Kentucky*, Part 9 (Chicago: Gravure Illustration Co., 1903); and R.C. Riebel, *Louisville Panorama: A Visual History of Louisville*, Published to Commemorate the 100th Anniversary of Liberty National Bank and Trust Company, Louisville, Kentucky 1954, page 160.
6 Harland Bartholomew & Associates, *A Major Street Plan for Louisville, Kentucky* (Louisville: City Planning Commission, 1929), page 15.
7 Carl Kramer, Ph.D., "Frederick Law Olmsted & His Louisville Legacy," *Louisville's Olmstedian Legacy: An Interpretive Analysis and Documentary Inventory* (Louisville Friends of Olmsted Parks, September 1988), pages 7-8.
8 For a history of land purchases and donations, including acquisitions from the Alexander, Barret, Barringer, Belknap, Bonnycastle, Cochran, McFerran and Reynolds families, please see "Cherokee Park Bridges Study," Louisville Olmsted Parks Conservancy, 2008, pages 12, 34, 68, 82 and 116; "Douglas Park and Boulevard," *The Courier-Journal*, May 13, 1906; and Judith Hart English, *Louisville's 19th Century Suburban Growth* (University of Louisville, 1972), pages 84-89.
9 *Art Work of Louisville, Kentucky*, Part 8 (Chicago: The Charles Madison Company, 1897), page 10.
10 "J.B. M'Ferran's Busy Life Ends," the *Louisville Herald*, February 14, 1920; "Rural Schools Father is Dead," *The Courier-Journal*, February 14, 1920; and "Historic Estate to be Put on Block," the *Louisville Herald*, June 7, 1921. See also R. Scott Gill, "Glenview, Kentucky," unpublished research paper, 1976.
11 Jefferson County Deed Book, 1890, page 395 (courtesy Samuel W. Thomas).
12 For the complete Olmsted records pertaining to John B. McFerran's Alta Vista subdivision, see File Unit 02064 at the Frederick Law Olmsted National Historic Site, Brookline, MA (www.rediscov.com/olmsted).
13 *Louisville's Olmstedian Legacy: An Interpretive Analysis and Documentary Inventory* (Louisville Friends of Olmsted Parks, September 1988); and "The Master List of Design Projects of the Olmsted Firm, 1857-1950," National Association for Olmsted Parks, in conjunction with the Massachusetts Association for Olmsted Parks. See also www.nps.gov/applications/frie/search.htm.
14 Charles E. Beveridge and Arleyna Levee, *Louisville's Olmsted Park Legacy: Cherokee, Iroquois and Shawnee Parks and the Parkways – A History* (The Louisville Olmsted Parks Conservancy, 1992), pages 41-42.
15 Elmer G. Sulzer, "'Commuters' Narrow Gauge' Water Works to Prospect (Louisville & Interurban Railroad)," *Ghost Railroads of Kentucky* (Bloomington: Indiana University Press, 1967), Chapter 12, pages 93-95; and –"Glenview – Salubrious Suburbia," the Louisville *Herald-Post*, October 28, 1936.
16 See "Historical Inflation," www.inflationdata.com.
17 See "U.S. Federal Individual Income Tax Rates History, 1913-2011," Tax Foundation, Washington, DC. www.taxfoundation.org.
18 For the growth of automobile registrations, please see Harland Bartholomew & Associates, *A Major Street Plan for Louisville, Kentucky* (Louisville: City Planning Commission, 1929), page 18.

PART ONE: CHEROKEE PARK

NORTON HALL

1 Samuel W. Thomas in John E. Kleber, ed., *The Encyclopedia of Louisville* (Lexington: University of Kentucky Press, 2000), 569-660. See also "Norton, Texas," in *The Online Handbook of Texas* (www.tshaonline.or/handbook/online).
2 For the complete Olmsted records pertaining to Norton Hall, see File Unit 02063 at the Frederick Law Olmsted National Historic Site, Brookline, MA (www.rediscov.com/olmsted).
3 For the complete Olmsted records pertaining to John B. McFerran's Alta Vista subdivision, see File Unit 02064 at the Frederick Law Olmsted National Historic Site, Brookline, MA (www.rediscov.com/olmsted).
4 See *Design Map for Alta Vista, The Property of John B. McFerran Esq., Louisville Kentucky, Showing Subdivision into Roads and Building Sites, Olmsted Brothers Landscape Architects, Brookline Mass. March 1900*, Frederick Law Olmsted Historic Site, Brookline, MA, job #02064; also *Louisville Title Co.'s (Incorporated) New Map of Louisville and Jefferson County, Kentucky* (Louisville: Louisville Title Company, 1913), Map 30 (courtesy University of Louisville Digital Collections).
5 Shepley, Rutan & Coolidge appear to begin work for Norton in 1899, per the archival records maintained by Shepley Bulfinch Richardson and Abbott, Boston, MA (successor firm to Shepley, Rutan & Coolidge).
6 Julia Heskel, *Shepley Bulfinch Richardson and Abbott, Past to Present* (Boston: Shepley Bulfinch Richardson and Abbott, 1999), page 19.
7 Hannah Muldoon, "Norton Hall Cherokee Park," undated notes accompanying photo albums of Norton Hall in a private collection.
8 From the ledger books held in the company archives of Shepley Bulfinch Richardson and Abbott, 2 Seaport Lane, Boston, Massachusetts.

ROSEHEIGHTS

1 Deed dated March 7, 1947, Deed Book 2214, pages 13 to 16 (Citizens Fidelity and Trust Company, Executor of the will of Marcia S. Hite, deceased).
2 "Material compiled at the request of President Kent because of the will of Allen R. Hite, making the University of Louisville residuary legatee of his estate," 1941 (est.), pages 15, 17, 19 and 30.
3 Jennifer Recktenwald, "Independent Expression: The Allen R. Hite Institute at 50" (*U of L Alumni Magazine*, Fall 1996).
4 Letter from Allen R. Hite to Olmsted Bros., November 18, 1901 (Private collection); for the complete Olmsted records pertaining to *Roseheights*, see File Unit 02277 at the Frederick Law Olmsted National Historic Site, Brookline, MA (www.rediscov.com/olmsted). (Letters held at the Library of Congress).
5 Letters from D.X. Murphy to Jacob Hoertz, April 30, 1902, and May 9, 1902 (Filson Historical Society); as well as letters from Olmsted Brothers to Cecil Fraser, August through December 1901 (Private Collection, see also Frederick Olmsted National Historic Site).
6 Letter from Olmsted Brothers to Cecil Fraser, December 2, 1901 (Private collection, see also Frederick Law Olmsted National Historic Site).
7 "Allen R. Hite Lost to City," *The Louisville Times*, June 26, 1941.
8 Janice Pope Meyer, "Comfortable And Homelike," *The Courier-Journal Magazine*, May 15, 1960; and "Bellarmine show house has been decorated by designers – and history," *The Courier-Journal*, August 14, 1986.

COLONIAL HALL

1 "Once the Home of a Leading Louisville Financier," *The Louisville Times*, January 19, 1956; and "Ann E. Barret, Widow of Banker, Passes Away," *The Courier-Journal*, December 31, 1915.
2 D.X. Murphy correspondence files, The Filson Historical Society, Louisville, Kentucky.
3 "Descriptive Inventory, MSS 46 Barret Family Papers," Manuscripts, Department of Library Special Collections, Kentucky Library, Western Kentucky University; and John E. Kleber, ed., *The Encyclopedia of Louisville* (Lexington: University Press of Kentucky, 2001), page 106.
4 Ibid., "Descriptive Inventory, MSS 46 Barret Family Papers," and "Former chief Engineer for L. & N. Dies," *The Courier-Journal*, February 8, 1931. See also *ThePeerage.com* for a complete genealogical history of the Montfort family.
5 "For Sale! 'Colonial Hall'," an advertisement from the Paul Semonin Company, unknown source, but likely *The Courier-Journal*, May 20, 1951. See also *Louisville Title Co.'s (Incorporated) New Map of Louisville and Jefferson County, Kentucky* (Louisville: Louisville Title Company, 1913), Map 30 (courtesy University of Louisville Digital Collections). The Abe Cohen house is included on page 214 of *Kentucky Houses of Stratton Hammon* by Winfrey P. Blackburn, Jr. and R. Scott Gill (Louisville: Butler Books, 2007).
6 Ibid., "For Sale! 'Colonial Hall'."

AYRSTEAD

1 E. Polk Johnson, *A history of Kentucky and Kentuckians: The leaders and representative men in commerce, industry and modern activities* (New York: Lewis Publishing Co., 1912); Douglas I. Stern, "Cowan, Andrew," in John E. Kleber, ed., *The Encyclopedia of Louisville* (Louisville: Kentucky Press, 2000), page 228; and William Elsey Connelley and Ellis Merton Coulter, *History of Kentucky*, Vol. IV (Chicago and New York: The American Historical Society, 1922), pages 104-105.2
2 Mark Alan Hewitt, *The Architect and the American Country House* (New Haven: Yale University Press, 1990), page 77.
3 Ibid
4 Ibid., page 53
5 Ibid.
6 Ibid., page 52
7 "Seneca Park," in *City of Seneca Gardens, Louisville, Kentucky* web site (www.cityofsenecagardens.com).
8 "Alloway House" (no author cited) (Louisville Landmarks Commission, 1980).

GARDENCOURT

1 For the complete Olmsted records pertaining to Norton Hall, see File Unit 03030 at the Frederick Law Olmsted National Historic Site, Brookline, MA (www.rediscov.com/olmsted).
2 See *Design Map for Alta Vista, The Property of John B. McFerran Esq., Louisville Kentucky, Showing Subdivision into Roads and Building Sites, Olmsted Brothers Landscape Architects, Brookline Mass. March 1900*, Frederick Law Olmsted Historic Site, Brookline, MA, job #02064; also *Louisville Title Co.'s (Incorporated) New Map of Louisville and Jefferson County, Kentucky* (Louisville: Louisville Title Company, 1913), Map 30 (courtesy University of Louisville Digital Collections).
3 " 'Maxwell Court,' A Residence and Gardens in the Italian Style at Rockville, Connecticut," *House & Garden* (October 1903, Vol. IV, No. 4).
4 Brochure, "Gardencourt – A Special Place, A Part of the University of Louisville," (n.d.); John M. Mulder, "In the Garden," *The Courier-Journal* (September 24, 1987???); and Jean Howerton, "A Mansion for Music – U. of L. School of Music is operating in its new home," *The Courier-Journal Magazine* (April 13, 1947).
5 Press release from Denise Fitzpatrick, Public Information Office, University of Louisville, April 6, 1987, "U of L to Sell Gardencourt Campus at Public Auction"; and "Gardencourt Celebrates 100 Years," article in the Louisville Presbyterian Theological Seminary website (www.lpts.com) dated July 31, 2006.

ROSTREVOR

1 See *Design Map for Alta Vista, The Property of John B. McFerran Esq., Louisville Kentucky, Showing Subdivision into Roads and Building*

Sites, Olmsted Brothers Landscape Architects, Brookline Mass. March 1900, Frederick Law Olmsted Historic Site, Brookline, MA, job number 02064; also *Louisville Title Co.'s (Incorporated) New Map of Louisville and Jefferson County, Kentucky* (Louisville: Louisville Title Company, 1913), Map 30 (courtesy University of Louisville Digital Collections).

2 For an excellent presentation of the complete works of Carrère & Hastings, including *Rostrevor*, see Mark Alan Hewitt, Kate Lemos, William Morrison and Charles D. Warren, *Carrère & Hastings Architects*, Volumes I and II (New York: Acanthus Press, 2006). Also note that the architects designed two subsequent projects in Louisville: the War Memorial Auditorium in 1924 and an amphitheatre for Judge Robert Worth Bingham at *Melcombe* in Glenview in 1929. Both projects were constructed and are extant.

3 "J. Ross Todd To Build Fine Suburban Home," *The Courier-Journal* (March 28, 1908), courtesy the Louisville Landmarks Commission.

4 For excellent descriptions, including plans and photographs, of *Bagatelle*, see Mark Alan Hewitt, *The Architect & the American Country House, 1890-1940* (New Haven: Yale University Press, 1990), pages 28-29; Mark Alan Hewitt, Kate Lemos, William Morrison and Charles D. Warren, *Carrère & Hastings Architects*, Volume II (New York: Acanthus Press, 2006), pages 121-127; and Robert B. Mackay, Anthony K. Baker and Carol A. Traynor, eds., *Long Island Country Houses and Their Architects, 1860-1940* (New York: W.W. Norton & Company, 1997), page 104.

5 Excerpt from David Gray, *Thomas Hastings, Architect* (Boston: Houghton Mifflin Co., 1933), page 72, in Robert B. Mackay, Anthony K. Baker and Carol A. Traynor, eds., *Long Island Country Houses and Their Architects, 1860-1940* (New York: W.W. Norton & Company, 1997), pages 104-105.

6 John David Myles, "1141 Rostrevor Circle," from The Filson Historical Society annual house tour, 9-28-08.

7 *The American Architect*, Vol. XCVIII, No. 1804, July 20, 1910. Early publications also include "The Home of Mr. and Mrs. J Ross Todd" in "Beautiful Homes of Louisville," *The Sunday Herald-Post*, Louisville, Kentucky September 23, 1928; and Nancy Ballentine, "Rostrevor A Treasure Trove," *The Courier-Journal Magazine*, May 10, 1959. It was also featured on pages 864-869 in *Antiques in Kentucky*, a reprint from *The Magazine Antiques*, March and April 1974.

8 For the complete Olmsted records pertaining to Todd, see File Unit 045104 at the Frederick Law Olmsted National Historic Site, Brookline, MA (www.rediscov.com/olmsted).

9 "J. Ross Todd To Build Fine Suburban Home," *The Courier-Journal*, 1908 (Louisville Landmarks Commission).

10 "James Ross Todd Dies Unexpectedly," *The Courier-Journal*, July 21, 1952; and "James Todd (1821-1890)," *ancestry.com*.

11 Roy A. Hampton III, "Rostrevor: A Brief Summary of its History and Architecture," draft paper, September 6, 1993 (Louisville Landmarks Commission)

12 Simpson Lawson, "Todd Estate To Be Converted Into Subdivision," *The Courier-Journal*, Section 5, January 26, 1964, pages 1 and 2.

ANOATOK

1 The date of 1905 is based on a survey of the parcel by Stonestreet & Ford dated May 18, 1905 (Frederick Law Olmsted National Historic Site, Brookline, MA, Job #03076); the Bullitt attribution is based on the *Design Map for Alta Vista, The Property of John B. McFerran, Esq.*, prepared in March 1900 by the Olmsted Brothers (Frederick Law Olmsted National Historic Site, Job #02064).

2 *Preliminary Plan for Estate of Frank Fehr Esquire*, Olmsted Brothers, Brookline, MA, January 25, 1906 (Olmsted National Historic Site, Job #03076).

3 See Olmsted National Historic Site, Job #03811.[4] "Beautiful Homes of Louisville: 'Anoatok,' the Home of Mr. and Mrs. Frank Fehr," the *Herald-Post*, March 3, 1929.

5 For the complete files related to the Frank Fehr estate, please reference the Olmsted National Historic Site, Job #03076.

6 For biographical information on the Fehr family, please see "Frank Fehr Passes Peacefully Away at 9:30 O'clock Yesterday Morning," *The Courier-Journal*, March 16, 1891; (www.beercollections.com/breweries/kentucky/frank_fehr_brewing); and the records of Cave Hill Cemetery.

7 For a biography of William Frederick Behrens, please see the Architectural Foundation of Cincinnati, *Biographical Dictionary of Cincinnati Architects, 1788-1940*, William Behrens (www.architecturecincy.org/dictionary/B.html). For references to Behrens' work on the Kentucky State Capitol, please see http://historicproperties.ky.gov/hp/capitol/history/complete+history.

8 "One of Louisville's Most Beautiful Homes – the Residence of Mr. and Mrs. Frank Fehr on Cherokee Drive in beautiful Braeview," *Crescent Hill Beautiful: A Souvenir of Louisville's Most Beautiful Suburb - Official Program of Crescent Hill Big Day, Held Under the Auspices of the Crescent Hill Forward Club, June 26, 1915.* (Reprinted August 2004 by the Crescent Hill Community Council.)

9 For information on the Goldberg house, please see Winfrey P. Blackburn, Jr. and R. Scott Gill, *Kentucky Houses of Stratton Hammon* (Louisville: Butler Books, 2007).

EDGECOMBE

1 For an interesting view on Sackett's role as Ambassador to Germany, see Bernard V. Burke, *Ambassador Frederic Sackett and the Collapse of the Weimar Republic, 1930-1933* (Cambridge: Cambridge University Press, 1994).

2 Biographical information: "Sackett, Frederick Mosley, (1868-1941), *Biographical Directory of the United States Congress, 1774-Present* (http://bioguide.congress.gov); John William Leonard, Editor, *Who's Who in Finance and Banking – A Biographical Dictionary of Contemporaries, 1920-1922* (New York: Who's Who in Finance, Incorporated, 1922), page 596; and "Ex-Senator F. M. Sackett Dies in East," *The Courier-Journal*, May 19, 1941.

3 See *Design Map for Alta Vista, The Property of John B. McFerran Esq., Louisville Kentucky, Showing Subdivision into Roads and Building Sites, Olmsted Brothers Landscape Architects, Brookline Mass. March 1900,* Frederick Law Olmsted Historic Site, Brookline, MA, job #02064; also *Louisville Title Co.'s (Incorporated) New Map of Louisville and Jefferson County, Kentucky* (Louisville: Louisville Title Company, 1913), Map 30 (courtesy University of Louisville Digital Collections); and Elizabeth Patterson Thomas, *Old Kentucky Homes and Gardens* (Louisville: Standard Printing Co., 1939), page 144.

4 As no plans or other documentation confirming Hutchings' role as architect seem to exist, we relied on correspondence suggesting such a relationship: Letter to Olmsted Bros. dated Sept. 10th, 1912, from John Bacon Hutchings (signed by E.T. Hutchings), Manuscripts Division, Library of Congress; and letter to Olmsted Bros. dated Oct. 3, 1912, from F.M. Sackett, Manuscript Division, Library of Congress.

5 For the complete Olmsted records pertaining to Sackett, see File Unit 04092 at the Frederick Law Olmsted National Historic Site, Brookline, MA (www.rediscov.com/olmsted).

6 A. Carter Goodloe, "In Southern Gardens, The Log of a Wandering Through Some of the Old and New Gardens of Louisville," *House & Garden Magazine* (October, 1917); "Beautiful Homes of Louisville," *The Herald-Post* (October 21, 1928); Elizabeth Patterson Thomas, *Old Kentucky Homes and Gardens* (Louisville: Standard Printing Co., 1939), page 144.

7 "Mrs. Sackett Estate Set At $3,390,000," *The Courier-Journal* (December 28, 1948).

COLD SPRING

1 Kathleen Jennings, "The Speed Family. Chapter VII.," *Louisville's First Families – A Series of Genealogical Sketches* (Louisville: The Standard Printing Co., 1920) (on line at www.kygenweb.net).

2 Biographical information in James J. Holmberg, "Speed, Joshua Fry," in John E. Kleber, ed., *The Encyclopedia of Louisville* (Louisville: Kentucky Press, 2000), pages 843-844. See also Robert Crosby, *The Highlands at a Glance* (University of Louisville Archives, 1974), who places the date of *Cold Spring* at closer to 1870.

3 *The Trow (formerly Wilson's) Copartnership and Corporation Directory of the boroughs of Manhattan and the Bronx* (New York: Trow Directory, Printing & Bookbinding Co., March 1906), page 320.

4 Alwin Seekamp and Roger Burlingame, eds., *Who's Who in Louisville* (Louisville: The Louisville Press Club, 1912), page 125; and *The Southern Reporter*, Volume 201 (West Publishing Company, 1918), page 489.

5 The Townsend & Fleming plans for the expansion and renovation of the house are in the private collection of the present owner.

6 *Jefferson County Journey: Tours Through the Historic Community* (Louisville: Jefferson County, 1992), item 67; see also the project roster from the D.X. Murphy File at the Filson Historical Society.

7 An undated site plan showing a version of the expanded house, the gardens and drives is available from the Department of Manuscripts and University Archives, 101 Olin Library, Cornell University, Ithaca, NY 14853. Reference #1380, Bryan Fleming Papers, Henning Estate, Louisville, KY.

8 Interview between the author and Mrs. Laurice Samuels, February 15, 2010.

9 *Louisville Title Co.'s (Incorporated) New Map of Louisville and Jefferson County, Kentucky* (Louisville: Louisville Title Company, 1913), Map 30 (courtesy University of Louisville Digital Collections).

10 Interview between the author and Mrs. Laurice Samuels, February 15, 2010.

BARNARD HALL

1 "New Home of Louis Seelbach Being Erected," *The Courier-Journal*, August 11, 1912.

2 "In June she married Tom Buchanan of Chicago, with more pomp and circumstance than Louisville ever knew before. He came down with a hundred people in four private cars, and hired a whole floor of the Muhlbach [Seelbach] Hotel, and the day before the wedding he gave her a string of pearls valued at three hundred and fifty thousand dollars." From F. Scott Fitzgerald, *The Great Gatsby*, first published in 1925.

3 "L. Seelbach, Sr., is Dead at Hotel – Native of Germany Succumbs after Illness of More than a Year," *The Courier-Journal*, March 19, 1925; and Jack Hamann, "Sniffing out history – and ghosts: Louisville's Seelbach Hotel a grand reminder of city's past" (CNN.com, August 18, 2000).

4 See *Design Map for Alta Vista, The Property of John B. McFerran Esq., Louisville Kentucky, Showing Subdivision into Roads and Building Sites, Olmsted Brothers Landscape Architects, Brookline Mass. March 1900,* Frederick Law Olmsted Historic Site, Brookline, MA, job #02064; also *Louisville Title Co.'s (Incorporated) New Map of Louisville and Jefferson County, Kentucky* (Louisville: Louisville Title Company, 1913), Map 30 (courtesy University of Louisville Digital Collections).

5 "When I saw the plans for my own home, as prepared by the Olmsteads [sic], I was satisfied that they were the best that could be gotten. I even had a dispute with Mrs. Seelbach on the subject, but her ideas finally prevailed, and after the house was built, Mr. Olmstead [sic] himself admitted it would have been a mistake to have built it the way he suggested." – Louis Seelbach quoted in, "Gift for Park – Frank Fehr to Erect Bridge in Father's Memory," *The Courier-Journal*, July 2, 1913.

6 Catalogue of the First Exhibition, Louisville Chapter of the American Institute of Architects, 1912 (republished in 2008 by Applewood Books, Bedford, MA). The Hunter Raine house, completed before Seelbach, was quite similar to its Louisville sibling in terms of massing, architectural detail and the use of a large central living hall.

7 For the complete Olmsted records pertaining to Barnard Hall, see File Unit 05456 at the Frederick Law Olmsted National Historic Site, Brookline, MA (www.rediscov.com/olmsted).

8 Mary Poynter Hedgepeth, Director of Research, the Louisville Landmarks Commission, "Barnard Hall" in the program for the Bellarmine College Women's Council-Louisville, Kentucky Designers' Show House of May 15 to May 31, 1982.

9 The Duke K. McCall Presidential Records of the Southern Baptist Theological Seminary, courtesy of Stephen Jones, Archives and Special Collections Assistant, James P. Boyce Centennial Library.

10 John David Myles, "715 Alta Vista Road," for The Filson Club Historical Society house tour of September 26, 1999 and Yvonne Eaton, "Seelbach's house, opulent like his hotel, being shown," *The Courier-Journal*, May 17, 1982, page B7.

HOMEWOOD

1 Carolyn Kelly, "Great Estates: Homewood Museum in Baltimore, Maryland," *The Magazine Antiques* (September 10, 2009); and Laurie Ossman, *Great Houses of the South* (New York: Rizzoli, 2010) pages 60-65.

2 For biographical information on Bishop Dudley, please see John E. Kleber, Ed., *The Encyclopedia of Louisville* (Lexington: University of Kentucky Press, 2000), page 256; and for Mrs. Dudley,

Prominent Families of New York (New York: The Historical Company, 1897), Page 386; and Evelyn Crady Adams, *Cooke Hall Replica of Homewood in Baltimore, School of Church Music – Cooke Hall – Southern Baptist Theological Seminary, Louisville, Ky.* (Archives of the Southern Baptist Seminary, n.d.).

3 Jean Field Marlowe, "Homewood of Louisville," a paper submitted in partial fulfillment of requirements for graduation summa cum laude (University of Louisville, May, 1995), page 42.[4] See "General Plan for Braeview, Louisville, Kentucky," Olmsted Brothers, Brookline, MA, revised April 1912 (Olmsted National Historic Site, Job #03811). Mrs. Dudley acquired lots 1, 38, 39 and 40.[5] "Beautiful New Home Built for Mrs. Dudley Near Cherokee Park," *The Louisville Evening Post*, April 24, 1915.

6 "P. H. Callahan, Crusader and Industrialist, Dies At 74," *The Courier-Journal*, February 5, 1940; and P. H. Callahan Leaves Estate Of $110,000," *The Courier-Journal*, February 17, 1940.

7 "Magnifying the Ministry of Music," *Southern Seminary News*, September 1943.

8 See also "Louisville's Ecumenical Mansion," a non-dated paper (author unknown); "Mrs. Donald Winters Interview, a non-dated paper (author unknown); and Evelyn Crady Adams, "Cooke Hall Replica of Homewood in Baltimore, School of Church Music – Cooke Hall – Southern Baptist Theological Seminary, Louisville, Ky.," a non-dated paper; all in the archive collections of the Southern Baptist Theological Seminary, Louisville, KY.

ALLIS

1 For more about Douglass Park and Douglass Boulevard, see "Douglass Park and Boulevard," The Courier-Journal (May 13, 1906).

2 Kathleen Jennings, "The Prather Family. Chapter III," Louisville's First Families – A Series of Genealogical Sketches, (The Standard Printing Company: Louisville, 1920), online at www.kygenweb.net.

3 See "House, Dr. M. E. Johnston, Lexington, KY," Architecture (October, 1918): Plates CLXII-CLXIV.

4 Lionel Moses, "Simplicity The Key-Note of Modern Architectural Design," The Art World (October 1917): pages 75-77.

5 "The Residence of Mrs. Ernest Allis At Cherokee Park, Louisville, Kentucky," House & Garden (December 1915).

6 Ibid., House & Garden.

7 "House of Mrs. Ernest Allis, Louisville, KY," The American Architect (December 8, 1915); "House, Mrs. Ernest Allis, Louisville, KY," Architecture (October, 1918): Plates CLVIII-CLXI; "The Residence of Ernest Allis," The Architectural Review (December 1919): 92; Charles S. Keefe, The American House, Being a Collection of Illustrations and Plans of the Best Country and Suburban Houses Built in the United States during the Last Few Years (New York, 1924); "Beautiful Homes of Louisville," Herald-Post (February 2, 1930).

8 Interview between the R. Scott Gill and Mrs. Barbara Castleman, daughter of Marvin and Eleanor Beard, January 20, 2010.

KANAWHA

1 Elizabeth Patterson Thomas, *Old Kentucky Homes and Gardens* (Louisville: The Standard Printing Company, 1939), page 144; and "Architectural landmarks of Charleston," www.whycharlestonwv.com. See the "Craik-Patton House:" "*Built in 1834 in the American Greek Revival style, The Craik-Patton House is the home to Rev. James Craik and his family. The house was originally built in a plot of land along the banks of the Kanawha river that Rev. Craik inherited from Dr. James Craik, the personal physician and close friend of George Washington.*"

2 Samuel W. Thomas, *Crescent Hill Revisited* (Louisville: George Rogers Clark Press, 1987), page 117.

3 Purchase of *The Poplars*: Samuel W. Thomas, page 118; purchase of *Kanawha*: Jefferson County Deed Book 720, page 313, per letter from Samuel W. Thomas to Winfrey P. Blackburn, Jr., February 20, 2009.

4 The site of the "Akers Place" was listed as 23.787 acres by *Louisville Title Co.'s (Incorporated) New Map of Louisville and Jefferson County, Kentucky* (Louisville: Louisville Title Company, 1913), Map 30 (courtesy University of Louisville Digital Collections).

5 Jefferson County Deed Book 720, page 313, per letter from Samuel W. Thomas to Winfrey P. Blackburn, Jr., February 20, 2009; and *The Southerner* (New Orleans: Southern Editors Association, 1945), page 382.

6 *Catalogue of the First Exhibition – Louisville Chapter American Institute of Architects*, first published in 1912, reprinted by Applewood Books, Bedford, Ma, 2008.

7 Kathleen Jennings, *The Courier-Journal*, May 26, 1912, per letter from Samuel W. Thomas to Winfrey P. Blackburn, Jr., February 20, 2009: "Mr. and Mrs. Matthew L. Akers have a handsome place with stable already up and landscape garden work completed, but the house has not yet been erected."

8 "Topographical Map of Environs of Proposed Residence for W.S. Speed, Esq.", n.d., drawing in the private collection of the owners of *Kanawha*.

9 Jefferson County Deed Book 786, page 508, per letter from Samuel W. Thomas to Winfrey P. Blackburn, Jr., February 20, 2009; and "Funeral Plans Await Arrival of Akers' Son, the *Herald-Post*, June 5, 1926.

10 John David Myles, "516 Altagate," description for The Filson Club Historical Society house tour of September 26, 1999.

11 Mark Alan Hewitt, *The Architect & the American Country House* (New York: Yale University Press, 1990), page 61.

12 Robert B. MacKay, Anthony Baker and Carol A. Traynor, eds., *Long Island Country Houses and their Architects, 1860-1940* (New York: W.W. Norton, 1997), page 348.

13 Keith N. Morgan, *Charles A. Platt, The Artist as Architect* (Cambridge: MIT Press, 1985), page 127.

14 MacKay et al, page 350.

15 Charles A. Jencks writing in the Foreword of Keith N. Morgan, *Charles A. Platt, The Artist as Architect* (Cambridge: MIT Press, 1985), pages xii-xiii.

16 MacKay et al, page 351.

17 Hewitt, page 64.

18 CaveHillCemetery.com; and John David Myles, "515 Altagate Road," description for The Filson Club Historical Society house tour of September 26, 1999.

19 John David Myles, "515 Altagate Road."

FOUR COURTS

1 Sources: "Distinguished Member Answers Call of Death," *Louisville Board of Trade Journal* (July 1921); "Colonel Taylor Taken by Death," the *Louisville Herald* (July 2, 1921); and Mike Veach writing in the "History of the Old Charter line of bourbon," www.straightbourbon.com, (April 23, 2007).

2 For sketches of the various garden proposals, see the archives of the National Park Service, Frederick Law Olmsted National Historic Site, Brookline, MA, job #07012.

3 C. Julian Oberwarth, FAIA, and Scott, William B., Jr., *A History of the Profession of Architecture in Kentucky* (Louisville: Gateway Press, 1987), 178.

4 History courtesy of Four Courts at Cherokee Park, a Signature HealthCARE facility.

CASA MIA

1 Source: Interview between R. Scott Gill and Mrs. John Morton Kimberly, the granddaughter of Alexander P. Witty, January 10, 2010.

2 For a detailed description of *Black Point*, see Gary Lawrance and Anne Surchin, *Houses of The Hamptons, 1880-1930* (New York: Acanthus, 2007), pages 193-206.

3 The Bingham-Hanna house, as it is now known, survives as part of the Western Reserve Historical Society campus in Cleveland, Ohio.

4 Source: Interview between the author and Mr. Paul Jones, the grandson of Alexander P. Witty, January 10, 2010.

5 For the complete Olmsted records pertaining to *Casa Mia*, see File Unit 07617 at the Frederick Law Olmsted National Historic Site, Brookline, MA (www.rediscov.com/olmsted).

6 "'Casa Mia' – The home of Mr. and Mrs. Alexander P. Witty, Cherokee Park," Beautiful Homes of Louisville, the *Herald-Post* (May 19, 1929).

7 "Third Fire Strikes Vacant Mansion On Red Fox Road; Arson Suspected," *The Courier-Journal* (October 18, 1970).

DANESHALL

1 See deed dated April 25, 1923, between P. L. Atherton and Cornelia A. Atherton and Mamie P. Jones, Jefferson County Court Clerk's Office, Deed Book 1089, page 167.

2 See deed dated July 8, 1925, Jefferson County Court Clerk's Office, Deed Book 1154, page 481.

3 See deed dated June 26, 1937, Jefferson County Court Clerk's Office, Deed Book 1639, page 613.

4 For biographical information on A. Gilmore Ouerbacker and his father, see, among others, Gilmore's obituary in *The Courier-Journal*, March 17, 1966; and E. Polk Johnson, *A History of Kentucky and Kentuckians, Vol. III* (Chicago and New York: Lewis Publishing Company, 1912), page 1157.

5 *The New York Times*, May 26, 1935; and Glenn Stout and Richard A. Johnson, *Red Sox Century* (New York: Houghton Mifflin, 2005).

6 For the complete Olmsted records pertaining to *Daneshall*, see File Unit 09507 at the Frederick Law Olmsted National Historic Site, Brookline, MA (www.rediscov.com/olmsted).

7 Mary Poynter Hedgepeth, Director of Research, the Louisville Landmarks Commission, "Barnard Hall" in the program for the Bellarmine College Women's Council-Louisville, Kentucky Designers' Show House of May 15 to May 31, 1982.

8 From a discussion between Winfrey Blackburn and Marea Gardner, daughter-in-law of Emma Austin Yawkey Gardner Ouerbacker, 2010.

9 Anne Means, "Daneshall in the Bluegrass Country," *Arts & Decoration – The Spur*, March 1941 (reprinted by Clare J. Hoffman–Interiors).

10 "Bulletin of The Woman's Club of Louisville" (The Woman's Club of Louisville Kentucky, December 1939).

11 "Homes Extend Hospitality," *The Courier-Journal*, April 21, 1968.

12 "Ouerbacker Estate Sold – To be subdivided after big house resold, buyer says," *The Courier-Journal*, February 9, 1964.

PART TWO: THE BLUFFS OF THE OHIO RIVER

LANSDOWNE

1 Dedication poem by George M. Davie, from "Laying of the Corner Stone at *Lansdowne*, May 20, 1899," the private collection of Mrs. George W. Norton, III.

2 "The Lure of Lansdowne," from the brochure prepared for the Bellarmine Women's Council Decorators' Show House, 1976.[3] Kathleen Jennings, *Louisville's First Families – A Series of Genealogical Sketches* (Louisville: The Standard Printing Company, 1920), page 118.

4 "Mrs. S. Thruston Ballard Dies Unexpectedly of Heart Attack," *The Courier-Journal*, February 28, 1938; and Kathleen Jennings, *Louisville's First Families – A Series of Genealogical Sketches* (Louisville: The Standard Printing Company, 1920), pages 117-118.

5 *The Courier-Journal*, February 11, 1920.

6 R. Scott Gill, "Glenview, Kentucky," research paper completed in 1976.

7 "Lansdowne In Ashes," *The Courier-Journal*, March 3, 1906.

8 "Will Rebuild Lansdowne," *The Courier-Journal*, March 4, 1906.

9 "Lansdowne In Ashes," *The Courier-Journal*, March 3, 1906.

10 "Will Rebuild Lansdowne," *The Courier-Journal*, March 4, 1906.

11 "A Beautiful Home on the River Road," *The Courier-Journal Illustrated Sunday Magazine*, August 8, 1909.

12 Glenview, Salubrious Suburbia," the *Herald-Post*, October 28, 1936. See also A. Carter Goodloe, "In Southern Gardens – The Log of a Wandering Through Some of the Old and New Gardens of Louisville," *House & Garden Magazine*, October 1917; and "Beautiful Homes of Louisville – 'Lansdowne,' The home of Mrs. S. Thruston Ballard at Glenview," the *Herald-Post*, December 9, 1928.

13 *The Louisville Times*, November 23, 1965; and www.chanceschool.org. The Ballard School survives today as the private Chance School.

14 "Glenview mansion will be razed to make way for new subdivision," *The Courier-Journal*, May 25, 1976.

THE ALLEN HOUSES

1 Donna M. Neary, *Historic Jefferson County* (Louisville: Jefferson County Fiscal Court, 2000), #JF546, page 31; William Elsey Connelley and Ellis Merton Coulter, *History of Kentucky* (Chicago and New York: The American Historical Society, 1922), Vol. IV, page 35; *Antiques in Kentucky* (New York: *The Magazine Antiques*, March and April 1974), page 863; and "The Funeral of Maj. Allen," *The Courier-Journal*, June 9, 1911.

2 Interview between R. Scott Gill and Mrs. Charles W. Allen, Jr., 1976.

3 *Art Work of Louisville, Kentucky*, Part 8 (Chicago: The Charles Madison Company, 1903).

4 *Antiques in Kentucky* (New York: *The Magazine Antiques*, March and April 1974), page 864.
5 *The Southerner* (New Orleans: Southern Editors Association, 1945), page 70.
6 Interview between R. Scott Gill and Mrs. Charles W. Allen, Jr., 1976.
7 "Handsome Homes To Be Built on The River Road," *The Jeffersonian*, August 31, 1911.
8 William Elsey Connelley and Ellis Merton Coulter, *History of Kentucky* (Chicago and New York: The American Historical Society, 1922), Vol. IV, page 48; "The History of Mengel Box Company," www.mountainlumber.com/index.php/learn/histories_deail/mengel_box_company; and "Arthur Allen, Civic Leader And Artist, Dies," *The Courier-Journal*, April 9,1949.
9 "Handsome Homes To Be Built on The River Road," *The Jef fersonian*, August 31, 1911.
10 Interview between R. Scott Gill and Mrs. Charles W. Allen, Jr., 1976.
11 For the complete Olmsted records pertaining to *Cobble Court*, see File Unit 09484 at the Frederick Law Olmsted National Historic Site, Brookline, MA (www.rediscov.com/olmsted).

RIO VISTA
1 William Elsey Connelley and E.M. Coulter, Ph.D., authors, Judge Charles Kerr, editor, *History of Kentucky*, Vol. V (Chicago and New York: The American Historical Society, 1922), page 21; and Alwin Seekamp and Roger Burlingame, Eds., *Who's Who in Louisville* (Louisville: The Louisville Press Club, 1912), page 78.
2 "Artistic Entrances and Hallways in Some New Louisville Homes," *The Courier-Journal*, February 25, 1900.
3 For the complete Olmsted records pertaining to the early Caperton estate, see File Unit 00246 at the Frederick Law Olmsted National Historic Site, Brookline, MA (www.rediscov.com/olmsted).[4]
4 *Art Work of Louisville, Kentucky*, Part 8 (Chicago: The Charles Madison Company, 1903); and "Views of a Handsome Suburban Home," *The Courier-Journal Illustrated Sunday Magazine*, November 3, 1907.
5 "John H. Caperton Dies of Apoplexy in Havana, Cuba," *The Louisville Times*, January 26, 1923.
6 "Beautiful Home of a Louisvillian –'Rio Vista,' the Residence of Mr. John H. Caperton on River Road," *The Courier-Journal Illustrated Sunday Magazine*, September 12, 1910.
7 *Catalogue of the First Exhibition, Louisville Chapter, American Institute of Architect* (Reprint: Applewood Books, Bedford, MA, 2008).
8 "John H. Caperton Dies of Apoplexy in Havana, Cuba," *The Louisville Times*, January 26, 1923.
9 "Caperton Leaves $1,500,000 Estate To His Only Son," *The Louisville Times*, February 2, 1923; and "J.H. Caperton Critically Ill," *The Louisville Herald*, January 25, 1923.
10 "Beautiful Homes of Louisville," *The Louisville Herald-Post*, October 7, 1928
11 Interview between Winfrey P. Blackburn, Jr., and John Caperton, son of Hugh Caperton, October 2010.[12] Winfrey P. Blackburn, Jr., and R. Scott Gill, *Kentucky Houses of Stratton Hammon* (Louisville: Butler Books, 2007), pages 192-195.

WINKWORTH-BOXHILL
1 *Louisville Title Co.'s (Incorporated) New Map of Louisville and Jefferson County, Kentucky* (Louisville: Louisville Title Company, 1913), Map 7.
2 Timothy T. Orwig, Ph.D. candidate in American Studies at Boston University, notes pertaining to a forthcoming dissertation on Joseph Everett Chandler, April 15, 2009. Mr. Orwig, noting that Chandler's papers were destroyed shortly after his death in 1945, cites two sources to support Chandler as the possible architect: (1) Chandler appears in the Olmsted records in connection with Chess once, when the W.E. Chess job is listed on Chandler's client/architect card (original on file at the Olmsted National Historic Site, Brookline, MA); and (2) Chandler's diaries (1919-1941) include a note on March 11, 1930, that "It must be about 22 yrs ago that I stopped…on my way north from Louisville, Ky., where I had been with the Chess'es [sic]…" There is no other evident documentation of Chandler as the architect of *Winkworth*.
3 "Sketch showing existing conditions, W.E. Chess place, Louisville, Ky," December 18, 1906, File Unit 03214 at the Frederick Law Olmsted National Historic Site, Brookline, MA (www.rediscov.com/olmsted).
4 A special note of appreciation for this observation is due to John David Myles for his piece about *Boxhill* written for The Filson Club Historical Society house tour of October 6, 1996.
5 "Sketch showing existing conditions, W.E. Chess place, Louisville, Ky," December 18, 1906; and "Topographical Map, Property of W.E. Chess, Esq., Woodside, KY," December 7, 1906 (Olmsted National Historic Site).
6 "W.E. Chess, Esq., Woodside, KY. Preliminary Plan to Accom pany Report," December 28, 1906 (Olmsted National Historic Site).
7 We make this assertion, despite a lack of concrete evidence, for primarily two reasons: (1) the citation in *House & Garden* mentioned below ("The Buffalo landscape artist who designed this garden…") and (2) the designs bear an uncanny resemblance to Townsend & Fleming's other work, especially that for Robert Carrier in Louisville of 1913 and, much later, at *Cheekwood* in Nashville of 1932.
8 A. Carter Goodloe, "In Southern Gardens, The Log of a Wandering Through Some of the Old and New Gardens of Louisville," *House & Garden*, Vol. 32, 1917.
9 "W.E. Chess Dead At London Home," the *Herald-Post*, July 31, 1926.
10 Mary Jean Kinsman, "Winkworth," *Kentucky Historic Resources Inventory*, Site No. JF-533 (Louisville: Jefferson County Office of Historic Preservation and Archives, 1977, rev. 1983).
11 These assertions are the result of (1) our examination of the Olmsted "existing conditions" survey of 1906 (see endnote #3) which indicate a rear terrace but no rear porch, (2) the article, "Beautiful Homes of Louisville, 'Boxhill' – Residence of Mr. and Mrs. Henning Chambers on Upper River Road" in *The Louisville Herald-Post*, dated September 16, 1928, which shows the second floor in place above the kitchen wing, the two-story rear porch and a photograph of the "swimming pool and pergola" and (3) our assumption that such major modifications – to the name and the structure – would likely not have been made by a Chess family member during the brief time between 1917, when Chess gave the estate to his daughter, and 1920, when father and daughter relocated to London.
12 "History of the Fifth Annual Decorators' Show House, 'Boxhill'," a two-page document printed in 1978.
13 "Remodeling for Mr. & Mrs. Joshua B. Adams, Upper River Road, Louisville," architectural drawings (Job No. 5608) by Stratton O. Hammon and Neal O. Hammon, architects and engineers, September 15, 1956 (Filson Historical Society, Louisville, KY).
14 Linda Stahl, "A Great Room – Former porch is party-perfect at Lansings' Boxhill home," *The Courier-Journal*, April 25, 1996.

BUSHY PARK-MELCOMBE
1 "A Summer Home at Fincastle," *The Courier Journal* (July 22, 1900).
2 For a history of the Fincastle Club, see "A Summer Home at Fincastle," *The Courier-Journal*, July 22, 1900; "Fincastle Club-House and Cottages, *The Courier-Journal*, September 6, 1896, page 4; and Samuel W. Thomas, *The Architectural History of Louisville, 1778-1900* (Louisville: The Filson Historical Society, 2009), pages 173 and 188.
3 "Rites for Mrs. Mina B. Ballard, Civic Leader, Arranged Friday," the Louisville *Herald-Post*, November 2, 1933.
4 Edith Bingham, "Talk to Glenview Garden Club," (March 3, 1994), page 2.
5 Kathleen Jennings, *Louisville's First Families - A Series of Genealogical Sketches* (Louisville: The Standard Printing Co., 1920); and E. Polk Johnson, *A History of Kentucky and Kentuckians: The Leaders and Representative Men in Commerce, Industry and Modern Activities, Volume II* (Chicago-New York: The Lewis Publishing Company, 1912), pages 950-951.
6 "Handsome Home on the River Road – 'Bushy Park' is the Name Given the New Home of Charles T. Ballard at Glenview," *The Courier-Journal*, March 3, 1911; and reprint of the *Catalogue of the First Exhibition, Louisville Chapter of the American Institute of Architects, 1912* (Bedford, MA: Applewood Books, 2008).
7 Edith Bingham, "Talk to Glenview Garden Club," page 4.
8 A. Carter Goodloe, "In Southern Gardens – The Log of a Wandering Through Some of the Old and New Gardens of Louisville," *House & Garden Magazine*, October 1917.
9 For a history of Robert W. Bingham and the Bingham family, see, among numerous other publications, Susan E. Tifft and Alex S. Jones, *The Patriarch: The Rise and Fall of the Bingham Dynasty* (New York: Summit Books, 1991); David Leon Chandler with Mary Voelz Chandler, *The Binghams of Louisville – The Dark History Behind One of America's Great Fortunes* (New York: Crown Publishers, 1987); and Sally Bingham, *Passion & Prejudice: A Family Memoir* (New York: Applause, 1991).
10 Interview with Barry Bingham, Sr., by R. Scott Gill, November 10, 1975.
11 Cowell's original drawings, entitled "Planting Plan for Greek Theatre, Judge R.W. Bingham" and dated August 1930, are in the private collection of the Bingham family.
12 Edith Bingham, "Talk to Glenview Garden Club," page 9.
13 "Melcombe Bingham at Glenview, Kentucky – The Country Estate of the Honorable Robert Worth Bingham, United States Ambassador to Great Britain," *Country Life*, October 1933.

LADLESS HILL FARM
1 "A. Brandeis, 74, Passes Away," *The Louisville Times*, August 8, 1928; "Rites, Cremation are Arranged for Brandeis," *The Louisville Times*, August 9, 1928; and William Elsey Connelley and E.M. Coulter, Ph.D., authors, Judge Charles Kerr, editor, "Alfred Brandeis," *History of Kentucky Volume IV* (Chicago and New York: The American Historical Society, 1922), pages 68-69.
2 *A Photographic Tour of The Country Estates of River Road Historic District* (Louisville: 1998), feature #3; and *Louisville Title Co.'s (Incorporated) New Map of Louisville and Jefferson County, Kentucky* (Louisville: Louisville Title Company, 1913), Map 7 (courtesy University of Louisville Digital Collections).
3 Susannah M. Wilson, "Kentucky Talents – Past and Present Artisans Showcased in Louisville," *Southern Accents Magazine*, September/October 1988; and "Handsome Homes To Be Built on The River Road," *The Jeffersonian*, August 31, 1911.
4 Mary Jean Kinsman, *Kentucky Historic Resources Survey Site No. JF-532, Ladless Hill*, Jefferson County Office of Historic Preservation and Archives, 1977 (rev. 1983).
5 A. Brandeis, 74, Passes Away," *The Louisville Times*, August 8, 1928.
6 John T. Berry, "Beautiful Homes of Louisville – 'Ladless Hill Farm,' the country estate of Mrs. Alfred Brandeis, Upper River Road," the *Herald-Post*, July 6, 1930.
7 Note on the drawings, "Remodeling for Mr. & Mrs. Owsley Brown II, Longview Lane," Stratton O. Hammon / Neal O. Hammon, Architects – Engineers, March 13, 1983.

LINCLIFF
1 "Mr. W.R. Belknap, Visit by Mr. John C. Olmsted, 25th September, 1905," from the diary of John C. Olmsted, Library of Congress. For the complete files related to *Lincliff*, please reference the Frederick Law Olmsted National Historic Site, Job #03069.
2 Ibid., "Mr. W.R. Belknap, Visit by Mr. John C. Olmsted, 25th September, 1905."
3 "Handsome Homes To Be Built on the River Road," *The Jeffersonian*, August 31, 1911.
4 Ibid., "Mr. W.R. Belknap, Visit by Mr. John C. Olmsted, 25th September, 1905."
5 "Residence for William Maxwell, Rockville, Conn. – Charles A. Platt, Architect," *The Architectural Review*, Vol. XIV, No. 12, December 1909.
6 Steve Wiser, AIA, "The Belknap Twins: A Faded Louisville Legacy," paper dated May 11, 2007; "W.R. Belknap Passes Away," *The Courier-Journal*, June 2, 1914; and Memorandum of Family of William Burke Belknap, private paper for Lafon Allen, 1936, page 20.
7 Hugh B. Foshee, "2115 Douglass Boulevard," *Kentucky Historic Resources Inventory* #JF 2906 – 056 (Louisville: Louisville Landmarks Commission, October 17, 1979); and "History of the Sixth Annual Decorators' Show House, 'Pelham'," 1979.
8 Susan E. Tifft and Alex S. Jones, *The Patriarch: The Rise and Fall of the Bingham Dynasty* (New York: Summit Books, 1991), page 66; and David Leon Chandler with Mary Voelz Chandler, *The Binghams of Louisville – The Dark History Behind One of America's Great Fortunes* (New York: Crown Publishers, 1987), page 114.
9 Mary Burns, "Lincliff: Showcase for designers," *The Concord*, April 29, 1983.
10 "A Story of Stewardship: The Life and Legacy of Mr. and Mrs. Charles Edwin Gheens," the Gheens Foundation (n.d.).

ROCKLEDGE

1 "George Wheeler Babcock," *Bonnycastle Genealogy* (http://genealogy.kolthammer.org/Bonnycastle-o/p3543.htm).

2 "Handsome Homes To Be Built on The River Road," *The Jeffersonian*, August 31, 1911; and *Louisville Title Co.'s (Incorporated) New Map of Louisville and Jefferson County, Kentucky* (Louisville: Louisville Title Company, 1913), Map 7 (courtesy University of Louisville Digital Collections).

3 Gayle Sanders Knight, *Bryant Fleming, Landscape Architect: Residential Designs 1905 to 1935*, a thesis presented to the faculty of the Graduate School of Cornell University, August 1987, pages 24-26.

4 Knight, page 26.

5 "Beautiful Homes of Louisville: *Rock Ledge*, George W. Babcock's residence on the River Road," the *Herald-Post*, November 4, 1928.

6 John David Myles, "3 Rockledge Drive," descriptive text for the 2006 house tour of The Filson Historical Society, Louisville, KY.

7 *A Photographic Tour of The Country Estates of River Road Historic District* (Louisville: 1998), feature 8, "Rockledge."‡
Gayle Sanders Knight, *Bryant Fleming, Landscape Architect: Residential Designs 1905 to 1935*, a thesis presented to the faculty of the Graduate School of Cornell University, August 1987, pages 24-26.

SHORE ACRES-GREYSTONE

1 Luxurious Country Houses at the City's Skirts," *The Courier-Journal*, May 26, 1912.

2 Mary Jean Kinsman, "History of Property Transfers for 'Greystone' Starting with the Whitley Purchase in 1948," private research paper for Mr. Gar Davis, October 15, 2006.

3 Mary Jean Kinsman, "Wymond House," Kentucky Historic Resources Inventory No. JF-456, Jefferson County Office of Historic Preservation, October 2, 1979.

4 Wilbert R. Hasbrouck, *The Chicago Architectural Club – Prelude to the Modern* (New York: The Monacelli Press, 2005), page 216; and Ronald L.M. Ramsay, Architectural Historian, "Biographical Sketch for Lawrence Buck [1865-1929]," Plains Architecture, State University Station, Fargo, North Dakota, n.d.

5 "Handsome Bungalow on Upper River Road – Home of Louis H. Wymond," *The Courier-Journal*, April 14, 1912.

6 Reprint of the *Catalogue of the First Exhibition of the Louisville Chapter of the American Institute of Architects, 1912* (Bedford, MA: Applewood Books, 2008).

7 Mary Jean Kinsman, "Summary of Research for 'Greystone' 4801 River Road," private research paper for Mr. Gar Davis, October 14, 2006; "L.H. Wymond on Petition etc. to change location of portion of River Road," Jefferson County Court Minute Book No. 78, Page 529, filed April 19, 1913.

8 Each of these projects is covered elsewhere in this book. Note that the work for W.E. Chess is strongly attributed to Townsend & Fleming, as no direct supporting documentation exists.

9 Townsend and Fleming, Landscape Designers, Buffalo, NY, "Forecourt and Adjacent Features, Estate of L. H. Wymond Esq., Glenview KY," May 1914, Revised June 4 [1914]. Townsend and Fleming's drawings for the Wymond estate are held at the Division of Rare and Manuscript Collections, 2B Kroch Library, Cornell University, Ithaca, NY.

10 Mary Jean Kinsman, "History of Property Transfers for 'Greystone' Starting with the Whitley Purchase in 1948," private research paper for Mr. Gar Davis, October 15, 2006.

11 See "Shore Acres, the Home of Mr. and Mrs. Wright Barr, Upper River Road," in the "Beautiful Homes of Louisville" section of the *Herald-Post*, September 22, 1929.

12 Letter dated April 11, 1958 from Olmsted Brothers to Mr. and Mrs. M.G. Whitley. Source: Mary Jean Kinsman. For the complete Olmsted records pertaining to the Whitley project, see File Unit 09821 at the Frederick Law Olmsted National Historic Site, Brookline, MA (www.rediscov.com/olmsted).

THE MIDLANDS

1 "Handsome Homes To Be Built on The River Road," *The Jeffersonian*, August 31, 1911.

2 "Obituary Notes," *The New York Times*, September 27, 1902.

3 Steve Wiser, AIA, "The Belknap Twins: A Faded Louisville Legacy" (Unpublished paper, May 11, 2007).

4 A copy of the Townsend & Fleming plans, "Stable and Gardner's Cottage for Mrs. Morris Belknap," July 1, 1912, is held in the archives of the Filson Historical Society, Louisville, KY.

5 "Leading Architect Yields to Death," *The Courier-Journal*, January 18, 1916.

6 "Plan for Property of Mrs. Morris B. Belknap," landscape drawing by A. Vernon Cassel, Landscape Architect, Louisville, KY (1930), private collection.

7 "Mrs. Belknap Willed Charity Over Half-Million," *The Courier-Journal*, May 23, 1966.

8 "Poplar Hill Estate Purchased," *The Courier-Journal*, June 16, 1968; and Mary Jean Kinsman, *Kentucky Historic Resources Inventory Site No. JF 671 for the Jefferson County Office of Historic Preservation and Archives*, 1983.

CARRIER

1 "Handsome Homes To Be Built on The River Road," The Jeffersonian, August 31, 1911.

2 Official Report, Eighth Annual Convention of the National Lumber Manufacturers' Association, April 19 and 20, 1910, pages II and 119.

3 John E. Kleber, ed., (Lexington: The University of Kentucky Press, 2001), page 424.

4 Mary Jean Kinsman, "Hewett House / Albert R. Cooper," Kentucky Historic Resources Inventory No. JF-542 (Louisville: Jefferson County Office of Historic Preservation and Archives, 1977, rev. 1983).

5 Gayle Sanders Knight, Bryant Fleming, Landscape Architect: Residential Designs 1905 to 1935, a thesis presented to the faculty of the Graduate School of Cornell University, August 1987, page 3.

6 Gayle Sanders Knight, page 183.

7 From descriptive text, Filson Historical Society PC23.0182 boxed collection, "Woodside." (The Filson Historical Society, Louisville, KY)

8 Notes from Mary Jean Kinsman associated with Kentucky Historic Resources Inventory No. JF-542.

9 The Courier-Journal, July 30, 1920, section 1, page 4, col. 8.

MALVERN HOUSE

1 "Death Due to Paralysis – George Gaulbert Passes Away After Two Months' Illness," *The Courier-Journal*, March 27, 1908; "Life's Curtain Falls Gently – Col. Attilla Cox Dies After Long Illness," *The Courier-Journal*, June 8, 1909; William Elsey Connelley and E.M. Coulter, PhD, *History of Kentucky*, Vol. III (Chicago and New York: The American Historical Society, 1922), pages 378-9; and oral histories of George Gaulbert and Attilla Cox as related to the authors by his descendants.

2 Donna M. Neary, Registration Form, United States Department of the Interior, National Park Service, National Register of Historic Places, February 8, 2005.

3 Certain of Codman's drawings for the Cox residence are held in the collection of the archives of the Frederick Law Olmsted National Historic Site in Brookline, MA, under the Attilla Cox job number 06362.

4 See Edith Wharton and Ogden Codman, Jr., *The Decoration of Houses* (New York: Charles Scribner's Sons, 1897, and subsequent reprints under various publishers).

5 For the complete Olmsted records pertaining to the Attilla Cox estate, see File Unit 06362 at the Frederick Law Olmsted National Historic Site, Brookline, MA (www.rediscov.com/olmsted).

6 Unfortunately, apparently none of Hutchings' drawings survives, save a rendering of the north façade held in the Olmsted Archives in Brookline. The first floor plan included in this chapter was based on the 1959 renovation plans of Nevin & Morgan and the 1914 plan by Ogden Codman, with clarifying input from family members Mr. and Mrs. Lee W. Robinson.

7 C. Julian Oberwarth, FAIA, and William B. Scott, Jr., *A History of the Profession of Architecture in Kentucky* (Louisville: Gateway Press, 1987), page 178.

8 Client note cards of Anne Bruce Haldeman (including reference to Arthur Cowell), private collection of Dr. John and Lynn Walker.

9 "Attilla Cox, Attorney, Dies of Pneumonia," the *Louisville News and Enquirer*, November 25, 1935.

10 In 1952, the Collis family gave 51 acres of land in the alluvial plain to the north of the house to the city as the Carrie Rogers Gaulbert Cox Park in memory of Mrs. Cox.

FAIR ACRES

1 Bridget Williams, "Southern Belle, A historic Beaux-Arts beauty in Glenview," *Sophisticated Living* magazine, July/August, 2008; and Albert Russel Erskine, *History of The Studebaker Corporation*, 1918.

2 "Veteran Auto Dealer, Breaux Ballard, Dies," *The Courier-Journal*, February 6, 1961; and "Personalities, G. Breaux Ballard," the Louisville *Herald-Post*, July 26, 1928.

3 "The History of the Second Decorators' Show House, 'Breaux Ballard Estate,'" The Bellarmine Women's Council, 1975. Additionally, the stone foundation and irregular placement of windows in the eastern portion of the house would tend to support this assertion.

4 Telegram from Nevin-Wischmeyer & Morgan to Olmsted Brothers, July 21, 1927; "report of visit" by F.B. Smith of Olmsted Brothers dated July 22-23, 1927; and letter from Hermann Wischmeyer to F.B. Smith of Olmsted Brothers, September 26, 1927 (all Library of Congress, Olmsted Associates Records, Series B ("Correspondence Files")). For the complete Olmsted record pertaining to Fair Acres, see File Unit 07833 at the Frederick Law Olmsted National Historic Site, Brookline, MA (www.rediscov.com/olmsted).

5 "'Fair Acres,' The Residence of Mr. and Mrs. G. Breaux Ballard at Glenview," the Louisville *Herald-Post*, August 12, 1928.

6 "Mrs. Breaux Ballard Is Dead At Age 68," *The Courier-Journal*, May 1, 1961; and John David Myles, "5402 Snowhill Road," for the 1999 house tour of The Filson Historical Society.

BREEZE HILL

1 "Bruce Haldeman Succumbs at 87," *The Louisville Times* (November 29, 1948). For additional information about Bruce Haldeman, see also Dennis Cusick, "Déjà-Vu: The sibling rivalries behind the Bingham sale of *The Courier-Journal* were played out once before with the paper's original owners," *Louisville Magazine* (March 1986), pages 20-21; as well as *Kentucky Historic Resources Inventory*, Site No. JF-678, Jefferson County Office of Historic Preservation & Archives.

2 For an illustration and information about *Sabine Hall*, see Mills Lane, *Architecture of the Old South: Virginia* (Savannah: The Beehive Press, 1987), pages 45, 48-50; and Virginia and Lee McAlester, *A Field Guide to American Houses* (New York: Alfred A. Knopf, 2005), page 173.

3 For an illustration of the Nathaniel Russell house, see Mills Lane, *Architecture of the Old South: South Carolina* (Savannah: The Beehive Press, 1984), page 116.

DUNLORA

1 For an illustration of *Tulip Hill*, see Mills Lane, *Architecture of the Old South* (New York: Abbeville Press, 1993), page 101.

2 For an illustration of H. Boone Porter's *Ridgeley Farm*, see Samuel W. Thomas, *The Architectural History of Louisville, 1778-1900* (Louisville: The Filson Historical Society, 2009), page 48.

3 For the complete Olmsted records pertaining to the William C. Dabney estate, see File Unit 09485 at the Frederick Law Olmsted National Historic Site, Brookline, MA (www.rediscov.com/olmsted).

4 "W.C. Dabney, Sr., Civic Leader, Dies," *The Courier-Journal*, January 16, 1963.

CODA

FINCASTLE

1 For excellent illustrations of both *Rose Hill* and *Ridgeway*, see Rexford Newcomb, *Old Kentucky Architecture* (New York: William Helburn, 1940), pages 44-47, and 51-52.

2 Martha Thorne, Editor, *David Adler, Architect: The Elements of Style* (Chicago: The Art Institute of Chicago, 2002), page 89 (Adler house) and 198 (Reed house).

3 Richard Pratt, *David Adler* (New York: M. Evans and Company, 1970), page 131 (Crane) and pages 176-181 (Armour).

4 "WAVE's President Norton Dies," *The Courier-Journal*, February 14, 1964.

5 "Fincastle, An Estate of Exceptional Pedigree," *Sophisticated Living Magazine*, May/June 2010.

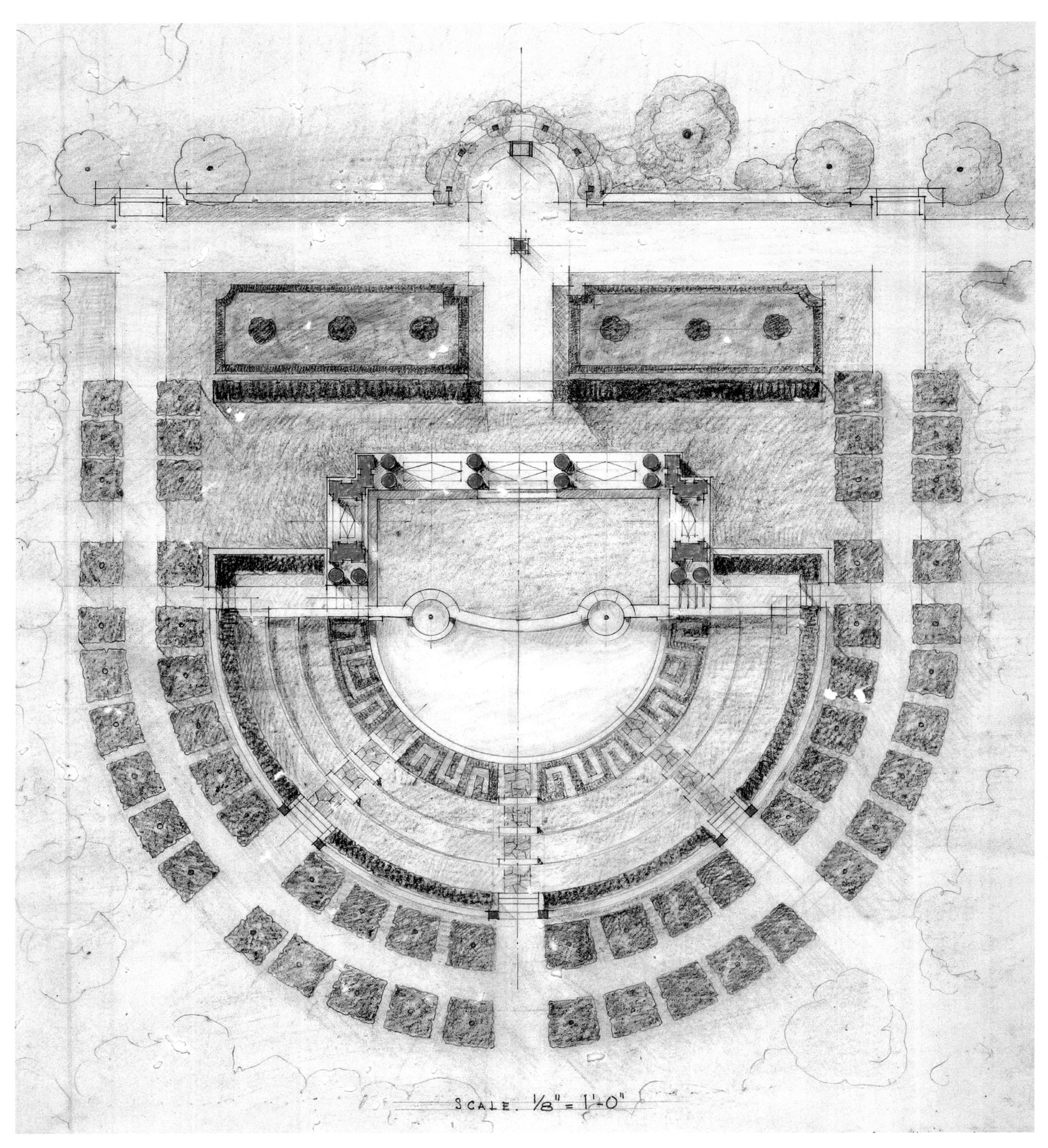

Landscaping plan for the Greek theatre at *Melcombe*, Carrère & Hastings, 1929. (Private Collection)

ACKNOWLEDGMENTS

We wish to give our special thanks to: Sam Thomas, Dean of Louisville historians; Mary Jean Kinsman, former member of the City & County Landmarks Commission; John David Myles, architectural historian; Steve Wiser, architect; and Tom Owen, Louisville historian.

In addition, special thanks to Christopher Bishop of the Don Meredith Company for his invaluable skill in reproducing the photos, maps and other materials, and to Jay Hollenburger for serving as our indefatigable proofreader.

A very special thanks goes to our consulting photographers, John Nation and Stephen Driver, for their skill and patience.

We wish to thank the following institutions and libraries: Bill Carner, Rachel Howard and Sue Finley, Special Collections, University of Louisville; T. Joseph Hardesty and Beverlee Marmion, Louisville Free Public Library; Kentucky Wesleyan College Library; Jason Fowler, Archives & Special Collections Librarian, The Southern Baptist Theological Seminary; Ana Guimaraes, Cornell University Library, Division of Rare and Manuscript Collections; Bruce Kirby, Library of Congress; Catherine Arthur, Director and Curator of Homewood Museum, The Johns Hopkins University; Kay Johnston and Kaye Crouch, Cheekwood Botanical Garden & Museum of Art; Robert J. Roche, Archivist, Shepley Bullfinch Richardson and Abbott, architects; Marla Smith and Linda Lally, Bellarmine University Library; T. Michele Clark, Archivist, Frederick Law Olmsted National Historic Site; Richard Jett and Darnell Farris, Landmarks Commission of Louisville; Nashville Public Library; Gail Gilbert and Kathy Moore, Margaret M. Bridwell Art Library, University of Louisville; Faith Harders and James Marcotte, Design Library, University of Kentucky; Mimi Zinniel, Director, Olmsted Parks Conservancy of Louisville; James Holmberg, Michael R. Veach, Robin Wallace, Sarah-Jane Poindexter, Jennifer Cole and Judy Miller, Special Collections, The Filson Historical Society of Louisville; Angela Morris and Ernest Miller, White Library, Louisville Presbyterian Theological Seminary; Young Library, University of Kentucky; Amy Inskeep, Librarian, *The Courier-Journal*; Mark Dennen, Historical Society of Kentucky; Jane Stahl and Martie Fahey, Four Courts at Cherokee Park, Signature Healthcare; Heather Bilodeau, Archivist, Walsh History Center, Camden, Maine, Public Library; Janet Parks, Curator, and Inna Guzenfeld, Drawings Assistant, Avery Library, Columbia University; and Ryerson and Burnham Libraries, Art Institute of Chicago.

We are especially indebted to Betsy Edwards, Diane L. Smith, Denise Ellis, Geralyn Ehley and Teresa Rice of Blackburn Domene & Burchett, PLLC, for their tireless efforts on our behalf.

We wish to thank all of the current owners of our featured houses for their invaluable assistance, cooperation and very considerable patience. Also, we express our gratitude to the following individuals who aided us tremendously in our research: Adath Jeshurun Synagogue; Allen Atherton; *Antiques* Magazine; Mary Louise Bickle; Richard Breen; Erica Bumba; John Caperton; Barbara Castleman; Rex Cecil; Ms. Helen Rechtin Combs; Danielle Devine, Gaela Erwin; Doug Farnsley; David Fenley; Jane Ferriell; Louise Fitzhugh; Marea Gardner; Jeff and Tricia Gill; Mrs. William Grant; Robert Griffith; Katie Haley; Neil Hammon, architect; Louise Hickox; Paul Higgs; Mrs. Roy L. Honeycutt; Betsy Hyslop; Emory Cowan Winston Jacobs; Mary Jennings; Flora Johnson; Ms. Larry Jones; S. Paul Jones; Mrs. John Morton Kimberly; Margaret Barr Kulp; James Lenihan; John Lenihan; Arleyn Levee; J. Sandford MacLean; John McCall; William McMahon; Charles Middleton; Larry Middleton; Mrs. Condict Moore; Pat Murphy, Murphy Camera; Charles S. Musson; Mrs. H. Shepard Musson; Tim Orwig; Joanne Owen; Lee Robinson; Meme Runyon, River Fields, Inc.; the Rev. Al Shands; John Speed; Mrs. James Stites; Walker Stites; Robert Tachau; Elizabeth Thompson; Louise Todd; Pat Updegraff; Roanne Victor; Tom Wallace; Joanne Weeter; Lee Wells; Tracey Williams; Juliet Willis; Susan and David Wood; Wilson Wyatt, Jr.; Mrs. Thomas J. Zimmerman.

We owe a special thanks to Carol Butler of Butler Books and Scott Stortz of Titan Design Solutions for making this book a reality.

Lastly, we thank Laura Porter Blackburn and Gionatan Surrenti, Bob Micou, Sallye Pence, Bill Stegeman, Elizabeth and Joe Walden, and Rob Young for their support and patience during this four-year project.

Library mantel detail, *Homewood*, 2009. (John Nation)

INDEX

Page numbers in bold refer to the chapters of the featured houses

D

E

F

G